Online News

Online News

Journalism and the Internet

Stuart Allan

Open University Press

Open University Press
McGraw-Hill Education
McGraw-Hill House
Shoppenhangers Road
Maidenhead
Berkshire
England
SL6 2QL

email: enquiries@openup.co.uk
world wide web: www.openup.co.uk

and Two Penn Plaza, New York, NY 10121–2289, USA

First published 2006
Copyright © Stuart Allan 2006

A catalogue record of this book is available from the British Library

ISBN 10 0 335 22121 1 (pb) 0 335 22122 X (hb)
ISBN 13 978 0 335 22121 9 (pb) 978 0 335 22122 6 (hb)

Library of Congress Cataloging-in-Publication Data
CIP data applied for

Typeset by YHT Ltd, London
Printed in the UK by Bell & Bain Ltd, Glasgow

Contents

Acknowledgements

'Information overload' is more than a buzzword for me. Enough material was accumulated in the course of researching this topic – over four years' worth of hunting, gathering and interviewing, to be precise – to make the challenge of transforming it into something readable a rather daunting one. While my computer's hard drive creaked and the number of filing cabinets grew, though, I was fortunate enough to incur more than a few debts along the way. For sharing their thoughts, as well as comments on large swathes of a first draft, I am grateful to Cynthia Carter, Andy Channelle, Simon Cottle, Donald Matheson, Lee Salter, Prasun Sonwalkar, Einar Thorsen, and Howard Tumber. Several other kind people similarly helped me to shape the perspective informing my approach here – my thanks to James Compton, Bob Franklin, Robert Hassan, Emma Hemmingway, Mark Lacy, Chris Paterson, Annabelle Sreberny, Ingrid Volkmer, and Barbie Zelizer. A number of ideas were tested out in conference venues, public lecture halls and seminar rooms – as well as in various newsrooms – dotted around welcoming places near and far. My appreciation to those who posed intriguingly awkward questions, some of which I hope this response begins to answer. Much of this book was prepared during my research leave from teaching and administrative responsibilities, generously funded by the Arts and Humanities Research Council and the University of the West of England, Bristol. Colleagues in media, cultural and journalism studies at UWE consistently inspire me with their passion for thinking anew about pressing issues, and the same goes for those who do most of the teaching about the internet – our students. At Open University Press, I am grateful to Chris Cudmore, Suzanne Renny, Malie Lalor, Jonathan Lee, and colleagues for their expert help in making the publishing process a pleasure. And for ensuring that the time spent writing was an interruption from the simple joys of everyday life, and not the other way around, my love to Cindy and Geoff.

1 Introduction

There are times when a seemingly minor, insignificant change can suddenly generate profound consequences. The term 'tipping point' is often used to characterize the precise instance when this occurs, when the rate of a process increases so dramatically that it creates surprising results. Various inflections of the term have been taken up in a diverse number of fields, such as sociology, engineering and mathematics, but it found its place in the popular lexicon with the publication of Malcolm Gladwell's (2000) *The Tipping Point: How Little Things Can Make a Big Difference*. Without doubt the book's influence – as well as its status on the bestseller charts – was enhanced by former US President Bill Clinton, who evidently mentioned it at a press conference as that 'now-famous book that everybody is reading'. For Gladwell, tipping points help to explain the social dynamics underlying the 'mysterious changes that mark everyday life', that is, the 'magic moment' when ideas, messages or behaviours 'cross a threshold, tip and spread like wildfire'. Despite the reservations expressed by some critics (in an otherwise approving review, *Publishers Weekly* calls the book a 'facile piece of pop sociology'), the term itself seems to have tipped, becoming something of what Gladwell himself would describe as a 'word-of-mouth epidemic' spreading 'just like viruses do'.

It is certainly striking to observe how frequently the notion of a 'tipping point' (together with variations such as 'milestone', 'watershed' or 'breakthrough') informs current debates about online news. Indeed, I shall begin this book's discussion by examining two such points which have been heralded for their impact in transforming the way we regard journalism in a digital environment. In the first instance, our attention turns to a speech delivered in the Spring of 2005 by media mogul Rupert Murdoch, chair and chief executive officer of News Corporation, to an audience of newspaper editors. In the view of some who were there, his comments signalled the moment when time was effectively called on the newspaper, at least in its familiar paper and ink format, thereby ushering in a radical rethink of its very future. Murdoch's intervention, the *Economist* magazine predicted, 'may go down in history as the day that the stodgy newspaper business officially woke up to the new realities of the internet age' (*The Economist*, 21 April 2005).

The newspaper is dead, long live the newspaper

The speech in question was Rupert Murdoch's address to the annual meeting of the American Society of Newspaper Editors (ASNE) in Washington DC on 13 April 2005, in which he outlined what he perceived to be the 'fast developing reality' confronting the newspaper industry, and its startling implications for the future. 'Scarcely a day goes by without some claim that new technologies are fast writing newsprint's obituary', he began. 'Yet, as an industry, many of us have been remarkably, unaccountably complacent.' In conceding that he personally had not done as much about it as he should have done 'after all the excitement of the late 1990's', he admitted that he thought of himself as a 'digital immigrant', someone still 'searching for answers to an emerging medium that is not my native language'. As he proceeded to elaborate:

> I wasn't weaned on the web, nor coddled on a computer. Instead, I grew up in a highly centralized world where news and information were tightly controlled by a few editors, who deemed to tell us what we could and should know [. . .] The peculiar challenge then, is for us digital immigrants – many of whom are in positions to determine how news is assembled and disseminated – to apply a digital mindset to a set of challenges that we unfortunately have limited to no first-hand experience dealing with. (Murdoch 2005)

Describing his two daughters as 'digital natives', that is, young people who will 'never know a world without ubiquitous broadband internet access', he underscored his contention that a generational shift was underway. 'We need to realize that the next generation of people accessing news and information, whether from newspapers or any other source, have a different set of ex-pectations about the kind of news they will get', he declared. This includes, in turn, 'when and how they will get it, where they will get it from, and who they will get it from'. Ever the businessperson, Murdoch saw in this looming crisis for the newspaper industry a critical set of difficulties, but also an op-portunity to 'improve our journalism and expand our reach' in a manner consistent with his larger corporate interests.

From Murdoch's perspective, the 'dramatic revolution taking place in the news industry today' revolves around the fact that 'technology-savvy young people' are becoming increasingly likely to turn to the web as their news medium of choice. Drawing upon audience data from a report by Merrill Brown (2005) for the Carnegie Corporation of New York, a philanthropic foundation, he explained why he considered certain 'ominous' findings to be especially 'alarming' for the viability of newspapers. Although local television news may be the most accessed source of news for consumers between the ages of 18 and 34, the study suggests, internet portals (such as 'the Yahoos, Googles, and MSNs') are fast becoming their favoured destination for news: '44 percent of the study's respondents said they use a portal at least once a day for news, as compared to just 19 percent who use a printed newspaper on a daily basis', he stated. Looking forward over the next three years, the study 'found that 39 percent expected to use the internet more to learn about the news, versus only 8 percent who expected to use traditional newspapers more'. Hence, in light of figures such as these, Murdoch's belief that a 're-volution' is underway with respect to how young people access their news. Moreover, he is convinced, they also do not 'want to rely on a god-like figure from above to tell them what's important. And to carry the religion analogy a bit further, they certainly don't want news presented as gospel.' Rather, in marked contrast, young people prefer 'news on demand' or, to put it another way, they 'want control over their media, instead of being controlled by it'. Highlighting an array of examples to illustrate his argument, not least the impact of blogs, he contends that young people need news that is con-tinuously updated because they want 'a point of view about not just what happened, but why it happened. They want news that speaks to them per-sonally, that affects their lives.'[1]

Recrafting newspaper journalism in light of these 'revolutionary' factors will entail the disruption of centuries-old traditions. Certainly this dynamic conception of young people as digital natives – individuals who actively question, probe and seek out different angles in the news online – throws into sharp relief some of the more familiar assumptions that typically guide in-dustry judgements about how best to extend the reach of newspapers via the internet. In issuing this call for media orthodoxies to be reconsidered, Mur-doch is insisting that 'we must challenge – and reformulate – the conventions that so far have driven our online efforts'. In other words, while the speed of technological change is a pressing concern, even more worrisome for Mur-doch is 'our ability to make the necessary cultural changes to meet the new demands'. To succeed in effecting a 'complete transformation of the way we think about our product' will entail recognizing, in turn, that 'too many of us editors and reporters are out of touch with our readers'. Rather than asking 'Do we have the story?', the question should be 'Does anyone want the story?' It is in facing certain unpleasant truths, then, that new ways forward can be found. There is much cause for optimism, in Murdoch's view, so long as operations are 'streamlined' and more 'nimble', but also – crucially – by be-coming much more responsive to the views of audiences. 'We may never become true digital natives,' he states, 'but we can and must begin to as-similate to their culture and way of thinking.' There is little doubt in his mind that this 'monumental, once-in-a-generation opportunity' cannot be missed; 'if we're successful,' he declared, 'our industry has the potential to reshape itself, and to be healthier than ever before.'

Reactions to Murdoch's intervention were remarkably muted, judging at least from the scant newspaper coverage it generated. By and large, details of the speech were much more likely to figure in opinion columns than in straight news reports. Maureen Dowd in *The New York Times* referred to Murdoch as a 'media big shot' who had given the ASNE 'some bad news about young people in the age of the Internet, blogging and cable news' (*The New York Times*, 20 April 2005). Across town, in *The New York Observer*, Richard Brookhiser suggested that he thought Murdoch was 'being polite', adding: 'What he was telling his colleagues was: Newspapers are dead' (*The New York Observer*, 2 May 2005). David Shaw, writing in *The Los Angeles Times*, re-affirmed several of the speech's points, but took issue with Murdoch's interpretation of data ostensibly indicating young people desire a 'point of view' in their news. He wrote:

> If that 'point of view' is evenhanded analysis, we all benefit. If it's opinion masquerading as news, as one sometimes sees on Fox News, it helps no one. Murdoch also says the young 'want news that speaks to them personally, that affects their lives.' True – and not just the young. But local TV stations have tried this 'news you can use' approach for years, and it has largely trivialized or replaced real news in many cities. Not all news can (or should) be personally, instantly useful to everyone. There is some information that every citizen should be familiar with, its immediate non-utility notwithstanding. We might all have better understood what led to the Sept. 11 terrorist attacks, for example, if most news organizations – the television networks in particular – hadn't cut back so much for so long on their international coverage and had spent more time examining the Arab world and less on Michael Jackson and Princess Di. (*The Los Angeles Times*, 1 May 2005)

Nevertheless, Shaw conceded that Murdoch deserved credit for recognizing the 'problems posed by the paradigmatic shift in the nation's news-consuming habits', suggesting that newspaper editors would be well advised to join him in the quest to search for answers. This point found its echo in the UK newspaper commentary. 'For a media magnate,' stated Roy Greenslade in *The Guardian*, 'it was a very humble speech.' Praising it for being 'intelligent and challenging', and 'rich in content', he recommended that every journalist read it (*The Guardian*, 18 April 2005). Even online, otherwise critical voices were suitably impressed. 'I'm no fan of Rupert Murdoch,' stated Dan Gillmor in his *Bayosphere* blog, 'a press (robber) baron whose greed and overtly one-sided journalism have been a malevolent force in the media sphere.' And yet, he continues, the speech 'said a bunch of things that needed saying – and for that, he's done a real public service'. In Gillmor's judgement, it was 'essential reading for anyone in the news business', demonstrating that

Murdoch 'and the people who are briefing him on this stuff are attuned to the emerging world, and in a profound way' (*Bayosphere*, 14 April 2005).

In the light of these types of remarks, the near-absence of hard news coverage of the speech in the press is arguably all the more telling. Then again, perhaps newspaper editors do not need to 'awaken to these changes', being all too aware that the industry is at serious risk of being 'relegated to the status of also-rans', to quote again from Murdoch. It may be that the real argument to be conducted is over what to do about it. That is, whether to embrace Murdoch's vision of the brave new world of the internet, to boldly reject it outright, or to find some way to negotiate favourable terms for a steady – if uneasy – truce of sorts between 'old' and 'new' media rivals. We shall return to these and related issues in later chapters. Presently our focus shifts to a second 'tipping point' for online news, one that took place on the beaches of South East Asia a few months prior to Murdoch's intervention.

The citizen journalist

It was at 7:59 am local time on 26 December 2004 that a portion of undersea crust off the coast of Sumatra suddenly shifted beneath an adjacent one, engendering a massive earthquake (registering 9.3 on the Richter scale) near the surface of the seafloor. Instantly set in motion were a series of awesomely destructive waves – a tsunami – along a 750-mile-long fault line, many of which had reached heights of more than 50 feet by the time they smashed onto the shorelines of 12 different countries.[2] The consequences were catastrophic. 'People caught in the waves became small ingredients in an enormous blender,' Barry Bearak (2005) wrote in *The New York Times*, 'bludgeoned by concrete slabs and felled trees, stabbed by jagged sheets of glass, tangled up in manacles of wire.' In time it would be estimated that some 232,000 people were either dead or reported missing. More than two-thirds of the victims had been living in the Indonesian province of Aceh, situated 155 miles from the earthquake's epicentre – a distance covered by the ensuing waves within a mere 30 minutes as they swept across the Indian Ocean.

Western news organizations scrambled to find reporters to press into service, given that so few of them were situated anywhere nearby. Much of the early coverage, as a result, tended to prioritize various aspects of the administrative response to the crisis. By the time rescue workers from First World countries began to arrive in numbers, however, journalists were there to bear witness. This front-page account published by the *Washington Post* describes what some encountered in vivid terms:

> LAMNO, Indonesia, Jan. 4 – From the skies above Aceh's devastated western coastline, no sign of civilization remains except for the

barren concrete foundations of houses sheared clean and wooden debris scattered like multicolored confetti.

But several miles inland, some isolated settlements were spared by the tsunami that devastated the tip of Sumatra island Dec. 26, killing more than 94,000 people in Indonesia alone. Villagers walk along the main roads toward the spots where U.S. Navy Seahawk helicopters have been dropping emergency supplies of food and water for the past three days.

The line between life and death was evident Tuesday looking down at the countryside from one of the Seahawks. [. . .] (*Washington Post*, 4 January 2005)

The report continues, focusing on the relief efforts underway, and the survivors encountered by the Seahawks' military personnel. In so doing, it provides important information, but necessarily only part of the story, and from a chosen perspective consistent with implicit judgements about access, news values, source credibility, and audience predispositions.

For press critic Danny Schechter (2005), however, this particular news item is a typical example of what he calls 'helicopter journalism'. In his view, it is 'like the foreign correspondent who flies into a conflict zone for an afternoon and gets most of his information from a taxi driver'. The limits of such forms of 'parachute' reporting are readily apparent, he argues, when one considers how distanced it is from what is actually happening on the ground away from the rescue helicopters. In this sense, the item in question may be considered broadly indicative of much Western news reporting of the tsunami's aftermath. In his words:

> When you watch the coverage, you see endless stories of Colin Powell touring the devastation or Kofi Annan arriving in Jakarta and speaking to the press. You hear the sound bites of the elite and high and mighty, who tend to look at the world from 30,000 feet – cruising in first class – and far from the pain of the real worlds below.
>
> And, yes, you also see US soldiers delivering aid, often dropping it from the skies. You hear about the UN Food program with enough food for 100,000 people. (When you read closer, you learn that the food supply will only last a week!)
>
> It looks so impressive – and in many ways it is. But the reporters on the ground say that there are still major problems reaching those most in need. And those people are dying and at risk from an epidemic of disease.
>
> They say the crisis is getting worse, not better.
>
> As the crisis deepens, the journalism has not. (Schechter 2005)

To reverse the priorities of 'outside-in' reporting, it follows, will require an entirely different set of principles to be upheld. 'Why is it so hard for western news organizations to connect with local journalists who often know the story best?' Schechter asks. 'What we need is "inside-out" and bottom up coverage – not just reporting from the clouds.'

It is precisely this issue of 'bottom up coverage' which I want to privilege for consideration here. Absent from Schechter's assessment – although he would be sure to recognize its significance – is the extraordinary contribution made by ordinary citizens offering their first-hand reports, digital photographs, camcorder video footage, mobile telephone snapshots or audio clips. Much of this material, whether taken up by news organizations seeking to augment their coverage or by individual bloggers seeking to counter-balance the excesses of 'helicopter journalism', proceeded to have a profound influence on audience perceptions of the crisis around the world. 'Never before has there been a major international story where television news crews have been so emphatically trounced in their coverage by amateurs wielding their own cameras', observed one British newspaper. 'Producers and professional news cameramen often found themselves being sent not to the scenes of disaster to capture footage of its aftermath, but to the airports where holidaymakers were returning home with footage of the catastrophe as it happened (*The Independent*, 3 January 2005). Many holidaymakers at beachfront resorts had recorded what they had witnessed, capturing in time something of the terrifying destructive power of the waves as they hit. Virtually all of the still images and video footage that would rapidly become a staple of the television news coverage were provided by 'amateurs' who happened to be on the scene, and who somehow managed to retain the presence of mind to record the horrors around them. This material, often sent via email and mobile telephones to friends and relatives before it was forwarded to news organizations, put human faces on the catastrophe.

This type of 'citizen journalism', to use the phrase suddenly appearing in mainstream news items, was being supplemented by other forms of reporting similarly made possible by digital media.[3] At the forefront were weblogs, or blogs, where individuals gathered whatever material they could and posted it, along with their own interpretation of its significance. 'We're getting out information that traditional media has not had access to', maintained Rohit Gupta working on a blog called SEA-EAT (The South-East Asia Earthquake and Tsunami). 'Certain areas have been cordoned off to traditional media by the Tamil Tigers', or Sri Lanka police. The blog, up and running from the first day of the tragedy, drew on over 50 people for its content from all over the affected areas. 'What we did not expect is the kind of traffic we're getting', Gupta added (cited in *InternetWeek*, 29 December 2004). Evidently the site's meter stopped at 100,000 visitors, testing the limits of their bandwidth allocation. Meanwhile, several mainstream news reports were calling attention to the importance of the internet for being the 'eyes and ears' of the disaster within local contexts. 'You can get a really good consensus picture of what's going on that's stronger than any one news organization could offer', Jimmy Wales, founder of the communal online encyclopaedia Wikipedia, was quoted as stating in one press account. 'So many people are on the ground in different places. And people pick up very quickly which are the bloggers to read, and they bring that information to the forefront and amplify it.' The volunteers behind Wikipedia had moved quickly to establish a page dedicated to collecting users' material of all descriptions. 'It's a place for people to synthesize all of the information and sort through it', Wales maintained (cited in *San Jose Mercury News*, 31 December 2004).

According to Technorati.com, which monitors blog activity, some 55,000 tsunami-related blogs appeared over the first three days, with tens of thousands more to follow. Much of the material presented, as one would expect, was as chilling as it was illuminating. Examples drawn from personal blogs by those on the scene include this one from 'Fred' in Jaffna, Sri Lanka:

> The sheer brute violence of that single wave is staggering. Every house and fishing boat has been smashed, the entire length of the east coast. People who know and respect the sea well now talk of it in shock, dismay and fear. Some work to do this week. (*This Way Please*, 26 December 2004)

The blog's next entry, posted two days later, begins:

> Well, hello world.
> Here is another picture from Point Pedro, which is the northernmost point of Sri Lanka to be hit by the tsunami. Thank you on behalf of the hard-hit people here for your concern and interest in this situation. I'm sorry not to have kept you posted, but I have been busy. I promise the next photograph will be of something more positive.
> I would counsel against watching the news over and over. We all know it's numbing. And please remember that the pictures you are seeing are from the areas that happen to be accessible and happen to be where holiday-makers go. The other places are pretty messy too, unfortunately, and were generally a lot humbler to start with. [. . .]

About his own role as a blogger, 'Fred' writes:

> On a personal note, I can say that this may be an unexpected challenge and responsibility, and it hurts to see people in pain, but it's also a remarkable experience to be on hand to do something modest

but useful in the aftermath of a disaster. (*This Way Please*, 28 December 2004)

Bloggers such as 'Fred', regardless of their relative investment in any sense of 'citizen journalism', were making a vital contribution. In addition to other qualities, bloggers' reports provided a degree of depth and immediacy that mattered. 'As individual voices,' newspaper reporter Bobbie Johnson observed, 'these eyewitness accounts made horribly compelling reading. As part of a wider network of stories, they brought a sense of scale to a story when the whole world was watching' (*The Guardian*, 6 January 2005). Similarly, video bloggers ('vbloggers' in web parlance), typically faced with the challenges of copyright, bandwidth demands and the expenses being incurred, often struggled and persevered because of a shared drive to tell the story. 'When you see it, and you see how it's happening to just ordinary people, it brings home the enormity of it', Kevin Aylward of Wizbangblog.org commented. 'That is the fascination with the videos' (cited in *Wall Street Journal*, 3 January 2005).[4]

Nevertheless, it was a relatively small number of online news organizations that made effective use of 'user-generated' items – MSNBC.com, for example, offered a 'Citizen Journalists' Report' page – with most tending to rely primarily on comments posted from users about stories. As a general rule, these sites seemed content to allow television news to take the lead. 'What's holding mainstream editors back this time?' enquired Steve Outing in Poynter Online about US news sites. 'Probably their long-held reticence to host any content that drives people off their websites to third-party offerings, and overall skepticism and fear about the wisdom of carrying citizen reporting' (Poynter Online, 6 January 2005). In contrast, several UK-based sites featured reporting aggregated from blogs, arguably the most successful of which was BBC News Online. It created space for survivors to post first-person accounts, photographs, and video items, as well as message boards for those hoping to post appeals for information about relatives, friends and colleagues. Evidently by the end of the first week, the site had received approximately 50,000 emails. Spokesperson Hannah Howard described how the emails could be divided into four main categories: 'People from the UK trying to get information on friends and family in South East Asia; people in Asia e-mailing in to say they were safe; people sharing their stories and experiences; and appeals for help'. Moreover, the site's message board had received over 400,000 visitors in the same period. 'The very moving postings contributed a first-hand account of how those involved in the tragic events felt and the things they had experienced', she added (cited in Srinivas 2005).

From today's perspective, the ways in which ordinary members of the public – 'accidental journalists' in the view of some – engaged in impromptu news-gathering can be interpreted as signifying a tipping point for online news, not least by opening up for redefinition what counts as 'news' and who can be a 'journalist' in ways which continue to reverberate today. 'This is journalism. Raw, unedited, but still journalism', Jonathan Dube, MSNBC.com managing producer, maintained at the time. 'Hearing about individual experiences directly from the people who survived the tsunami offered readers a different, more personal perspective on the human side of the tragedy than most of the articles published by news organizations' (cited in *National Geographic.com*, 28 January 2005). As such, it went some distance toward providing viable alternatives to the 'helicopter journalism' described above. Although *Guardian* blogger Neil McIntosh does not use the term 'tipping point' when making his assessment, he describes the transformative shift at stake in eloquent terms nonetheless:

> It would be obscene to remember this tsunami as anything other than a huge natural disaster, a human tragedy on an unimaginable scale. But for those watching this small, comparatively insignificant world of media, this may also be remembered as a time when citizen reporting, through the force of its huge army of volunteers and their simple type and publish weblog mechanisms, finally found its voice, and delivered in a way the established media simply could not. (Guardian Unlimited News Blog, 4 January 2005)

Citizen reporting had indeed 'found its voice' when confronted with the misery and suffering produced by the tsunami, and in so doing signalled its promise to dramatically recast journalism's familiar protocols in unanticipated ways.

Points of departure

The two 'tipping points' discussed above usefully frame the broad parameters shaping this book's engagement with online news. Taken together, they are indicative of a communication continuum that stretches between the interests of multinational news corporations (where online news is first and foremost a commodity defined by profit-maximization), at the one end, and the spontaneous actions of ordinary citizens compelled to adopt the role of a journalist in order to participate in the making of online news, at the other.

Here I wish to point out, though, that my use of the term 'tipping point' is merely intended to be suggestive, to tease out certain pertinent issues for closer scrutiny, and as such is not meant to bear too much conceptual weight. This is not deny that it would be possible to write a history of online news that sought to identify a distinct trajectory of such points, each shown to be revolving around a radical disjuncture from past practice. While this type of approach would likely generate some interesting insights, it would be difficult to avoid the danger of reifying these 'magic moments' – to use Gladwell's (2000) phrase – into self-contained, isolated events. This when the stuff of journalism, as we all know, is far messier than such an approach might otherwise concede. In the discussion that follows on these pages, I will necessarily dwell on certain formative instances, but I wish to emphasize from the outset that each of them needs to be seen as being indicative of a complex – and always contradictory – array of interrelated imperatives. To the extent that it is possible to discern the contours of these imperatives, especially with respect to the economic, political and cultural dynamics which imbue their logics, it is likely that they will be more apparent in retrospect than they were at the time. In other words, when examining them from the vantage point of today, it is a challenge to appreciate the socially contingent, frequently contested nature of their lived negotiation. Hence the need to be alert to the countervailing pressures of experience, innovation, transformation and appropriation while, simultaneously, resisting any sense of inevitability where these formative processes are concerned.

Guiding the course of this book's exploration of online news, principally in its US and British contexts, are several questions which may be briefly highlighted here as follows: Which reportorial innovations have attracted public attention to online news, and why? To what extent have the forms and practices – as well as epistemologies (ways or methods of knowing) – widely held to be characteristic of online news become conventionalized? What factors (technological, but also economic, political and cultural) are shaping the gradual consolidation of these conventions? And, lastly, in what ways will online news have to develop in order to further enhance its reportorial integrity? Bearing these questions in mind, our attention turns in the next chapter to 1995, the year when 'cyber-journalism' became front-page news in the mainstream press.

2 The rise of online news

'Welcome to Cyberspace' was the bold salutation splashed on the front cover of *Time* on 1 March 1995. This special issue of the news magazine was devoted to exploring precisely what this new-fangled concept of 'cyberspace' meant, offering an overview of the state of internet technology and various assessments of its growing impact on everyday life (telecommunications giant AT&T was the issue's sole sponsor with 28 pages of advertising). From one section to the next, *Time* marshalled together a range of perspectives, addressing topics such as the seemingly imminent arrival of the global village, net-based commerce, computer crime, the wiring of schools, online dating and digital television, all with a view to illuminating the emergent terrain of cyberspace for its readers. Here it is worth recalling, of course, that in 1995 only a relatively small number of these readers could have been expected to possess first-hand experience of the internet.

With the benefit of hindsight, *Time*'s special issue can be recognized as a significant intervention, representing a formative moment when the esoteric realm of cyberspace was deemed sufficiently newsworthy to warrant in-depth treatment by a mainstream news publication. In its opening essay, Philip Elmer-Dewitt (1995) sets the scene by explaining that the origins of the 'cyberspace' concept could be traced back to science fiction writer William Gibson's (1984) dystopian novel *Neuromancer* with its chilling depiction of a virtual reality existing behind the computer screen. Elmer-Dewitt points out that the concept has since been taken up to describe the 'shadowy space where our computer data reside', thereby joining words such as 'the Net, the Web, the Cloud, the Matrix, the Metaverse, the Datasphere, the Electronic Frontier, [and] the information superhighway'. In prophesying that Gibson's coinage would likely prove the most enduring of these alternatives, he highlights its multiple inflections in different contexts. 'Now hardly a day goes by without some newspaper article, some political speech, some corporate press release invoking Gibson's imaginary world', he observes. 'Suddenly, it seems, everybody has an E-mail address.'

Of particular interest to Elmer-Dewitt, however, is the way in which cyberspace is being characterized in news reports as one of the driving forces – possibly the primary one – for economic growth in the years to come. In his words:

> All this is being breathlessly reported in the press, which has seized on cyberspace as an all-purpose buzz word that can add sparkle to the most humdrum development or assignment. For working reporters, many of whom have just discovered the pleasures of going online, cyber has become the prefix of the day, and they are spawning neologisms as fast as they can type: cyberphilia, cyberphobia, cyberwonk, cybersex, cyberslut [...] The rush to get online, to avoid being 'left behind' in the information revolution, is intense. Those who find fulfillment in cyberspace often have the religious fervor of the recently converted. (Elmer-Dewitt 1995)

For all intents and purposes, he adds, 'the Internet is cyberspace', or at least it will be '[u]ntil something better comes along to replace it'. To understand what is at stake, he maintains, it is necessary to look beyond the polarizing extremes of typical sorts of press accounts, where 'hype and romanticism' are counterpoised against 'fear and loathing'. The internet is remarkable and, at the same time, far from perfect, in his view:

> Largely unedited, its content is often tasteless, foolish, uninteresting or just plain wrong. It can be dangerously habit-forming and, truth be told, an enormous waste of time. Even with the arrival of new point-and-click software such as Netscape and Mosaic, it is still too hard to navigate. And because it requires access to both a computer and a high-speed telecommunications link, it is out of reach for millions of people too poor or too far from a major communications hub to participate. (Elmer-Dewitt 1995)[1]

Still, in recognizing that the 'rough-and-tumble Usenet newsgroups' were slowly giving way to the 'more passive and consumer-oriented "home pages" of the World Wide Web', it was becoming increasingly apparent that fundamental changes were underway. Changes with an effect, in Elmer-Dewitt's estimation, 'likely to be more profound and widespread and unanticipated than anyone imagined – even the guys [and gals] who write science fiction'.

For those readers interested in the implications for journalism posed by the advent of cyberspace, several of the special issue's articles provide telling insights. An essay by *Time*'s managing editor James R. Gaines (1995) outlines his take on the 'cyberrevolution' and the pressing need to introduce the magazine's 'own brand of journalism' to new media forms. 'For the past 18 months,' he writes, 'each weekly issue of TIME has been available on the electronic newsstand of America Online, the fastest-growing of the commercial computer services.' This decision to go online has meant, in turn, that 'our editors, writers and correspondents have been familiarizing themselves with yet another new journalistic venue: the ongoing exchange of real-time computer messages with our readers – friend and foe alike'. This issue of interactivity between the magazine and its readers is similarly addressed by David S. Jackson (1995) elsewhere in the issue. In noting that *Time* was one of 450 publications (mainly magazines and newspapers) that had 'embraced the electronic option' by the end of 1994, he stresses the importance of making journalists an integral part of the online relationship. 'By offering message boards and forums, as well as by posting the E-mail addresses of reporters and editors', publications such as *Time* 'have started an electronic dialogue between journalists and their audiences.' This type of dialogue, he maintains, 'is having a subtle but important effect on both – and, inevitably, on the whole profession of journalism'. As a result, it seems, 'reporters, their sources and their readers find themselves all together in a new environment, in which the much criticized power and distance of the press looks entirely different'.

The realization that the 'information superhighway is a two-way street', where journalists could expect to encounter the viewpoints of their readers on a regular basis, brought with it a growing awareness that traditional rules and conventions were being rapidly rewritten. Slowly but surely, the participants in what would prove to be a lively, and frequently acrimonious, debate over whether 'real journalism' could take place in cyberspace were taking up their places. It is with this in mind that this chapter proceeds to examine several formative instances where the relative advantages and limitations of online news came to the fore when the web was in its infancy; specifically, the reporting of the Oklahoma City bombing, the crash of TWA Flight 800, the Heaven's Gate mass suicide, and the death of Princess Diana. Each of these respective instances will be shown to have contributed – to varying degrees and in different ways – to the rapid growth of a news provision online. At the same time, each instance will also be shown to help pinpoint its emergent ecology as a distinctive medium of journalism, that is, the ways in which the rudimentary conventions of online news underwent a gradual – and contested – process of consolidation.

Breaking news

For many online journalists today, the Oklahoma City bombing of 19 April 1995 continues to be regarded as a tipping point of sorts, namely the moment when the potential of news sites for providing breaking news became readily apparent to advocates and critics alike within journalism's inner circles. It was at 9:02 am that Wednesday morning when a rented truck, packed with some 4800 lbs of explosives, detonated in front of the Alfred P. Murrah Building, a nine-storey concrete office block housing a number of federal government agencies. The resultant blast, it was later claimed, could be felt over 15 miles away. Described by authorities at the time as the worst terrorist attack ever to take place on US soil, the bombing killed 168 people, including 19 children who attended a day-care centre on the second floor, and wounded more than 500 more. Approximately 90 minutes after the explosion, Timothy McVeigh was stopped by the police for driving without a licence plate near the town of Billings. Found to be carrying a concealed weapon, he was promptly arrested. Two days later, just as he was about to be released, he was identified as a bombing suspect. Also that day, Terry Nichols, a friend of McVeigh's, surrendered in Herington, Kansas. He and his brother, James Nichols, were held as material witnesses. Like McVeigh, Terry Nichols would be eventually indicted on 11 counts for the bombing. Both men pled not guilty at separate arraignments in Oklahoma City's federal courthouse in August of that year.

In 1995, a time when news websites were typically little more than repositories of reports previously published elsewhere, the role of the internet in creating spaces for information to circulate that fateful day in April has since been hailed as a landmark moment in online history. Worthy of particular attention was the immediacy of the news coverage, its volume and breadth. Minutes after the bombing, journalists and their editors at online news services were rushing to post whatever information they could about the tragedy. 'Within an hour of the blast', stated Beth Copeland, deputy managing editor at *Newsday Direct*, 'we had a locator map of Oklahoma City, the latest AP [Associated Press] story, [and] a graphic talking about various types of bombs used in terrorist attacks' (cited in Agrawal 1995). Elsewhere on the web, eyewitnesses posted their descriptions of the excavation scene, often with heart-rending details. Others transcribed news reports, especially with regard to the disaster-relief work underway. Listings of survivors, and the hospitals treating them (complete with telephone contact details), similarly began to appear. For people anxious to contact relatives but unable to get through on long-distance telephone lines, some Oklahoma City residents offered to make local calls for them. Discussion forums called 'newsgroups' appeared, where people gave expression to their rage, others to their grief, while still others offered emergency aid for victims. Such was also the case with online chatrooms; several Internet Service Providers (ISPs) opened multiple rooms dedicated to discussions about the bombing. CompuServe's Daphne Kent described the chatrooms she visited as the most emotional she had seen, apparently due to the fact children had been killed and 'it could have happened anywhere' (cited in *USA Today*, 21 April 1995).

As quickly as it could manage, the *Oklahoma City Daily* began to post related stories, as did local television station KFOR, 'where people could query station staff about events and inquire about the station's progress in getting word out to the rest of the broadcast media' (Oakes 1995). ISPs, such as America Online, created repositories devoted to the bombing, making available news feeds from the wire services. Prodigy and AT&T Interchange also offered their members news coverage of ongoing developments (as did CompuServe, although not on the first day). Evidently, within three hours of the explosion, *Newsday Direct* users were able to ask questions of an expert, author and retired Navy Seal Richard Marcinko, on the service's bulletin boards (Agrawal 1995). For many of the newspapers with an online presence, such as *The New York Times* with its @times site or *The Chicago Tribune*'s Chicago Online, it would be near the end of the day before a pertinent story was posted. Few offered much by way of provision for unfolding news events beyond copy taken from the wire services, preferring instead to post the daily's news items once they had been published. News photographs were particularly rare. The site associated with *The San Jose Mercury News*, along with that operated by *Time* magazine, were amongst the very few able to post photographs. ABC News made a video clip available to users of its service on America Online, although it apparently took 11 minutes to download what was a grainy, postage-stamp-sized, 15-second clip, even with the fastest modem connection available (Agrawal 1995). From the next day, the amount of online coverage improved, with some news sites also allowing users to access archived stories on terrorism, militia groups and related topics.

Confusion reigned over who was responsible for the bombing. Many mainstream news organizations, such as CNN, repeated unfounded rumours that 'three men of Middle Eastern extraction' were the prime suspects. Other experts, called upon to conjecture, pointed out that 19 April was the second anniversary of the disastrous assault by Federal agents on the Branch Davidian compound near Waco, Texas, which ended in the death of 80 people (the agency blamed for the ill-fated operation had offices in the destroyed Oklahoma City building). In this whirl of speculation, where claim and counter-claim clashed, people were turning to the internet in numbers never seen before. There too, however, much heat was being generated, with little light. The capacity of the internet to place an astonishing amount of information at users' fingertips was not without its pitfalls. Talk of conspiracies concerning the bombing resounded across the web, especially in the case of sites used by members of right-wing militias, pro-gun groups, neo-Nazis, survivalists and similar conspiratorially inclined organizations. 'To those who've followed the coverage of the Oklahoma City bombing', observed Todd Copilevitz, 'it might seem like the tools of terrorism are teeming across the Net' (*Dallas Morning News*, 7 May 1995). Many analysts and politicians were incensed that technical instructions regarding how to make a copy of the bomb used to destroy the office building, which reportedly used a combination of ammonium nitrate fertilizer and racing fuel, were all too readily available. Was the internet responsible, some wanted to know, for inciting the violence of extremists? 'Fast-spreading computer technology' was being recurrently blamed for allowing disaffected individuals and groups to communicate with one another, and thereby spread their messages of hate. 'In the past, someone who held those views was in isolation, was disenfranchised', argued one commentator in a *Washington Post* article. 'With this technology', he added, 'they can gather. They couldn't even find each other before' (cited in *Washington Post*, 28 April 1995).

Separating out facts from supposition was difficult work. For journalists turning to the web for information, a particularly pressing concern was the need to ascertain whether a given source could be trusted, especially where verification was difficult to establish. 'There is something incredibly seductive about information that shows up on a computer screen', Theresa Grimaldi Olsen (1995) argued in the *Columbia Journalism Review*. As some journalists discovered in the aftermath of the bombing, she observed, 'it can make gullible neophytes out of people who should be professional skeptics'. A case in point revolved around the following message, which appeared on an internet newsgroup (identified as a site used by militia groups) the day after the explosion:

> If this turns out to be a bomb, expect them to tie it to the militia ... I have expected this to come before now. I will lodge a prediction here. They will tie it to Waco, Janet Reno is behind this, the campaign will succeed because the media will persuade the public. Expect a crackdown. Bury your guns and use the codes. (cited in Olsen 1995)

This comment, Olsen contends, was cited as evidence of extremists using the internet in an array of news outlets, such as *Newsday, The Dallas Morning News, USA Today, The Atlanta Journal and Constitution*, the *Huston Chronicle*, and the *Minneapolis Star Tribune*, amongst others. However, it would later be revealed that the posting was a prank, the playful invention of a University of Montana journalism student.

A further hoax occurred two days later, this one concerning McVeigh, who had been arrested and charged with the bombing. This time the claim was that the suspect had posted his personal profile in America Online's membership directory. Subscribers to the service could read a profile describing him as 'Mad Bomber', which stated: 'Let us take back the government ... or die trying. Boom.' Evidently the television programme *Dateline NBC* broke the story, which swiftly spread around the globe. In the UK, for example, the *Sunday Mirror* newspaper's headline declared: HELLO, I'M THE MAD BOMBER ... BOOM!; SICK MESSAGE FLASHED WORLDWIDE; OKLAHOMA BOMB SUSPECT LEAVES MESSAGE ON INTERNET. Later the same day, however, it was revealed that the profile was false; it had actually been created and posted on the service after McVeigh had been arrested. For Scott Rosenberg, all of the 'post-Oklahoma traffic between the on-line world and the news media represents a coming of age for relations between the two realms'. Cyberspace, he argued, was fast becoming a 'real place', one which acted as a 'kind of transnational meeting ground where people talk, rumors spread and news happens, and where reporters need to know the customs and pitfalls, or risk massive goofs' (*San Francisco Examiner*, 30 April 1995). In his view, the Oklahoma story created a type of 'feedback loop' between the news media and the online community, which possessed the potential to be either informative or treacherous depending on the amount of care used by reporters.

Scooping exclusives

In the aftermath of the national crisis engendered by the Oklahoma City bombing, advocates of the internet insisted that it had proved itself to be an indispensable news and information resource. Critics, in sharp contrast, were sceptical about the value of news sites, arguing that they were slow to react, and in the main offered news that was otherwise available in evening newspapers or on television. Others pointed to technical glitches, observing that several of the major news sites had ground to a halt because they were overwhelmed with demand in the early hours, when they would have been especially valuable (*The Seattle Times*, 30 April 1995).

Nevertheless, analyses of internet traffic in the first two weeks after the bombing discerned dramatic increases in the 'hits' registered by online news sites. 'Broadcast is no longer the only medium for breaking news', stated Bruce Siceloff, editor at NandOnet, the online service of *The News and Observer* in Raleigh, North Carolina. 'We didn't have to stop a press to replate', he added. 'There were no deadlines. No readers who lost out because they got an early edition.... Like CNN and radio, we can and did break and update and expand the story on a minute's notice – numerous times in a single hour' (cited in Agrawal 1995). According to Siceloff's figures, the number count of hits for the NandOnet site grew by about 300,000 a week for the first two weeks, reaching 2.37 million hits for the week that ended 30 April. Of particular interest to users, he argued, was the wealth of information from primary sources available online (such as the University of Oklahoma's student newspaper, the White House, relief agencies, pro- and anti-militia groups, and so forth), its instant availability, and also the opportunity to interact (Agrawal 1995).

News coverage of the ensuing judicial proceedings against McVeigh and Nichols was remarkably intense by any standard. Significantly, however, it was the decision taken on Friday, 28 February 1997 by *The Dallas Morning News* to break a major story associated with the ongoing trial of McVeigh on the web, some seven hours before the newspaper went to press for the Saturday edition, that had far-reaching implications for the emergent ecology of online news. Some commentators declared it to be a 'journalistic Bastille

Day', seeing in the decision the sudden liberation of newspapers from the time constraints associated with print, which meant that they were now empowered to break news straight away (Hanson 1997). The *Morning News* story in question contained details of what was claimed to be a jailhouse confession by McVeigh, where he allegedly admitted to his defence team that he had sought to ensure a 'body count' so as to put his political point across to the government. The suspect's lawyer, Stephen Jones, instantly denounced the report as a 'hoax', stating: 'If McVeigh said anything like that to the defense team, I think I would be aware of it' (cited in *Washington Post*, 1 March 1997). In his view, the *Morning News* was 'one of the most irresponsible newspapers in the country', simply intent on building its circulation in Oklahoma. The decision to post the story on the web, he added, was due to the fear that a district judge would issue a temporary injunction against publication. In response, Ralph Langer, the daily's editor, insisted: 'We put the story on the web site because it was, in our view, extraordinarily important and we got the story finished this afternoon and we felt we ought to publish, so we published' (cited in AP, 1 March 1997).

Langer's decision, in the eyes of some, amounted to the *Morning News* site effectively scooping the newspaper. 'Did we scoop ourselves? I don't think so', commented Dale Peskin, the daily's assistant managing editor for new media. 'This is a new age. We're all dealing with new opportunities to tell stories in lots of different ways and get them out there when they're most vital and valuable' (cited in AP, 1 March 1997). Across the media spectrum, journalists weighed in with different interpretations of the decision's significance. For some, the online report was an example of compromised reporting, a charge based on the fear that the media controversy (it was front-page news across the country the next day) would undermine McVeigh's right to a fair trial. As these sorts of anxieties began to fade, however, attention turned to the larger impact of the internet on newspaper publishing. Some participants in the ensuing discussion heralded the posting of the exclusive on the web as a landmark, one representing the crossing of a journalistic Rubicon (*The Guardian*, 4 March 1997). While other newspapers had stepped over similar thresholds by breaking news online before, none had involved such a major story. Within minutes of the posting, AP, CNN and Reuters contacted the *Morning News* in pursuit of further details; within hours, links to the story were appearing on the websites of the *Washington Post*, CNN and MSNBC. According to Peskin, the daily's own site – typically attracting as few as 100 users an hour at that time of day – was accessed by 40,000 visitors between 3:30 pm and 10:00 pm (*The Guardian*, 10 March 1997).

The 'scoop heard around the Internet', as it was aptly described at the time, was credited by some commentators with helping to chip away the rigid boundary separating newspapers from their online counterparts. Some of online journalism's strongest advocates sensed that progress was being made in the struggle for legitimacy. 'Perhaps the historic decision', Jon Katz (1997a) suggested in his *Wired News* column, 'will help to cool the irrational, sometimes bizarre mainstream media portrayal of the digital culture as de-civilizing, sexually degenerate, chaotic, and irresponsible'.

Of fact and fakery

Discussions about the potential of the internet as a news source assumed a far greater salience in journalism's inner circles in the months to follow the Oklahoma City bombing. For those in the newspaper industry, it was becoming increasingly obvious that they would not be able to compete with their electronic rival where breaking news was concerned. This was particularly so at a time of crisis, when people's need for information to provide context to rapidly unfolding events was of paramount importance. 'Information in the form of raw news, opinion, condolence and all else that spews from connected humans when their world goes haywire', Chris Oakes (1995) wrote at the time of the bombing. 'Perhaps more than any Web use, this Internet response to a national tragedy presages what the future of online will be.'

The reliability of the information available online increasingly became a matter of dispute in the months to come, however, particularly with respect to the circumstances surrounding the crash of TWA flight 800. On 17 July 1996, the Boeing 747 airliner, en route from New York to Paris, plunged into the Atlantic Ocean off eastern Long Island. All 230 people on board were killed. Beginning with the breaking news reports, speculation was rife as to who or what might have been responsible for the explosion, which took place about 20 minutes into the flight. A number of eyewitnesses offered their perspectives in these reports, several of whom were convinced that they had seen some type of object or streak of light closing in at high speed on the airliner. Several 'terrorism experts', called upon for their views, were quick to blame Arabs and Muslims for the explosion (echoes of Oklahoma City), contending that a bomb was surely involved (*Chicago Tribune*, 2 January 1997). Others insisted that its cause would likely prove to be due to some sort of mechanical failure or design flaw in the airliner, amongst other technical possibilities. In the ensuing rush to judgement, a number of mainstream journalists recurrently relied on anonymous sources, some of the more far-fetched of which were attributed to the internet. At the same time, however, the internet was also being recognized as an important resource for official inquiries into the crash. In the case of the Federal Bureau of Investigation (FBI), for example, its New York website address was regularly mentioned at press conferences, together with an appeal for help to determine the cause (both an email address and a toll-free telephone number were provided). The site reportedly received more than 1500 pieces of information in the days immediately following the crash, some of which was described as being 'extremely valuable' by a spokesperson (*Courier Mail*, 6 August 1996).

In the days that followed, as speculation about the reason for the crash became ever more intense, something resembling a consensus had begun to emerge across several online newsgroups. The preferred theory was that the TWA 800 had been accidentally shot down by a US navy cruiser engaged in exercises off the coast of Long Island, a tragic case of so-called 'friendly fire'. According to *Sunday Times* reporter James Adams, the theory first appeared in the alt.conspiracy.com newsgroup, from where it was copied and circulated to other newsgroups, such as activism.militia, survivalism.com and impeach.clinton.com. It was further amplified, in turn, by local television news stations, to the point where it began to surface in mainstream news reports around the world. 'Within a week of the crash', Adams wrote, 'the friendly fire story was the hot topic of Washington dinner parties and had already been investigated and dismissed by the Pentagon' (*Sunday Times*, 22 September 1996). The Pentagon's refusal to affirm the theory engendered, not surprisingly, allegations of a government cover-up. One popular explanation for the alleged cover-up 'making the rounds on the Internet', Dennis Duggan reported in *Newsday*, was that 'the plane was targeted because two Arkansas state troopers who were once part of Bill Clinton's security detail were on their way to Paris to tell all about Clinton's extra-curricular affairs to *Le Monde*' (*Newsday*, 24 November 1996). This story, he maintained, was printed in the *Miami Herald*.

For those following the conspiracy claims being made, events took an unexpected turn in November of the same year. Speaking at an aviation conference in Cannes, Pierre Salinger, a former ABC News correspondent (and one-time press secretary to President John F. Kennedy), made a startling announcement. To the astonishment of his audience, he claimed that he was in possession of evidence proving that TWA 800 had been shot down by US forces. His allegation, based on a report which he insisted had been obtained from a French intelligence agent, created a media sensation. Days later, however, Salinger was made to acknowledge what certain internet commentators had been pointing out from the start, namely that the report, with its apparently authoritative details, had been in circulation on the web for several weeks. Crash investigators at the FBI, as well as the National Transportation Safety Board, were scathing in their criticism, with one official from the latter describing the retired Salinger as a 'once-respected journalist' (cited in *Toronto Sun*, 12 November 1996). Much of the mainstream media criticism went beyond Salinger, however, focusing instead on the internet as a platform for delivering spurious information. Newspaper critics were particularly harsh, some contending that facts rarely get in the way of a good conspiracy on the internet.

Television journalists, typically much less troubled by the rise of the internet than their counterparts in the press, were strongly critical as well. 'Forgery, fakery, falsehoods – they're everywhere on the Internet', declared Leslie Stahl of CBS's popular news programme *60 Minutes*, in a story which addressed the alleged 'cover-up' concerning TWA 800. 'And rumors are so rampant', she added, 'that cyberspace is becoming a dangerous place' (transcript, *60 Minutes*, 2 March 1997). Less than a fortnight after the programme was broadcast, Salinger reiterated his allegations at a Paris news conference, this time releasing a 69-page document and radar images to support his contention. Assistant FBI Director James Kallstrom promptly derided the charges. 'It's the big lie', he stated. 'There's no facts. It's based on Internet gossip, hearsay, things that can't be substantiated, [and] faulty analysis' (cited in *Daily News*, 14 March 1997). Shortly afterwards, Maggie Canon, *ComputerLife*'s editor-in-chief, stated that she was one of several journalists who had received – and had decided to ignore – the same 'official military document' which Salinger interpreted as confirmation of his missile theory. 'The nature of the Internet leads people to more readily believe rumors too', she commented. 'The Internet is often viewed by its users as an unfiltered, primary source of information and not to be distrusted like the traditional news media. There is almost an immediate acceptance of information on the Internet.' This when in actuality, she argued, 'there are far more lies, rumors and hoaxes transmitted on the Internet than anywhere else' (cited in *PR Newswire*, 18 March 1997).

Nevertheless, the value of the internet was underscored by Ford Fessenden, a *Newsday* (Long Island) journalist, who won the Pulitzer Prize for his reporting of the crash. The newspaper's coverage, he observed, 'owes a deep debt to the technology of computer assisted reporting'. Describing his methods, he explained that 'hourly consultation of the Internet and daily querying of safety databases became routine' in the course of investigating the story. 'Computer-assisted reporting has the ability to transform public understanding of aviation safety' (cited in *The Guardian*, 10 July 1997). Reporters like Fessenden, although still very much in the minority, were making inroads in the struggle to change perceptions of this medium and its potential.

Immediacy, depth, interactivity

Notions such as 'new media', and with it 'computer-assisted reporting', were slowly becoming a part of the journalistic lexicon. For every journalist heralding the promise of new technological possibilities, though, there were likely to be several more calling for restraint to be exercised. Speaking on a CNN broadcast in December of 1996, *Washington Post* media columnist Howard Kurtz had argued:

...the thing we shouldn't lose sight of here is that, for a lot people this is still a toy. They surf around, they check out what's there. Nobody has made money on it yet. But the reason that all these big news organizations, including mine, are investing in going onto the net, is because of the feeling that in three or four or five years when you can get video and when it really becomes faster and more reliable, that this will be a more [serious] news player. (transcript, CNN 'Reliable Sources', 1 December 1996)

As the Salinger controversy waned, the situation appeared to be improving, but not nearly fast enough in the eyes of some advocates of online journalism. Katz (1997a), commenting in his *Wired News* opinion column, remarked that more than '700 newspapers have dumped their static, stale content online, to little effect. With a handful of exceptions – the *San Jose Mercury News*, *The Wall Street Journal* – papers' use of the Web as a news medium has been dull, expensive and counterproductive.' Old media, he argued, must embrace the changes created by new media, especially where the latter enable journalists to break the news first. 'Newspapers', he wrote, 'have clung beyond all reason to a pretense that they are still in the breaking news business they dominated for so long, even though most breaking stories are seen live on TV or mentioned online hours, sometimes days, before they appear on newspaper front pages.' To reverse their decline, one commentator after the next was contending, newspapers would have to recognize the speed-driven imperatives of the internet. Merrill Brown, editor-in-chief of the all-news network MSNBC (set up the year before), echoed this point, arguing that a key objective of Microsoft and NBC's joint venture was 'to break stories with frequency on the Internet' (cited in AFP, 5 March 1997).

Later that same month, a shocking incident took place that further pinpointed certain unique qualities that online journalism could contribute to the coverage of breaking news. The Heaven's Gate mass suicide, as it was promptly dubbed at the time, transpired over several days in an affluent neighbourhood in Rancho Sante Fe, near San Diego, California. The police arrived on the scene on 26 March, having been contacted by a fallen member of the Heaven's Gate cult who had received a videotape from its members. The cult's leader, along with 38 members, had taken their own lives by consuming applesauce pudding laced with phenobarbital, followed by vodka. Evidently it was their fervent belief that the passing of the Hale-Bopp comet was to be interpreted as a sign indicating that they were to leave behind their earthly bodies ('containers') and board a spacecraft travelling in the comet's wake. News of the suicide created an instant media sensation. Amongst the online news sites, the *Washington Post*'s helped lead the way. 'When this story broke at 8:00', recalled Jason Seiken, editor at the time of washingtonpost.com, 'we put it up immediately. Any time there was any sort of update, that went up immediately' (transcript, National Public Radio, 3 April 1997).

This immediacy, in Seiken's view, was one of three important advantages the site had over its press and television rivals. The second advantage was the capacity for greater depth in online reporting. 'There's really no limit on what you can put on a web site', he argued. 'So, whereas when publishing *The Washington Post*, we have to be very cognizant of how many pages we put out, when we're publishing washingtonpost.com, well, we currently have more than 40,000 pages.' In the case of the Heaven's Gate story, when it became apparent that the cult's own site was being overwhelmed with online traffic, Seiken made its contents (including a book they had written and transcripts of their videos) available for washingtonpost.com users from a copy derived from an America Online cache. This strategy allowed users to see for themselves what the cult members believed in their own words, as opposed to having to rely upon a journalist's interpretative summary. Seiken also arranged to have a timeline created. Interspersed throughout the descriptions of the different periods in the cult's history were links to members' primary source documents. Previous articles by *Washington Post* journalists were also made available so as to help contextualize events. A third advantage identified by Seiken was the capacity of online media for interactivity. 'We were able to find one of the world's foremost UFO experts and actually put him online and have him answer questions from our readers', he commented. This strategy, commonplace today, was novel at the time. When asked whether he could anticipate a future where online news would be better placed to cover breaking news than traditional news organizations, he replied: 'As the web becomes really interwoven into the fabric of more and more people's lives, it's just common sense that that's going to happen.'

Public interest in the Heaven's Gate suicides was so intense that media attention did not subside for quite some time. Weighing into the ensuing discussions about the significance of the events were those who felt they needed to be understood, at least in part, in relation to the growing influence of the internet on public life. Much had been made in news reports about the fact that the group was supported in the main by money earned by members who were professional webpage designers. Once again, Katz (1997b) was quick to offer pertinent insights:

> Wherever these people really went when they died, they left us with the first Web tragedy. For the first time, the dead are very definitely us, not them. Their lives, work, beliefs, and passing are woven into the machinery of the digital culture, already part of our archives and history. This wasn't some remote cult hidden away in some faraway jungle, to kill and die in private. Their messages, fingerprints, voices, and handiwork are ineluctably available on the World Wide Web,

easily and instantly accessible, a couple of clicks away on any browser. Web sites from Pathfinder to Yahoo! to Wired News threw up links, dug out postings, reproduced Web sites and pages within minutes; a medium within a medium, covering the destruction of part of itself. (Katz 1997b)

Adopting sharply contrasting positions, however, were other commentators already predisposed to regard the internet as posing an inherent danger to society. Many sought to characterize the Heaven's Gate members' involvement with the internet as evidence to support their criticisms. The web, they argued, was a recruiting ground for cultists. Young people, in particular, were at risk of being 'brainwashed' in their view, hence their demands for controls to be imposed over the type of information allowed to circulate on the web. Much of this criticism echoed emergent campaigns against the availability of pornography online, a growing threat to morality in the eyes of some.

Above dispute, however, was the role online news sites had played in making available resources to help contextualize the news story, thereby bringing to light dimensions otherwise not being addressed by their print and television rivals. Still, searching questions continued to be raised about the credibility of the new medium in journalistic terms. Would the primary role for online news sites be an ancillary one, that is, mainly to provide background information to supplement the reporting undertaken by these rival media? Or, alternatively, would these sites contribute to the elaboration of a different type of journalism altogether?

Confirming authenticity

Ongoing debates about these and related questions, not least regarding the relative quality of the information circulating on the web, took an unexpected twist in the aftermath of the news that Diana, the Princess of Wales, had been killed in a car crash in Paris. She died along with her lover, Dodi Al Fayed, and their chauffeur (a fourth person in the car, a bodyguard, was seriously injured). The story broke in the early hours of 31 August 1997, with online journalists scrambling to post whatever information they could gather. Matt Drudge of the online *Drudge Report* would later claim to have been the first to break the news to US audiences (transcript, National Press Club Luncheon, 2 June 1998). In any case, the BBC's fledgling online news site, as well as that of *The New York Times*, ABCNews.com, CNN.com and Yahoo!'s Current Events, amongst others, rapidly posted stories after television reports announced the initial details. Even before Diana's death had been officially announced at a news conference at Paris's Hospital de la Pitie Salpetriere, online news coverage encompassed the globe.

Just as television news has long been considered to have had its legiti-macy confirmed by the coverage of US President John F. Kennedy's assassi-nation and funeral in 1963, some felt that a parallel of sorts could be drawn with the online reporting of Princess Diana's demise. For those looking for updates on breaking developments, yet impatient with the repetitive cycles of television news, once again the web came into its own (CNN.com apparently attracted some 4.3 million page views on the Sunday, an extraordinary figure for the time: see *CNET News*, 2 September 1997). Some news sites made available links to audio and video files, as well as to related websites, such as those of the charities with which she was involved. Timelines were widely used, as were story archives and bulletin boards. 'Perhaps the key benefit of the Net as a news-delivery mechanism', observed Bruce Simpson at the time, 'is the way that users can do their own research and scan huge amounts of information [in] such a short space of time – while users of other media are "spoon-fed" whatever the news-editors feel appropriate' (*Aardvark News*, 1 September 1997). This capacity to enable users to pursue their own paths of enquiry was underscored by the extent to which other media focused, almost exclusively for hours on end in the case of some television networks, on the officially sanctioned details of the Diana story. Much of the television re-porting adopted a reverent, even deferential tone, with newsreaders serving as the 'mourners in chief', as described by *The New York Times* television critic.

In contrast, certain voices on the web were posing awkward questions, and in so doing raising difficult issues. 'I welcome the opportunity to be franker and quicker in this medium', Andrew Ross, managing editor of *Salon*, remarked. 'The traditional media felt the need to be more stately and official and to parrot conventional wisdom' (cited in *CNET News*, 2 September 1997). Elsewhere on the web, users went online to express their viewpoints in a collective response widely described, as noted in *The Sunday Times* a week later, as an 'unprecedented electronic outpouring of grief'. Heartfelt memorial pages appeared, allowing mourners to pay their respects, share their mem-ories, and offer condolences. Similar sentiments were expressed across hun-dreds of chatrooms and discussion forums. At the same time, debates raged over topics such as the possible implications for the monarchy's future status, whether a boycott of the tabloid press should be organized, and the conduct of the paparazzi in the events surrounding the high-speed crash. In the case of *Newsweek Interactive*'s 'My Turn Online', for example, one day's topic was: 'Princess Di vs. the Press. Princess Diana's car crash apparently happened as she was trying to elude news photographers. Did the press kill her? Did we, its readers?' (cited in *Modesto Bee*, 9 September 1997). Meanwhile, proponents of contending conspiracy theories posed their 'unanswered questions' on dif-ferent newsgroups (e.g., alt.conspiracy.princess-diana), seeing in the crash sufficient grounds to suspect foul play.

Interestingly, from the very outset of the online coverage, various commentators were predicting that photographs of the accident scene would find their way on to the web. The Paris police had moved quickly to try to confiscate the film shot by the paparazzi (one of whom was beaten by angry witnesses at the scene), and a number of newspapers made it clear to their readers that they would refuse to pay for images depicting the accident's victims. Still, there seemed to be little doubt that a story of this magnitude would generate photographs online before too long. 'The 'Net always contains the most scandalous, dubious and exploitative information you might possibly want or stumble into', commented 'Web expert' J.C. Herz at the time. 'There's no mechanism for suppression of information on the Internet, and while that's part of the beauty of the medium, [it is] also the downside' (cited in *Network World*, 8 September 1997). Less than a week after these remarks were made, a photograph ostensibly depicting Diana in the crashed Mercedes surfaced on the web. Specifically, the image appeared on a site providing 'an archive of disturbing illustration' operated by an anti-censorship group called Rotten Dot Com. Based in California, the group claimed to have received it via an email from an undisclosed source (no credit line for the photograph was provided). While the image shows the aftermath of a very serious car accident, it was unclear whether the bloodied, blonde-haired woman trapped in the twisted steel was actually Diana. The group's own stance was ambiguous at first, neither confirming nor denying the photograph's authenticity. The image was posted, the homepage stated, 'for political reasons, to make people think, and to make them upset'. If indeed this was the group's intention, it succeeded. The number of visitors to the site – many of whom responded with emails expressing their outrage – was such that the available bandwidth was insufficient, forcing the group to remove the image so as to allow the site to continue to operate.

'Group posts picture purporting to show dying princess' was the Agence France-Presse (AFP) headline for the wire service story that broke the news. The Italian news agency ANSA, along with several newspapers, including the Paris daily *France-Soir*, also put the unverified photograph into public circulation. Various news sites promptly linked to the Rotten Dot Com site, although in at least one instance the pertinent ISP proceeded to delete the image in response to what was fast becoming an ethical controversy over the relative appropriateness of its use (*CNET News*, 18 September 1997). Within 24 hours, French authorities were being quoted in news reports as stating that the photograph was indeed a fake. Certain inconsistencies were identified, including the fact that the rescue workers depicted were not wearing French emergency service uniforms, nor were the emergency telephone numbers on their equipment the correct ones for France (999 being the British emergency code). A number of embarrassed newspaper journalists, not surprisingly, placed the blame for the hoax directly on the internet. The editor-in-chief of *France-Soir*, Claude Lambert, told Amy Harmon of *The New York Times*:

Not very adroitly, perhaps, we did it to put a spotlight on the excesses of the Internet [. . .] There were heated arguments about the decision in the office on Friday, and not everybody on the staff agrees we executed it properly. Maybe the headline should have said 'Diana, the Phony Internet Photo,' but we still would have gone ahead and published it. (cited in *The New York Times*, 22 September 1997)

If the incident was a test of the internet's credibility as a news source, as some said, then in the eyes of many it had failed. While examples of photographic hoaxes abound in journalism's history, the capacity of internet users to disseminate misleading material so far and so quickly deeply troubled some critics. For Harmon, the controversy surrounding the Diana photograph 'underscores the public's apparent eagerness to give the Internet's indiscriminate electronic press the benefit of the doubt. Or at least its tolerance for the often sensational appeal of material it carries.' In other words, one might be tempted to reply, much like the public response to the mainstream media.

A further criticism of the proliferation of rumours in cyberspace featured in a televized speech made by respected BBC News foreign correspondent Fergal Keane in October of that year. Delivering the Huw Weldon Memorial Lecture to the Royal Television Society, he argued that the fundamental obligation of the reporter is to the truth (broadcast on BBC1, 20 October 1997). Pointing to the 'hundreds of conspiracy theories floating around about the death of Diana', he expressed his concern that 'calm and considered reportage' was at serious risk of losing out to 'the sensational and the spectacular', especially where 'the generation growing up on a diet of the X-Files' was concerned. At issue, he feared, was a 'dangerous retreat from rationality', whereby 'truth-telling' that is 'artful, fearless and intelligent' all but disappears into the swirl of 'trivia, gossip and celebration of the banal'. Growing technological pressures – compounded by those from the market – must be resisted, he reasoned, in order to better protect the interests of truth. 'I am worried about the potential of the internet to devalue the role of the reporter', Keane revealed, before wondering aloud about what the future might portend. 'What a pity', he mused, 'if technology, far from pushing us into another age of enlightenment, was to return us to the rumour-ridden gloom of the Middle Ages'.

3 Brave new media worlds: BBC News Online, the Drudge Report, and the birth of blogging

Played out across the media around the world, the trial of 19-year-old British nanny Louise Woodward in Cambridge, Massachusetts was sensational by any measure. Matthew Eappen, an 8-month-old child in her care, had died on 10 February 1997. The prosecution alleged that Woodward had shaken him in a fit of temper, causing a head wound and fatal brain injuries. Woodward protested her innocence, insisting that she had never used excessive force. The medical evidence was inconclusive, which meant that much of the ensuing trial revolved around perceptions of the relative credibility of her testimony. On 30 October of that year she was found guilty of second degree murder by the jury. During the sentencing hearing the next morning, Woodward – still maintaining her innocence – was told that she faced a mandatory sentence of life imprisonment (with the possibility of parole in 15 years). Attention then turned to Judge Hiller Zobel, who under Massachusetts law possessed the power to overturn the verdict, or to reduce the charge to manslaughter, in the event that he believed the conviction should not be upheld. What happened next astonished everyone. 'The judge in the Louise Woodward trail stunned the world last night', *The Mirror* newspaper declared, 'by deciding to reveal her fate only on the Internet' (*The Mirror*, 5 November 1997).

In what was widely proclaimed to be an unprecedented move for a criminal judgement, Judge Zobel informed the trial's participants that he would post his ruling on the website of a law magazine titled *Lawyers Weekly*. Critics wasted little time in condemning the decision, branding it a cheap ploy to attract even greater publicity for the trial (one Labour MP called the move an 'astonishing gimmick'). Some went even further, labelling the judge an 'Internut', and making much of the apparent fact that he did not own a television set. Comments from those close to Woodward similarly received widespread attention in the press. 'This is a disgrace. I wanted to see his face as he announced his decision', said one friend to reporters in the nanny's hometown of Elton, England. 'What kind of a legal system allows a judge to tap his verdict onto a computer screen and press the button?' (cited in *Daily*

News, 5 November 1997). Others, in sharp contrast, discerned in the decision a desire to circulate the judgement to the world's media in a manner that was both fair and inexpensive. 'This makes perfect sense given that we have the kind of sophisticated technology we have today', observed a technology columnist for *The New York Times*. 'Why shouldn't he put the information directly in the hands of people today?' (cited in AP, 4 November 1997). Free speech advocates interpreted it as a step forward in democratizing the legal system, pointing out that anyone with internet access would be able to read the document for themselves, and thereby make up their own minds about its significance. In the meantime, Woodward faced an agonizing wait – possibly for as long as 60 days – to learn what the judge's verdict would be.

Plans to restrict the release of Zobel's ruling to the chosen website – *Lawyers Weekly* – were promptly abandoned when it experienced a 'massive overload' following the initial publication of its address. A further 25 sites were added to help cope with the anticipated demand. Moreover, in light of concerns about fakery, it was agreed that the Massachusetts Superior Court would contact legal organizations and news sites in advance of the verdict so as to alert them that a genuine email was about to be sent. Here it is significant to note the extent to which the internet had already figured in the case from the outset. As the proceedings got underway, the judge had extended the customary instruction to the jury to avoid news reports of the trial (lest their impartiality be compromised) by forbidding them to surf the internet as well. 'May I stress that the Internet is now a medium of communication', he stated, 'and that you may not draw information from there, either' (cited in *Daily News*, 10 November 1997). Campaigners for the defence and, to a lesser extent, the prosecution had already mobilized to stake their claim in cyberspace, and to draw attention to what they considered to be the important issues. More than 200 'Free Louise' pages were operated by supporters, several with email addresses to send messages, online petitions to sign, links to make financial donations, and details about where protests were being held, amongst other features. An electronic yellow ribbon picture was made available for people to download and distribute, as were clips from Court TV Online (the phenomenon of television cameras in the courtroom, then as now, all but unheard of in Britain). Message boards, chatrooms and discussion groups, provided by services such as Usenet, Prodigy and America Online, created forums for people to share their views – which they did in the thousands with remarkable passion and insight (see Senft 2000).

Opinions about the news reporting of the unfolding trial were hotly contested, not surprisingly. A considerable number of websites (official and otherwise) had appeared in order to provide commentary on the daily coverage, as well as to make available various background resources – such as timelines, biographical details about the participants, overviews of the legal and medical issues (such as 'Shaken Baby Syndrome') involved, and so forth.

Major news organizations were rapidly recognizing the significance of sustaining an internet presence. A small number of television stations made video items accessible online, albeit more with an eye to principle than practice given that download speeds were likely to engender considerable frustration for most users. Some newspapers – such as the *Boston Globe* – posted stories and links to previous ones in its archive. At each turn, news organizations were answering questions such as: 'What is the Internet?' for their audiences, taking care to explain the attendant terminology to the uninitiated (still assumed to be the majority of readers at the time).

Brian MacArthur, writing in *The Times*, sought to consider the apparent implications for the press. National newspaper editors, he pointed out, had regarded the guilty verdict to be the most significant news story for over a week. 'Viewed from an editor's chair,' he wrote, 'it was a human interest story of sensational proportions.' More than the back and forth of the murder case itself was the fact that it revolved around a 'British woman at bay in an American courtroom and a suspicion that she was found guilty simply because she was British'. The intense interest generated by the case could similarly be linked, in his view, to the anxieties nagging 'the conscience of every working man and woman who places their children in the care of a nanny, au pair or childminder'. Nevertheless, of particular concern to MacArthur was what coverage of the trial signalled for the future of newspapers:

> [W]hat we have witnessed in the past week (as we did in the week after the death of Diana, Princess of Wales) is a global news story in which newspapers are not [...] the primary source of news.
>
> The trial in Cambridge, Massachusetts, was broadcast live on British television, and the jury's verdict was reported on radio, television and the Internet hours before it was published in the newspapers. The news itself is now happening on the Internet and on television, with newspapers following behind.
>
> It is in this threatening environment – in which the villagers of Elton, Cheshire, speak directly to Cambridge, Massachusetts, without any intervention from Fleet Street, the *Liverpool Echo* or the *Ellesmere Port Pioneer* – that editors must now fight for the survival of newspapers into the next millennium. (*The Times*, 7 November 1997)

In MacArthur's view, the viability of newspapers in 'the new media world' will be threatened unless they can continue to attract and retain their readers in the face of the rising competition from broadcasting and the internet. In this way, the trial was throwing into sharp relief difficult questions about the 'new role of newspapers within the emerging news environment' deserving of close attention.

Woodward's wait for the verdict ended on the morning of 10 November, when Judge Zobel ordered that her sentence be reduced to involuntary manslaughter. In seeking a 'compassionate conclusion' to the case, he maintained that she had not acted in malice in his view. His ruling that she serve 279 days in prison – the same amount of time she had already spent in custody – meant that she was promptly set free (although forced to remain in the state pending a possible appeal). The keenly anticipated 'Internet milestone' was not to be, however, due to an electric power outage in Brookline, Massachusetts that brought the email server used by the court to a halt. US television newscasts, some of which were drawing on apparent leaks from court staff, broke the news before anything could be posted to the web. The ABC, CBS and NBC networks each interrupted their normal programming to report the verdict. Shortly thereafter, several of the major news sites were 'gridlocked' by demand – a less than auspicious moment for online news reporting. Meanwhile, others in the press were expressing their reservations about the growing influence of the internet on public perceptions of justice. 'Now that the Internet has entered fully into judicial territory,' Edward Rothstein wrote in *The New York Times*, 'some will praise its virtues: helping to create a broadly informed public, eliminating privilege and secrecy, and opening up new forums for self-expression and influence – all of which are partly true.' Nevertheless, he cautioned, 'the Internet is also expanding an already enormous range of social institutions whose very purpose is to second guess, disagree, rant, express and dissent'. Alarmed by what he feared might happen to 'reasoned argument' in the face of the controversy and disagreement spread by the internet ('the Internet abhors consensus'), he made apparent his concern that nothing short of the judicial system's 'controlled consensus based on fact' was at risk (*The New York Times*, 24 November 1997).

From the vantage point of today, there can be little doubt that the Woodward case signalled a profound shift was underway with regard to the changing nature of journalism in a digital age. What consequences were being set in motion would soon become apparent.

The launch of BBC News Online

For anyone casting their eye over the list of websites chosen to break the news of Zobel's judgment, there were few surprises. Virtually all of them were based in the US, with the three exceptions being British – the first two were the news agency sites of the Press Association and Reuters, respectively. The third site, however, may have raised eyebrows. It belonged to the new BBC News Online service officially launched on 4 November 1997, a week before the judge's announcement that he would be issuing his decision on the internet.

BBC News Online represented a significant initiative within the Corporation's strategy to reaffirm its public service ethos in a multi-channel universe, and thereby be better placed to challenge commercial rivals such as CNN, MSNBC, EuroNews, and News Corp. 'We are this autumn only at the starting block', stated Tony Hall, chief executive of BBC News, the day before the launch. 'My ambition is, first, to ensure that we preserve and build a public service in news for the next generation. And, second, to ensure that BBC News develops as a global player' (cited in *The Guardian*, 3 November 1997). Widely perceived to be late on to the scene, arriving long after both British and international competitors had established their online presence, the initiative nevertheless represented a bold move. 'Our basic aim is to extend our public service remit on to the Web', Bob Eggington, the director of project, said at the time. 'The design is simple and it is easy to use.' The decision to proceed was justified, in his view, 'because that's where young people are going [.] We have to be there because the Web audience is increasing by 10 per cent every month' (cited in *The Times*, 5 November 1997). Much of the press commentary was focused elsewhere, however, namely on the other initiatives being unveiled around the same time. Easily the most significant of these was the Corporation's 24-hour rolling news channel, BBC News 24, which went to air with considerable fanfare the following week. Where the online commitment was generally regarded as being overdue, this venture invited a far more sceptical response. In the words of Damian Whitworth writing in *The Times*, 'dear old Auntie, always regarded as a little dotty, appears to have gone completely bats. As she celebrates her 75th birthday, she has suddenly decided to embark on some new adventures. The question is: is she up to it?' (*The Times*, 7 November 1997).

Not surprisingly, this question was answered rather emphatically in the affirmative by senior managers in the Corporation. 'This has been the most significant month in the history of BBC News', Hall declared at the BBC News Online launch (cited in *European Media Business and Finance*, 17 November 1997). 'BBC News Online will, for the first time, put the entire wealth of BBC journalism at your fingertips', he maintained. 'You will get the news you want and the news you need 24 hours a day' (cited in *Electronic Media*, 17 November 1997). Earlier in the year, Hall had highlighted key aspects of the rationale to transform the news-gathering operation in a presentation at a Freedom Forum conference in London. Journalism was in danger of becoming too parochial, he argued, not least because of the way budget-cuts were undermining international news coverage. 'At a time when most of our futures are decided globally, the readership of our newspapers and the audience of our broadcast programmes appear to be less interested in the world. And journalism, in response, seems less interested, more introspective too.' The growth of the internet was significant as a counter-measure of sorts, but brought with it further concerns. 'There is an awful lot which is flimflam, half-truths, speculation, and it may mislead', he maintained, before proceeding to make the case for the BBC's distinctive approach. 'Information without understanding is worthless. Because we are in the midst of an information revolution we are deluded into believing that we understand the world better than before. We don't', he insisted. 'What I think is happening is an "understanding gap" [and this] gap will grow unless it is checked by a journalism committed to making sense of the world' (cited in *The Guardian*, 30 May 1997). It is precisely this commitment, he suggested, that would characterize the new initiatives underway at the Corporation as it actively sought to recast what would count as quality journalism, including its development in an online environment.

At the time of BBC News Online's launch, the restructuring of the Corporation's news-gathering division meant that some commentators were wondering aloud whether diminished resources were being spread too thinly. Free of advertising, the site's financial costs were financed almost entirely by the licence fee (then an annual sum of £91 per household). An estimated £21 million was set aside to support the BBC's online activity overall, with about £3.5 million devoted directly to BBC News Online in its first year. Critics were quick to point out that because many users of the site were situated outside the UK, they were in effect being subsidized by British users. In the eyes of some, this represented a departure from the BBC's original mission. Others felt that the monies would be better spent on broadcast programming, in keeping with the interests of the majority. Universality, an organizing tenet of the public service tradition, could only be applied to a small minority. About 4 million people in the country enjoyed access to the internet, although the rate of growth was widely projected to be about 100 per cent per year. Other critics were more concerned about the possible impact of this level of investment on commercial alternatives – especially at the local level – struggling to find a viable business model. In response, BBC spokespersons affirmed that the Corporation was dedicated to making the internet accessible to members of the public, and to equipping them with the skills necessary to use it effectively (its web tutor for beginners was called BBC Web Wise). The site also pointed users to other sites outside of the BBC, thereby enhancing their profile.

The BBC, then as now one of the largest news-gathering organizations in the world, managed 42 foreign bureaus and 13 more around Britain generating around the clock coverage (the annual news budget totalled approximately £300 million). Where rival sites – both television and newspaper-based – typically relied on copy from the wire services to provide breaking news, BBC News Online could draw on the expertise of over 2000 members of staff and 250 correspondents across the globe. The online news team was composed of some 40 journalists, in addition to technical staff and graphic designers preparing news stories on the basis of reports provided by these correspondents. Staff members joined the site from other divisions within the BBC, as well as from other news sites outside the Corporation. 'It is easier to teach old media journalists new tools than to teach techies journalism', ob-served one of the site's reporters (cited in Perrone 1998). Daily editions of the *Nine O'Clock News* were made available in Real Video Format, together with hourly audio bulletins from the BBC World Service using a RealAudio player. News items were also presented in languages other than English, including Arabic, Cantonese, German, Mandarin, Russian and Spanish, and archived editions made accessible. A range of experiments were conducted to de-termine how best to present and package stories, a sense of standard practice being the subject of daily renegotiation. It was decided at the beta-stage, for example, to avoid flashy, resource-intensive graphics so as to facilitate downloading. Given that the new site was judged to have received about one million hits on its first day, this precaution quickly proved sensible.

Described within the BBC as 'the third broadcast medium', BBC News Online was charged with the responsibility of helping to take the 'core values' of the Corporation's 'brand' forward into the digital era. 'The BBC reinvented itself once, when television was invented, and now we feel we have got to do it again', stated Edward Briffa, the controller of Online and Interactive for BBC. 'It is not that radio and television are going to diminish, but it is that people's time is going to be taken up, in increasing amounts, with this third opportunity' (cited in *The Scotsman*, 17 December 1997). Important here was the need to demonstrate how it could forge a new relationship with licence-fee payers. 'It's very exciting indeed', BBC News Online editor Mike Smartt remarked shortly after the launch. 'This medium is now our third broadcast service alongside radio and TV, and we believe it could take over as the main way people receive BBC journalism in the UK and around the world' (cited in *PR Week*, 21 November 1997). Smartt, who years earlier had travelled to CNN and ABC's online newsrooms to gain insights into how best to set up BBC News Online, recognized the synergies to be gained by close collaboration with a television counterpart. Online staff worked closely with colleagues from BBC News 24 to collect material, especially picture stills as well as audio and video clips. Journalists – in contrast with those at some of the major US sites – were expected to be multi-skilled, that is, to package their stories up to and including the post-production stage, in addition to writing copy in the first place. As conventions gradually evolved through the trialling of ideas – new and borrowed ones alike – efforts were similarly made to incorporate feedback from users via devices such as online questionnaires to help shape form and practice. 'We don't have a set of rules because we're learning as we go along', Smartt commented. 'I don't think anybody in the business knows precisely how to do this' (cited in Perrone 1998).

By early 1998, BBC Online had been confirmed as the leading British internet content site, with BBC News Online recording 8.17 million page impressions in March according to the Audit Bureau of Circulations (BBC Online overall recorded some 21 million page impressions from direct requests by over 900,000 users that month). Considered to be a 'strong driver of traffic', the news site was fast gaining a reputation for its immediacy – where the deadline is 'always now' – and the depth of its coverage. Interestingly, one of the first exclusives achieved by the site occurred when a Massachusetts police officer who arrested Louise Woodward and testified at her trial accused her of 'absolute child abuse' in an email to the 'Talking Point' section of the site. Specifically, Detective Sergeant William Byrne, who felt he could no longer resist expressing his feelings, wrote:

> Why is it so hard for many people to realise that this is absolute child abuse? It happens every day here in America and in England. If this girl [Woodward] was a big, unattractive woman with no teeth and tattoos, would the public have had a different opinion as to whether or not she was guilty? (cited in *The Times*, 23 June 1998)

BBC journalists confirmed his identity with the police department before posting the email, which promptly sparked widespread attention in the press. To some extent, this scoop helped to overshadow the fact that shortly after Judge Zobel had announced that he would be posting his verdict on the web, the fledgling site was rendered inoperable by the sheer volume of interested users trying to access it.

By June that year, BBC Online offered over 140,000 pages of content, some 61,000 of which consisted of news. Considered a great achievement by most commentators – and begrudgingly acknowledged as the leader in the field by rivals – its growing provision steadily improved, albeit not without the occasional instance of technical teething problems. 'We have found that [producing online content] is not as simple as we thought', Dave Brewer, managing editor for the site, observed. 'The Web audience is sophisticated and will not stand for a simple reversioning of what was put on the TV or radio. We needed to learn to write for the Web and that meant starting from scratch' (cited in *The Australian*, 1 September 1998). This commitment to thinking afresh clearly played a significant role in defining the site's distinctive approach to public service, as well as the cultural authority of the journalism it sought to embody.

Drudge's dredging

To the extent that BBC News Online represents one end of the journalistic spectrum where web-based reporting is concerned, then it is reasonable to suggest that the Drudge Report represents the other end. Likening himself to a Walter Winchell of the internet era, Matt Drudge's website has been variously characterized as an 'online gossip rag', 'a newsmaker's tip sheet', 'a daily bulletin of rumor and oddball news' or 'a strange brew of media, political and showbiz tidbits', amongst other, more colourful descriptions.

No stranger to controversy, Drudge himself has courted press attention for his personal brand of reporting since February 1995. Years before, having in his words 'barely' graduated from high school, he had travelled from Takoma Park, Maryland, across the country to Los Angeles, where eventually he secured a job at CBS Television, first as a runner and later in the gift shop in Studio City. There he occasionally heard 'little morsels of studio rumors' which he promptly circulated via email to various internet newsgroups. Over seven years he became manager of the shop, by which time he had saved enough money – and established a sufficiently robust network of contacts – to quit and devote his energies to the Drudge Report on a full-time basis. Working from his apartment near Hollywood and Vine, he rapidly established an online following for his postings, despite making no pretence of being a journalist. Described in a newspaper profile as a 'cheerful 29-year-old, looking out of place on the Boulevard of Broken Dreams', he explained how the site operated. 'I use a beat-up Packard Bell 486 desktop running Windows 3.1, with a 28.8 modem. And Netscape Navigator 1.1. I keep going back to earlier versions because they're easier to use.' In the same interview, he expresses his surprise about the growing interest in his site generated by the mainstream media. 'Here I am, I write this thing out in my boxer shorts with my cat, as if I'm passing notes in high school', he stated. Then, suddenly, 'I'm getting mentioned on Rush Limbaugh's radio show – that's 20 million listeners – and the *New York Times* are giving out my address too' (cited in *The Independent*, 29 July 1996). Some of the members of his email distribution list paid the voluntary $10 subscription fee, but those who refused nevertheless enjoyed equal access to it and the webpage version – Drudge being well aware from the outset of the value of interconnectivity across the web.

The Drudge Report site consists primarily of electronic links to other news sites, interspersed with occasional items or 'flashes' written by Drudge himself 'when circumstances warrant'. Several scoops were widely credited to it in its early days, including leaked details about the cast of television show Seinfeld's salary negotiations, the plotline of a forthcoming Hollywood film, the firing of newscaster Connie Chung from CBS News, and the choice of Jack Kemp as Republican Bob Dole's running mate in the 1996 presidential election, amongst others. At the same time, certain trumpeted exclusives were removed when they turned out to be false, and not always before they had been picked up by major news organizations. 'Sometimes I'll turn on CNN and they'll say "a source is saying," and it's me. And it's some piece of junk', Drudge commented. 'That bugs the hell out of me' (cited in *Washington Post*, 19 May 1997). Most of the site's information is derived from his near-constant monitoring of other internet sites, wire services, newspapers (especially those available online in the middle of the night), television newscasts and talk radio. Readers themselves, some of whom have proven to be surprisingly well placed in the corridors of power, are frequently forthcoming with emails containing hot tips, story leads or comments. 'It's about the whole new medium of no editor, no expense and mass distribution across international borders', he remarked. 'I do it all for the price of one phone call' (cited in *The Observer*, 10 August 1997).

Drudge has made no secret of his conservative politics, nor of his resolute determination to cause trouble for the Democratic Party whenever possible. A severe critic of then President Bill Clinton, he seized upon any sliver of innuendo with even a hint of scandal and promptly posted it. For *Newsweek* magazine reporter Michael Isikoff, this meant that certain elements of an investigative story he was pursuing – concerning the allegation that Clinton may have made an improper sexual advance to former White House aide Kathleen Willey – appeared on the Drudge Report site weeks before a proper determination had been made regarding their validity. Drudge went with whatever he received from his anonymous source, making no independent effort to confirm its accuracy, nor demonstrating concern for Willey, whom he identified by name in the process. 'He's rifling through raw reporting, like raw FBI files, and disseminating it', Isikoff complained. 'He doesn't conform to any journalistic standard.' Moreover, he added, this 'is not harmless fun; it's reckless and ought to be condemned. He ought not to be treated as an impish character. It's hard to do real reporting in an atmosphere that's been polluted like this.' For his part, Drudge refused to concede that any damage was being done. Isikoff 'has a right to be furious', he acknowledged, 'but life's not fair. The new technology lets someone interrupt the flow.' Besides, he added, 'I seemed to have about 80 percent of the facts' (cited in *Washington Post*, 11 August 1997). Further proof that he was justified in posting his allegations, at least to his way of thinking, was revealed by the intense interest in the breaking story evidently demonstrated by the Clinton administration. Responding to his critics, Drudge asserted: 'Logs show that the DRUDGE REPORT web site was visited more than 2,600 times by the gatekeeper.eop.gov Internet domain – the White House – in the 12 hours after the World Exclusive was first posted.' In the first hour alone, he claimed, 'more than 400 separate accesses were served, records show' (cited in *The Boston Globe*, 11 August 1997). Willey herself insisted that she had 'a good relationship' with Clinton, but her account would change dramatically during her deposition in the Paula Jones sexual harassment case against the president the following year.

The reputation of Drudge's 'one-man news bureau' was significantly bolstered by his revelations, which stood in sharp contrast to *Newsweek*'s inconclusive, deliberately open-ended report (albeit one based on several months' research). While Isikoff insisted that much of what Drudge reported was wrong, there could be no denying that the site was first with the news that Willey had been subpoenaed by Jones's lawyers. Within a fortnight, however, Drudge's self-described status as a 'citizen reporter' suffered a dramatic reversal, following a posting that once again had the White House in its sights. Specifically, the site claimed in an item posted on 10 August 1997 that Clinton aide Sidney Blumenthal 'has a spousal abuse past that has been effectively covered up'. The allegation had been rendered on the basis of information ostensibly provided by anonymous sources described as 'top GOP operatives' – information which Drudge himself could not be bothered to properly double-check – and posted by the AOL service (Drudge received a monthly royalty payment of $3000 from AOL at the time). Presented with a letter from the Blumenthals' council the next day denying that such violence had ever occurred, Drudge quickly posted a retraction of the story on his site and via email to his subscribers. 'I apologize if any harm has been done', Drudge stated shortly afterwards. 'The story was issued in good faith. It was based on two sources who clearly were operating from a political motivation.' As critics sharpened their invective, he sought to explain how he got it so wrong. 'Someone was trying to get me to go after [the story] and I probably fell for it a little too hard', he admitted. 'I can't prove it. This is a case of using me to broadcast dirty laundry. I think I've been had' (cited in *Washington Post*, 12 August 1997). Drudge's earlier boasts about his freedom to write whatever we wanted, and the virtue of not having an editor, had caught up with him. 'He seems to feel he's outside the journalistic rules', the Blumenthals' attorney stated. 'But nobody's exempt from the rules. If you're going to be on the Net, these rules apply to you, too' (cited in *Washington Post*, 15 August 1997). Denouncing the Drudge Report's item as 'contemptible drivel', he soon after announced that a $30 million libel lawsuit against Drudge and AOL was being prepared (the case would be eventually settled before trial).

Evidently being a 'renegade cyber-journalist', as some were labelling Drudge, meant being first with the story, regardless of whether or not it happened to be factually correct. Despite this latest setback, an unabashed Drudge remained dismissive of his critics. 'To me, you don't get a license to report', he told one newspaper. 'I think that's a faulty theory that's built up in the last half of the century. Anyone can report anything' (*USA Today*, 14 August 1997). Little did anyone appreciate at the time quite how significant such a claim would be. Everything changed on 17 January 1998, however, when Drudge posted a 'blockbuster report' that would propel the Drudge Report into the global spotlight, and decisively undermine the Clinton presidency over the months to come.

BLOCKBUSTER REPORT: 23-YEAR OLD, FORMER WHITE HOUSE INTERN, SEX RELATIONSHIP WITH PRESIDENT

World Exclusive

Must Credit the DRUDGE REPORT

At the last minute, at 6 p.m. on Saturday evening, NEWSWEEK magazine killed a story that was destined to shake official Washington to its foundation: A White House intern carried on a sexual affair with the President of the United States!

The DRUDGE REPORT has learned that reporter Michael Isikoff developed the story of his career, only to have it spiked by top NEWSWEEK suits hours before publication. A young woman, 23, sexually involved with the love of her life, the President of the United States, since she was a 21-year-old intern at the White House. She was a frequent visitor to a small study just off the Oval Office where she claims to have indulged the president's sexual preference. Reports of the relationship spread in White House quarters and she was moved to a job at the Pentagon, where she worked until last month.

The young intern wrote long love letters to President Clinton, which she delivered through a delivery service. She was a frequent visitor at the White House after midnight, where she checked in the WAVE logs as visiting a secretary named Betty Curry, 57.

The DRUDGE REPORT has learned that tapes of intimate phone conversations exist.

The relationship between the president and the young woman become strained when the president believed that the young woman was bragging about the affair to others. [...] (www.drudger-eport.com/ml.htm).

The report continues, revealing that *Newsweek* and Isikoff were intending to name the young woman alleged to be involved. It also refers to the 'blind chaos in media circles' – *Time* magazine and the *New York Post* are also mentioned – ignited by the story's impending release shortly after President Clinton's scheduled testimony in the Paula Jones sexual harassment case. The report pauses to offer complimentary words about Isikoff's past reporting on related developments before proceeding to state that he was not available for comment on this story, and nor was anyone from *Newsweek*. The White House, meanwhile, 'was busy checking the DRUDGE REPORT for details'.

The White House intern in question was Monica Lewinsky, of course, who found herself at the centre of a media maelstrom widely referred to as the 'Lewinsky scandal' or 'Monicagate' by the world's press. One of the first to investigate how the story had unfolded was Howard Kurtz of the *Washington Post*, who questioned *Newsweek*'s editors for an explanation as to why they had 'failed to publish the story that stunned the nation', having 'pulled the explosive piece from this week's issue' at the last moment. The editors, it seemed, were responding to a request from independent counsel Kenneth Starr to put the story on hold so as to avoid the risk of compromising his investigation. 'On the basis of what we knew Saturday, I am comfortable that we didn't go ahead with the story', *Newsweek* president Richard Smith was quoted as stating. 'Given the time that was left, we had the ability to get some very sensational charges out there', he continued. However, 'when the clock ran out, I wasn't prepared to air an allegation that a young White House intern had an affair with the president without more independent reporting on her'. The Drudge Report had not hesitated to post its take on *Newsweek*'s story, however, which was then taken up first by the *Washington Post* on 20 January, three days later, and virtually every other news organization thereafter. Drudge himself could celebrate his second snatching of an exclusive from *Newsweek*, and that his typical 43,000 'hits' per day had reportedly spiked to over 300,000, effectively overwhelming the site. 'Lightning did strike twice', he told Kurtz. 'There's something in the culture of Washington where reporters share their stories, and now there's an outlet, meaning me. Before we all talked about it, but who's going to print it?' (cited in *Washington Post*, 22 January 1998). Drudge's admission that '[t]his thing just fell into my lap' was little consolation to *Newsweek*'s Isikoff, whose story was belatedly posted on the magazine's AOL site four days after it was pulled from publication (Isikoff claimed to have been aware of the Clinton-Lewinsky allegations 'for nearly a year').

In the days to follow, the Drudge Report became a household name. '[I]t was Drudge's dredging', the *Boston Globe* (22 January 1998) acknowledged, 'that triggered the game of media dominoes'. Casting himself in heroic terms, Drudge was widely quoted in different media reports as someone who considered himself to be engaged in a 'turf war with the establishment press', most of whom he believed were not giving him sufficient credit for his scoop. 'I'm concerned with the *Newsweek* approach of not running the story', Drudge told one interviewer. 'I think to treat the American people like babies, like they're not prepared to talk about these issues, is very disturbing' (cited in the *Philadelphia Inquirer*, 23 January 1998). In the view of critics, he was more aptly described as the 'Bad Boy of Web journalism', if not a symbol of 'the evils of the Internet' (one likening him to a virulent 'computer virus' polluting cyberspace), in his flagrant disregard for the conventional norms of news reporting. Viewed from any perspective, the 'digital age muckraker' was quickly becoming 'the lightning rod of controversy' for the growing debate about the internet's perceived impact on journalistic standards and credibility. 'This is very exciting for the Web', Dan Froomkin, political news developer for washingtonpost.com, stated. 'It's the beginning of a whole new era in journalism, like it or not' (cited in *The Seattle Times*, 24 January 1998). Beyond dispute was the fact that several major news sites were recording dramatic increases in the number of users accessing their pages – a leap of

more than 20 per cent at *The New York Times* site – in the immediate aftermath of Drudge's revelations. 'The Internet is growing by such leaps and
bounds that every major story becomes a watershed', web analyst Mike
Godwin pointed out. 'We are finding that people are using this channel to
keep track of a breaking story, just as they often now use CNN', he observed.
'The Internet turns every news operation into a 24-hour channel if they want
to be' (cited in *The Orange County Register*, 30 January 1998).

Much less straightforward to assess was the longer-term ramifications of
this emergent 'new frontier' in journalism. 'The Internet made this story',
wrote Michael Kinsley in *Time* magazine. 'And the story made the Internet.
Clinterngate, or whatever we are going to call it, is to the Internet what the
Kennedy assassination was to TV news: its coming of age as a media force.'
Then again, he added, 'some might say media farce' when recognizing the
'comic seediness' of the scandal as a 'telling comment on the new medium'
and its drive to 'lower standards' (*Time*, 2 February 2002). Drudge was well
aware that his relaxed attitude to fact-checking invited scorn, but he saw
much of the criticism as being elitist in nature, steadfastly refusing to take the
blame for an erosion of standards. 'I'm a citizen first and a reporter second',
he insisted. 'The people have a right to know, not the editors who think they
know better. You should let people know as much as you know when you
know' (cited in AP, 1 February 1998). This familiar argument, well rehearsed
over the course of journalism's history, was suddenly striking a different
chord – in the view of some, a deeply disturbing one – in the era of 'instant
news' being ushered in by the internet.

Birth of the blog

Matt Drudge may have been the most famous pioneer in the earliest years of
the democratization of journalism, Howard Rheingold (2003) has remarked
since, but at the same time he failed to establish a sterling example of new
media's promise. Indeed, the Drudge Report, in Rheingold's view, 'serves as a
cautionary tale for those who would fall victim to the magical thinking of
assuming stronger democracy is the necessary result of the democratization of
publishing'.

Certainly of major significance in this regard was the emergence of
blogging as a citizen-based form of journalism, yet its early development was
very much overshadowed by sites such as the Drudge Report (with which it
shares some characteristics). Weblogs, or blogs for short, may be aptly described as diaries or journals written by individuals seeking to establish an
online presence. The initial formula, recalls Rebecca Blood (2000, 2002), one
of the progenitors of the weblog movement, was 'Links with commentary,
updated frequently'. The typical format revolves around a shared practice

whereby each new entry is placed at the top of the page, its posting being instantly time- and date-stamped. Not only is this reverse-chronological ordering expedient for the 'Web enthusiast' turned weblogger (sometimes called a 'public diarist' or 'journaller' in the early days), it also makes it possible for users to see at a glance whether or not the weblog had been updated since their last visit. This format quickly caught on because of its ease of use, enabling regular postings (often daily) to appear in a logical sequence. When the number of posts became too large for convenient scrolling, they could then be archived for future reference. The majority of early weblogs were 'personal' weblogs, that is, authored by a single person (as is the case today), although some 'portal-like' or 'content aggregator' weblogs involved the collective efforts of a group of like-minded individuals making fresh contributions.

Debates regarding which weblog should be heralded as the first one to appear continue to attract attention. Much depends, of course, on how 'weblog' is defined. For some, the first website may be considered to be the first weblog, in which case the site built by Tim Berners-Lee at CERN (http:// info.cern.ch/) is deemed deserving of proper recognition. Other contenders for this status include the ubiquitous 'What's New' pages, such as the one hosted by the National Center for Supercomputing Applications (NCSA) page. Still others nominate certain 'microportals', or even the 'web musings' – rumoured to have been written by Netscape creator Marc Andreeson – that began to appear on a regular basis in 1993. Justin Hall, a student at Swarthmore College, created 'Justin's Links from the Underground' in January 1994. Another early prototype was Dave Winer's first weblog, a forerunner of sorts to 'Scripting News', in February 1996. Also appearing were Jorn Barger's 'Robot Wisdom WebLog', Jesse James Garrett's 'Infosift', Steve Bogart's 'Nowthis.com', Cameron Barrett's 'CamWorld', and Rob 'CmdrTaco' Malda's 'Slashdot', amongst others. The 'weblog revolution', it seemed, was set to transform the world of 'old media'. Andrew Sullivan, recounting his personal history as a weblogger, calls to mind the fervour for change which accompanied the arrival of this new challenge to global media. 'If the Drudge Report pioneered the first revolution of his kind', he observed, 'then bloggers are the vanguard of the second wave' (*Sunday Times*, 24 February 2002).

There appears to be something of a consensus – to the extent it is possible to discern one in the blogosphere – that credit for the invention of the term 'weblog' itself belongs to Jorn Barger of Chicago. His 'Robot Wisdom' first coined the term in December 1997 as a means to describe a format that was slowly being formalized into a daily net journal (thereby displacing an earlier rendering of 'weblog' as a term meaning the record of the traffic for a web server). The 'log' in 'weblog' was generally interpreted as referring to the way such sites effectively provided a log or record of their owner's surfing in the form of a collection of links to other locations online. Certain other webloggers were disinclined to be terribly concerned either way, sometimes for fear of being caught up in the growing hype. 'I rarely use the term "Weblog." I say it's just a site with links to stories that I find interesting', stated James Romenesko. 'I want to remain obscure' (cited in *Chicago Tribune*, 7 September 1999). Variations on this sort of comment appear in a number of other accounts about the origins of weblogs, thereby underscoring the point that weblogs emerged in form and practice – however unevenly – prior to the arrival of the term itself.

'A few months back', Cameron Barrett commented on 26 January 1999, 'I heard the term *weblog* for the first time'. Unable to recall who said it, or where it came from, he posted an enquiry on his own website: 'Is CamWorld a weblog?' The reply from users was 'yep', an affirmation Barrett understood to be based on the site's rudimentary characteristics. More specifically, it was updated daily; possessed a user-friendly interface; held to a unifying theme ('Random Thoughts + Web Design + New Media'); facilitated user interaction with one another (via a mailing list and by contributing links); and fostered a sense of community by encouraging repeat visits. Barrett's CamWorld, like most first-generation weblogs, required considerable technical knowledge to establish and to maintain. The effort involved in hand-coding pages, or uploading files in order to add a new link or comment, meant that only the savvy could cope. The first webloggers were typically programmers or web designers, people who were conversant in hypertext markup language – HTML – with the resources, and time, to apply their site-building skills. 'Among the earliest blogging practitioners,' John Foley observed, 'are code-in-the-blood techies, such as the Unix and open-source programmers whose days aren't complete without a visit to www.slashdot.org.' In essence, he writes, weblogs are: 'Web pages with some common characteristics: commentary, sometimes lengthy, but often only a sentence or paragraph per subject; hyperlink connections to other Web pages; discussion threads; a search-engine function; maybe even advertising' (*InformationWeek*, 22 July 2002).

In addition to linking to other types of electronic material, weblogs will typically point to other weblogs so as to share information and commentary. Given that most of the early bloggers held internet-related jobs, topics tended to reflect their collective concerns – from sharing industry news to debates about copyright law. Jesse James Garrett, content editor for Ingram Micro's Web site and editor of the weblog jjg.net, likens weblogs to 'the pirate radio stations of the Web'. That is to say, they constitute:

> personal platforms through which individuals broadcast their perspectives on current events, the media, our culture, and basically anything else that strikes their fancy from the vast sea of raw material available out there on the Web. Some are more topic-focused than

others, but all are really built around someone's personal interests. Neither a faceless news-gathering organization nor an impersonal clipping service, a quality weblog is distinguished by the voice of its editor, and that editor's connection with his or her audience. (cited in Katz 1999)

This interlinking of sites, sending users far and wide across the web, was a standard feature of weblogs from the outset. In so doing, they broke the unwritten rule of commercial sites – that is to say, where a financial logic dictated that users be discouraged from leaving a particular site, a weblog actively encouraged users to go elsewhere on the understanding that they would eventually return to the original weblog in question. 'We are always sending people away from our sites', Blood stated. 'I think that Web logs represent a much more profound understanding of the Web itself than I've seen on any commercial site' (cited in *The New York Times*, 28 December 2000).

By and large, the more popular weblogs revolved around a specific topic or theme, carving a niche that allowed them to build a dedicated following. Most of them, as one might expect, were devoted to one aspect of the computer industry, or a particular set of technical or programming issues. 'An individualistic community with a common purpose', Jon Katz (1999) commented at the time, 'sites like this attract focused, like-minded participants, programmers and developers whose shared experience was mastery of a complex operating system, a willingness to endure technical hurdles, and an almost secret common language'. Gradually, as its rudimentary features began to consolidate, the weblog acquired its familiar form. 'Weblogs', Katz continued, 'are a perfect example of the biological evolution of electronic communities' (see also Katz 1998). The 'audience' of mainstream media, so often characterized as being effectively duped into passivity by the sheer volume of information being generated, become an active, participatory and engaged 'public' in this formulation. Much of the excitement generated by weblogs revolved around their perceived potential as a means to counteract the excesses of corporate media. Blood's (2000) experience as a blogger, for example, convinced her of their power to transform people's capacity for critical evaluation. 'Weblogs are no panacea for the crippling effects of a media-saturated culture', she observes, 'but I believe they are one antidote'.

Crossing thresholds

If weblogs were generating a certain amount of hype for some web users, mainstream news organizations were largely oblivious. In the case of newspaper reporting, instances of pertinent reports are scarce. One of the first references to the actual term appears in Miles Kington's opinion column in *The Independent*, published in London. In a humorous aside, he remarks: 'This is a new Internet word I have made up, which I hope will catch on. If it does, I will work out a meaning for it later' (*The Independent*, 18 February 1998). Austin Bunn, writing in his 'Machine Age' column in the *Village Voice* in New York, briefly mentions Jorn Barger's Robot Wisdom WebLog, observing that it 'might not be pretty, but it's one of the best collections of news and musings culled from the Web – and updated daily'. Of particular interest to Bunn was a 'semi-scientific' study conducted by Barger on the 'visibility' of news sources online. Evidently Barger's findings, based on querying newsgroups, found News.com top of the list, with 8693 mentions. Next was the Drudge Report, which apparently edged out *The Wall Street Journal*, *USA Today*, and *Bloomberg* (*The Village Voice*, 8 September 1998). Interestingly, the following month sees Barger's weblog feature as one of *The Guardian* newspaper New Media Department's web picks. Described as a 'real gem', the weblog is characterized as 'a daily account of John's [sic] travels around the web'. *Guardian* readers were invited to: 'Watch a highly observant and thoughtful surfer at work' (*The Guardian*, 24 October 1998).

At the start of 1999, some 23 weblogs were said to be in existence (according to Jesse's 'page of only weblogs' cited by Blood 2000), attracting the attention of communities of users who sometimes numbered in the hundreds. Weblogger Peter Merholz was widely credited by fellow webloggers with coining the shorter version of the word, 'blog', in the Spring of that year. In effect, by advocating that the word 'weblog' be subdivided into 'we-blog', he facilitated the popular usage of 'blog' as a type of shorthand (and with it 'blogger' to refer to a weblog editor). Others simply regarded it as something of an in-joke abbreviation. Regardless of its precise origins, however, throughout the year it was becoming increasingly apparent that blogs were catching on with users scouring the web for news. Their growing popularity did not escape the attention of journalists elsewhere. 'Weblogs have become popular enough', Jim McClellan pointed out in *The Guardian* newspaper in June 1999, 'to draw fire from conventional journalists who dismiss them as parasitic and unoriginal' (*The Guardian*, 3 June 1999). Serious doubts were expressed that any sort of 'new journalism' would emerge from them that would be viable, let alone worthwhile. In marked contrast, though, webloggers themselves were becoming increasingly convinced that real possibilities were opening up. 'To me', Katz (1999) pointed out on Slashdot, 'weblogs may embody personalized media on the Net – enterprising geeks creating interesting new sites that set out to define news in different ways, to be both interesting, coherent, and more civil'. In this way, he adds, this is 'the complete opposite structure of conventional media, which is top-down, boring and inherently arrogant'.

It is difficult to generalize about the more news-oriented weblogs in the early days, given that they varied fairly dramatically in form and practice. That said, though, and as Katz's comment above suggests, many were informed by a shared ethos, namely that news-gathering and commentary needed to be democratized. By acting as 'unofficial' news sources on the web, these blogs were linking together information and opinion which supplemented – or, in the eyes of some advocates, supplanted – the coverage provided by 'official' news outlets. Only a relatively small number of these blogs provided actual news reporting, however. Rather, most bloggers were pulling together their resources from a diverse array of other sites, often in a way that resituated a given news event within a larger context so as to illuminate multiple angles. As Blood (2000), who began her weblog 'Rebecca's Pocket' in April 1999, elaborates:

> By highlighting articles that may easily be passed over by the typical web user too busy to do more than scan corporate news sites, by searching out articles from lesser-known sources, and by providing additional facts, alternative views, and thoughtful commentary, weblog editors participate in the dissemination and interpretation of the news that is fed to us every day. Their sarcasm and fearless commentary reminds us to question the vested interests of our sources of information and the expertise of individual reporters as they file news stories about subjects they may not fully understand. (Blood 2000)

Customarily the sources of the blogger's information are acknowledged explicitly, with the accompanying hyperlink enabling the user to negotiate a network of cross-references from one blog to the next, or to other types of sites altogether. In principle, the facts or claims presented in any one blog can be subjected to the relentless double-checking of users, some of whom may be even better informed about the events in question than the initial blogger. Any attempt by a blogger to present a partisan assertion as an impartial statement of truth is likely to be promptly recognized as such by other users. In practice, a small number of leading blogs receive a hugely disproportionate number of links from other blogs and so tend to dominate the so-called 'blogosphere', bringing little-read blogs to prominence, giving credence to criticisms and making some impact on wider public debate.

Communities of interest

It was over the course of 1999, with the launching of free build-your-own-weblog tools (first was Pitas.com by 29-year-old programmer Andrew Smales in Toronto, followed by Pyra Lab's release of Blogger, and then Groksoup and Editthispage), that the 'bandwagon-jumping turned into an explosion' (Blood 2000; Kahney 2000; Jensen 2003). This rapid influx of weblogs – now numbering in the hundreds – began to attract the interest of mainstream media commentary in a more substantive manner.

In the case of newspapers, coverage remains sparse, but when reading through it certain features become apparent. Frequently it is the case, for example, that the weblog is defined as a useful filtering tool to help users sift through the internet's 'flood of information' in a manner more effective than that provided by search engines with their 'seemingly random lists'. In June 1999, a piece by Dan Gillmor, a technology columnist for the *San Jose Mercury News*, discusses 'one of the most fascinating venues on the Web', namely a site called Slashdot ('News for Nerds. Stuff that matters') that is 'almost addictive in its drawing power'. Interestingly, he mentions that its homepage 'is presented in a format that's coming to be known as a "Weblog". Every day you'll find a dozen or so one-paragraph introductions to a variety of topics.' In considering Slashdot to be an 'archetype of the Internet-led communication revolution', Gillmor is intrigued by the fact that it offers both news and discussion in a way that 'transcends traditional genres and boundaries, creating something different from its mix of the old and new'. It is in assessing the possible impact of weblogs more widely, though, that he makes a remarkably prescient observation:

> I've heard Slashdot called a form of journalism. However defined, [it] makes us think about journalism's inevitable evolution as the Web takes hold. Traditional mass media have been lectures: We tell you what the news is from our perspective. Tomorrow's Web-enhanced journalism will include a conversation. (*San Jose Mercury News*, 17 June 1999)

Gillmor is in little doubt that weblogs, with their 'torrent of chatter', will become increasingly popular, representing as they do a 'model of convenience' for users. 'If you care about a particular topic', he writes, 'you can learn a lot' via this innovative format.

'Online digests' is the preferred term for weblogs used by Andy Wang of *The New York Times*, writing in August 1999. In his report on the 'emerging speciality of Net scavenging', Wang begins with an account of James Romenesko 'furiously surfing the Web' at 5:00 am in search of appropriate stories for the two 'digests of Web links' he publishes ('Mediagossip.com' and 'obscurestore.com', respectively) before leaving the house for his day job as a newspaper journalist. Romenesko, variously labelled a 'news hound' and a 'gatekeeper for gatekeepers', is credited with providing a useful 'electronic clipping service' that draws upon a diverse range of news sources. It is 'largely through grass-roots, word-of-mouse popularity', Wang observes, that 'sites like Romenesko's are catching on with a discerning crowd – including reporters and editors of many news organizations, who rely on the sites to help filter the welter of information on the Web' (*The New York Times*, 2 August 1999). Somewhat curiously, Romenesko also features in a *Chicago Tribune* item published about a month later. Here, in contrast with Wang, *Tribune* staff writer Julia Keller employs the term 'weblog' with reference to Romenesko's sites, while at the same time expressing her desire to resist formally defining its meaning so as to be 'true to the fluid, floating, idiosyncratic spirit of the enterprise'. Webloggers, in her judgement, 'are a self-selected group of mostly young (under 30), relentlessly verbal, fiendishly well-read, usually subversive folks who relish tying together the shoelaces of the stiffly homogenized corporate world'. Meanwhile, she informs her readers, Romenesko's 'Mediagossip.com' – described as a 'Weblog specializing in juicy tidbits about news-purveyors' – was about to adopt a new name due to its sponsorship by the non-profit journalism education foundation, the Poynter Institute, beginning the following month (*The Chicago Tribune*, 7 September 1999).

Much of the newspaper commentary on weblogs highlighted their usefulness for 'Internet surfers', albeit in a patronizing way at times. A focus of criticism was the apparent triviality of much of the content being hyperlinked across blogs, as well as the emphasis on links for their own sake. Professional journalists, in the perception of some of their online-oriented colleagues, were turning up their noses. 'From the day in 1994 that I first fooled around with the Mosaic browser', Scott Rosenberg (1999) recalled in Salon.com, 'I thought it was obvious that, on the Web, links are good. They're a service, a boon, a new kind of communication that distinguishes this strange new medium from its antecedents.' Rosenberg proceeds to make a case for the importance of weblogs, an intervention prompted by a desire to respond to a dismissive remark he attributes to a *Wall Street Journal* reporter speaking at a new media conference at the UC-Berkeley Journalism School earlier in the year. The reporter in question, Kara Swisher, allegedly referred to 'a new breed of Web journalists as "linkalists"', thereby provoking Rosenberg's ire. Although she later insisted that her choice of word was meant to be light-hearted, and that her intended point was that there were 'easy and sometimes too-seamless links between commerce and editorial on the Web' (Letter to the Editor, Salon.com, 28 May 1999), for Rosenberg it was indicative of a much deeper criticism. The message, he believed, was clear: 'People who provide links to other people are performing a low, menial task that any boob can handle, and that doesn't deserve comparison to the hallowed labors that constitute the august tradition of "journalism".'

Rosenberg's decision to place the word 'journalism' in quotation marks neatly underscores the source of the tension he was striving to identify. The reason why 'a phenomenon known as the weblog', in his view, 'is one of the fastest-growing and most fertile creative areas on the Web today', is because 'millions of Web users' place 'an extremely high value on the reliable, timely provision of useful – or quirky, or overlooked – links'. Journalists who are disdainful of this practice of providing links, he adds, may soon find themselves unemployed. Weblogs possess the potential to enhance the value of news available elsewhere on the web, providing a 'fundamental service' for users otherwise struggling to cope with 'the vast media terrain we all now inhabit'. To the extent that webloggers are helping to fashion the tools and strategies necessary to deal effectively with this 'information ecology', he believes, they are 'fulfilling the predictions by Internet visionaries of the rise of a new breed of personal journalism online – only instead of pounding the physical pavement, they forage for news on the Net itself'. And yet, as Rosenberg readily concedes, it is precisely this point that infuriates some journalists '"Reporting isn't just finding links!" they cry. "It's interviewing people. Checking sources. Digging for the truth"', to which he replies: yes, of course. 'No one's suggesting that weblogs are any sort of replacement for the old-fashioned virtues of good journalism', he maintains, 'but the defensive hostility of some journalists does make you think a bit about how much today's "professional" media are already behaving like the link-happy new medium they fear.' Pointing to the ways in which newspapers, magazines and television newscasts reprocess stories from one another, he adds: 'The big difference between online and offline news is that the offline press will "pick up" a story without bothering to credit it – let alone link you to the original source.'

By the end of 1999, the 'big idea' of the internet – namely, that a multitude of users could harness the power of distributed information to connect with one another in meaningful dialogue – was becoming increasingly consolidated. It was obvious to most that those commentators seeking to dismiss weblogs as 'the latest Internet craze' were wide of the mark in their criticism. 'Weblogs', Barrett posted in his CamWorld blog in November 1999, 'have established a small island of rationality and stability among the sea of information that the Internet has thrown at everyone'. While blogging was still very much a specialized activity on the margins, still relatively unknown among typical web users, the most popular blogs were generating enough hits to justify their place at the forefront of the 'New Journalism' in the view of advocates. It would take the tragic events of September 11, 2001, however, for them to demonstrate their remarkable potential in times of crisis to sceptical observers in the mainstream press.

4 Covering the crisis: online journalism on September 11

Less than ten minutes after the first passenger jet struck the World Trade Center on the morning of September 11 2001, eyewitness accounts began to appear on the web. People were desperate to put into words what they had seen, to share their experiences, even when they defied comprehension. 'This unfathomable tragedy', online writer Rogers Cadenhead observed, 'reminds me of the original reason the Internet was invented in 1969 – to serve as a decentralized network that couldn't be brought down by a military attack.' Cadenhead's comment was made to newspaper reporter Amy Harmon, who interviewed him on September 11 about the way his WTCattack email discussion list was circulating news about what was happening. 'Amateur news reporters on weblogs are functioning as their own decentralized media today', Cadenhead pointed out, 'and it's one of the only heartening things about this stomach-turning day' (cited in *The New York Times*, 12 September 2001).

In the immediate aftermath of the attacks, the country's major news sites had scrambled to post information as quickly as they could gather it from bewildered sources. If the day before these sites – such as CNN.com, MSNBC.com, ABCNews.com, CBS.com and FoxNews.com – had been counting their 'hits' in the hundreds of thousands per hour, suddenly they were experiencing millions of them. Online news managers, like their mainstream news counterparts, were caught completely off-guard by breaking developments of this speed and magnitude. Most of the sites were so besieged by user demand that they quickly became virtually inaccessible. MSNBC.com, for example, reportedly registered as many as 400,000 people hitting its pages simultaneously. In the case of CNN.com, 9 million page views were made per hour that morning. Where some 14 million page views would be ordinarily made over the course of an entire day, about 162 million views were made that day (*Editor and Publisher*, 19 September 2001). Each of the other major news sites could be reached only sporadically as efforts mounted to ward off the danger of the internet infrastructure undergoing a complete 'congestion collapse'. Criticisms levelled by some non-web journalists were sharp and to the point. 'At a time when information-starved Americans needed it as never before', *Detroit Free Press* newspaper columnist Mike Wendland (2001) admonished, 'the Internet failed miserably in the hours immediately following yesterday's terrorist attacks'.

Several online news commentators have since declared the atrocities committed that day to be 'the biggest story to break in the Internet Age'. Current estimates suggest that almost 3000 people were killed, a tragedy which left millions more in the US and around the world traumatized for some time afterwards. Rhetorical appeals to September 11 continue to permeate public life, not least – most regrettably – in the militarist discourses of the Bush administration, which has consistently invoked its significance as justification for the invasion of Iraq despite the absence of evidence to support any such connection (see Chapter 6). Meanwhile, close analyses of the news media's reporting on that fateful Tuesday have found much to admire, but have also pinpointed serious shortcomings due, in part, to a type of self-censorship which then CBS News anchor Dan Rather aptly attributed to 'patriotism run amok'.[1] This chapter will proceed to consider the online news coverage of the crisis as it unfolded in the early hours, where several pressing issues continue to be the subject of much discussion and debate.

Tangled wires

Before turning to examine the nature of the online news reporting, it is important to first recognize the extent to which certain logistical problems surrounding electronic communication were compounded by the destruction of the World Trade Center (WTC) itself. Long-distance telephone lines, quickly ascertained to be numbering in the thousands, were severed when the north tower collapsed. These lines formed a crucial component of the infrastructure connecting a range of major network sites to the internet. At the same time, several of the city's radio and television stations lost their transmitter towers with the Center's disintegration. Some stations were able to stay on the air, such as the local CBS affiliate once it switched to a backup antenna on the Empire State Building, while others were knocked off the airwaves completely. Included in the latter were the local affiliates of the ABC, NBC and Fox networks. An estimated 30 per cent of households in the area relying on over-the-air antennae were unable to receive signals from them, although cable television subscribers were unaffected (*The New York Times*, 12 September 2001).

Shortly after 9:00 am local time in New York, telephone communication came to a standstill in parts of the upper Eastern seaboard. As Nancy Weil reported, 'it became impossible to get a phone call out of or into New York and other major East Coast cities, including Washington, D.C., and Boston' (*Industry Standard*, 12 September 2001). Many people attempting to make telephone calls either to or from the affected cities heard only an 'All circuits are busy' recording. Text messaging, via cell phones, proved to be effective for some, mainly because such messages were sent over different networks than those carrying voice calls. Hours would pass before telephone traffic could be re-routed, making the networks accessible again. In the meantime, for those New Yorkers unable to communicate via wireless and landline telephones, the internet performed a vital role in providing other ways of making contact with relatives, friends and colleagues. Many went straight to email and instant messaging, posted messages to their online communities and mailing lists, or logged on to instant IRC (Internet Relay Chat) services. Most email services were largely unaffected by the sudden surges or 'spikes' in internet traffic and related technical breakdowns. Emailed 'I'm OK' messages were usually able to get through. One office worker in a building close to the WTC said that he sent email to 'everyone I could think of' after the attacks. He relayed the messages 'as soon as things got really bad because I knew people would worry about me. After that, the e-mails I got were from people worried about other folks in Manhattan, and news updates' (cited in *CNET News*, 11 September 2001).

The internet's main 'backbone' lines stayed functional, with the overall flow of data remaining stable. Nevertheless, the amount of network use was such that logjams formed at the hub, or server, computers responsible for routing traffic to and from websites (Glasner 2001). The sites of the airlines whose planes had crashed – American Airlines and United Airlines – were experiencing more traffic than they could manage. People searching for information about the tragedy, or seeking updates on transportation conditions, were likely to be frustrated in their efforts. Also experiencing difficulties were several of the law firms and small businesses located in and around the WTC, who were looking to the internet to post information about their status and what they were doing to cope with the situation. The website of one law firm, for example, posted the following message for employees' families and clients:

> Due to the tragic events that have occurred in New York and Washington this morning, we are closing all of our offices. We will keep you apprised of developments, as appropriate, via the Web site, voice mail and e-mails. Based on the information currently available to us, we understand that all of our personnel in the World Trade Center were evacuated safely. (cited in *CNET News*, 11 September 2001)

Some companies, of course, were not so fortunate. Their websites were used to report the deaths of colleagues. Emergency numbers were also posted for staff members to contact in the event that they had survived. Relief organizations similarly moved quickly to establish an online presence. The American Red Cross, for example, called upon technology companies to provide internet space for public appeals for blood donations for those injured in the attacks. Moreover, the organization's web-team sent its own reporters to New York and the Pentagon so that they could post breaking news at RedCross.org and DisasterRelief.org. The importance of keeping information continuously updated was emphasized by Phil Zepeda, the Red Cross's director of online media: 'It's an immediate medium. People expect to go there and find out what's happening now, not what happened six hours ago' (cited in *Washington Post*, 13 September 2001). Still other users were turning to police and fire fighter sites for details. It was possible to listen to dispatches between police officers on a NYPD scanner site, for example, as well as other audio feeds from related sites for emergency workers. The unofficial site of the NY firefighters provided information updates, photographs and archival links, such as to radio codes (Langfield 2001b). By mid-afternoon, however, most of these sites had also succumbed to internet congestion (Wendland 2001).

Alert to the pressures being brought to bear on mainstream sites, several members of the public responded by recasting their personal websites so as to open up points of contact. Science fiction writer William Shunn, for example, created a shared list to circulate information amongst his family and friends. In a matter of hours, however, the site promptly burgeoned into the first online 'survivor registry' for New Yorkers, affording everyone the space to post a brief note or contact details. As Shunn writes:

> Messages from across the country appeared in my inbox, some from users who had inadvertently posted the names of the missing as survivors. I worked as fast as I could to delete erroneous reports, to screen out profanity and hate speech, and to implement a much-requested search function.
>
> By midnight the URL had spread so far that high traffic rendered the board unusable. I had to close it down, freezing the list at 2,500 entries, and shift the burden of data collection to other unofficial registries.
>
> The next day, five hundred E-mails offered me thanks, blessed me, called me an American hero. A CNET reporter said my efforts were a mitzvah. Another hundred messages asked what I knew about missing loved ones, or begged me to reveal who had posted a son or daughter's name to the check-in list. Dozens more demonized me for the list's inaccuracies, or for the ugly jokes and racist diatribes that had sneaked on. [...]
>
> I came to believe what I built on Tuesday, imperfect as it was, was right and necessary for that moment in time. [...] Outbursts of terror and grief share the page with avowals of love, hope, and faith. Clots of insensitivity lodge among eloquent pleas for understanding, closed fists of hatred among prayers for surcease from pain. I find raw

eruptions of anger and confusion cheek by jowl with moments of brilliant, shining joy. (William Shunn.net/okay)

Shunn believed that the site received over a million hits that day and the next. His was one of several survivor registries that emerged, drawing readers in such numbers that they too struggled to remain operational. Some sites eventually gave way and crashed, while others began directing visitors to official sites, such as the Hospital Patient Locator System (*The New York Times*, 20 September 2001).

It is against a backdrop of these and related developments, then, that the contribution made by online news coverage needs to be contextualized. Pertinent insights into the logistics underpinning this coverage will be the primary focus of this chapter's discussion. In addition to focusing on the major news sites, attention also will be devoted to considering the part played by so-called 'amateur' or 'personal' reporters. Regarding the latter, the various roles and responsibilities they assumed raise interesting questions about how best to define 'news' – and who could rightly assume the status of 'journalist' – in an online environment. Leander Kahney (2001a) makes an important point in this regard. In conceding that the major sites experienced serious problems during the crisis, she rightly observes that 'under the radar, the Net responded magnificently; it was just a matter of knowing where to look'.

Redefining news

'It's a bad day for Internet media', Steve Outing argued, 'when it can't accommodate demand and the audience shifts back to traditional media sources' (Poynter.org, 11 September 2001). Judging from some of the personal recollections published in the days to follow, few online journalists would dispute the claim that television led the way in covering the attacks during the early hours. 'When the unexpected met the unimaginable', Wayne Robins maintained, the various newspaper sites available 'were no match for the numbing live and taped pictures of the catastrophe broadcast on TV'. This news story, he added, 'was war, an unnatural disaster, with horrific developments overlapping before your eyes with such speed that the brain – never mind the computer keyboard – couldn't process the information' (*Editor and Publisher*, 11 September 2001). Similarly, Nick Wrenn, an editor at CNN.com Europe, pointed out: 'To be honest, it showed that the web is not quite up to the job yet. It couldn't meet the demand and millions of viewers would've gone from the web to TV for updates' (cited in *The Guardian*, 17 September 2001).[2]

The dramatic footage of crashing jetliners was indeed such that individuals with access to television were much less likely to turn to the internet than those who were deskbound, such as office workers. Even the homepage of the popular Google.com search engine posted an advisory message which made the point bluntly:

> If you are looking for news, you will find the most current information on TV or radio. Many online news services are not available, because of extremely high demand. Below are links to news sites, including cached copies as they appeared earlier today. (Google.com, 11 September 2001)

A decision had been taken at Google to transfer duplicates of news items from the major news sites to a special page, thereby making them available to those otherwise unable to access them. As the site's co-founder and president, Sergey Brin, stated when interviewed: 'We took it upon ourselves to deliver the news, because the rest of the Internet wasn't able to cope as well' (cited in *Washington Post*, 13 September 2001).

Meanwhile, the major online news sites, painfully aware of their users' frustrations, struggled to make the best of a desperate situation. In the early hours of the crisis, efforts to cope with the huge upsurge in traffic were varied and met with limited success. Users turning to MSNBC were met with the message: 'You're seeing this page because MSNBC is experiencing high site traffic', and were unable to proceed beyond it (*Newsbytes*, 11 September 2001). Behind the scenes, the site's operators were responding as best they could manage. Across the array of major sites, pages were being stripped of their image-intensive graphics, and advertising content minimalized, so as to facilitate access.[3] CNN.com, for example, trimmed away all but the most essential graphics under its 'America Under Attack' title, allowing pages to be loaded much more efficiently. 'Viewed another way', commented Bob Tedsechi, 'CNN.com's home page before the events held more than 255 kilobytes of information; the slimmed-down version was about 20 kilobytes' (cited in *The New York Times*, 17 September 2001). ABC News.com adopted the same approach, while the homepage for CBSnews.com consisted of a grey page featuring a single hyperlink to one story, accompanied by a small photograph.

Further strategies to improve the capacity of websites to respond included expanding the amount of bandwidth available, bringing additional computer servers online, suspending user registration processes and temporarily turning off traffic-tracking software. *The New York Times* site promptly dispensed with its famous masthead to streamline the loading process. Others, such as *The New York Post*'s site, simply opted to point readers to an Associated Press (AP) story (Blair 2001). In light of these and related difficulties, many users were forced to look elsewhere on the internet for information about breaking developments. Those turning to the websites associated with the wire services, such as AP and Reuters.com, encountered similar technical difficulties.

The response time – if and when they actually loaded – must have seemed painfully slow. Some users came to rely on updates from less well-known news sources – such as the Drudge Report – because they were typically less burdened with web traffic. Such was also the case with 'specialty' news sites, such as those associated with business publications. The *Wall Street Journal*, its main office evacuated due to its proximity to the World Trade Center, made its website free of charge for the day. The stock markets having closed, Bloomberg.com, a financial news site, posted continuing updates while assessing the possible implications of the events for futures trading and interest rates. Meanwhile, news portals, namely sites that offer readers a range of links to newspaper and trade publications, also stepped into the breach. One such portal, Newshub, reportedly performed consistently throughout the day, offering information updates every 15 minutes (Wendland 2001).

Several non-news sites similarly stepped in to lend a hand, their operators racing to rewrite their pages so as to make information available as it emerged. In the case of a 'tech site' such as Slashdot.com ('News for Nerds. Stuff that matters'), for example, its editor posted this message 23 minutes after the first airliner struck the World Trade Center:

Word Trade Towers and Pentagon Attacked

Posted by Cmdr Taco on Tuesday, September 11,
@08:12AM [09:12 am EDT]
from the you-can't-make-this-stuff-up dept.

The World Trade Towers in new york were crashed into by 2 planes, one on each tower, 18 minutes apart. Nobody really knows who did it, but the planes were big ones. Normally I wouldn't consider posting this on Slashdot, but I'm making an exception this time because I can't get news through any of the conventional websites, and I assume I'm not alone.

Update We're having server problems. Sorry. Updated info, both towers have collapsed, pentagon hit by 3rd plane. Part of it has collapsed.

The site's founder, Rob 'Cmdr Taco' Malda, decided not to offer links to mainstream news sites. 'I couldn't get to CNN. MSNBC loaded but very slowly. Far too slowly to bother linking. I posted whatever facts we had' (cited in Miller 2001). Slashdot's staff of four people kept the site online throughout the day, according to Brad King (2001), even though at 60 page views a second it was experiencing nearly triple its average amount of traffic. Significantly, as online journalist Robin Miller (2001) later pointed out, '[w]hen media pundits talk about "news on the Internet" Slashdot is almost never mentioned, even though it has more regular readers than all but a few newspapers'. The secret of its success, he added, was that its contributors 'don't use the Internet as a one-way, broadcast-style or newspaper-like information distribution medium, but as a collaborative, fully interactive network that has the power to bring many voices together and weave them into a single web'.

On September 11, these kinds of alternative news sites, Jon Katz (2001) wrote at Slashdot.org, 'were a source of clarity and accuracy for many millions of people, puzzled or frightened by alarmist reports on TV and elsewhere'. Slashdot was joined by several other 'techie' or community-news sites which similarly provided *ad hoc* portals for news, background information and discussion. Staff working at Scripting.com, a site ordinarily devoted to technical discussions of web programming, set to work redistributing news items otherwise inaccessible at their original news site (Glasner 2001). Also posted on the site were personal eyewitness accounts and photographs emailed to the site by users, thereby providing readers with fresh perspectives on the crisis. As one of the site's writers stated in a note posted on the opening page the following day:

> The Web has a lot more people to cover a story. We, collectively, got on it very quickly once it was clear that the news sites were choked with flow and didn't have very much info ... There's power in the new communication and development medium we're mastering. Far from being dead, the Web is just getting started. (cited in Kahney 2001a)

Morpheus, a multimedia file-swapping service, was similarly transformed into an alternative news source. Posted on its start page was the notice: 'Now you can do your part to make sure the news will always be available to members of the Morpheus Users Network. Imagine the power of a news organization with 20 million reporters around the world. BE THE MEDIA!'.

Personal journalism

This invitation to 'be the media', and thereby to challenge traditional definitions of what counted as 'news' as well as who qualified to be a 'journalist', was answered in surprising ways across the breadth of the internet's virtual communities. Hundreds of refashioned personal websites began to appear over the course of September 11, making publicly available eyewitness accounts, personal photographs and in some cases video footage of the unfolding disasters.

Taken together, these websites resembled something of a first-person news network, a collective form of collaborative news-gathering. Ordinary people were transforming into 'amateur newsies', to use a term frequently heard, or instant reporters, photojournalists and opinion columnists. Many of them were hardly amateurs in the strict sense of the word, however, as they were otherwise employed as professional writers, photographers or designers. 'Anyone who had access to a digital camera and a Web site suddenly was a guerrilla journalist posting these things', said one graphic designer turned photojournalist. 'When you're viewing an experience through a viewfinder, you become bolder' (cited in *CNET News*, 12 October 2001). The contributions to so-called 'personal journalism', or what some described as 'citizen-produced coverage', appeared from diverse locations, so diverse as to make judgements about their relative accuracy difficult, if not impossible. These types of personal news items were typically being forwarded via email many times over, almost always by people who did not actually know the original writer or photographer. Presumably for those 'personal journalists' giving sincere expression to their experiences, though, the sending of such messages had something of a cathartic effect. In any case, the contrast with mainstream reporting was stark.

'[N]ot only was so-called citizen-produced coverage sometimes more accessible', argued Leander Kahney (2001b), 'it was often more compelling'. Her reading of diverse comments about 'personal journalism' posted by uses on different sites suggested that these forms of reporting were providing some members of the online community with a greater sense of connection to the crisis than that afforded by 'official' news reports. By way of example, she quotes one such post as stating: 'The news coverage thus far has been heavily skewed to talking heads, while the Internet has overflowed with (talkative) New Yorkers and DCites, telling the real story' (cited in Kahney 2001a). Such generalizations aside, of particular importance here was the crucial role played by weblogs, or blogs (see Chapter 2), in making these forms of journalism possible. 'Most of the amateur content', Kahney (2001b) noted, 'would be inaccessible, or at least hard to find, if not for many of the Web's outstanding weblogs, which function as "portals" to personal content'. Bloggers spent the day rapidly linking together any available amateur accounts and photographs onto their respective sites. 'Some people cope by hearing and distributing information in a crisis', wrote the owner of one popular blog. 'I'm one of those people, I guess. Makes me feel like I'm doing something useful for those that can't do anything' (cited in Kahney 2001a). Another blogger stated: 'I found that for me, posting videos and sharing these experiences was the best therapy. It's a modern way of a survivor of a disaster declaring, "I'm still alive; look at this Web site. I got out"'(cited in *CNET News*, 12 October 2001).

In stretching the boundaries of what counted as journalism, so-called 'amateur newsies' and their webloggers together threw into sharp relief the reportorial conventions of mainstream journalism. The bloggers, as online journalist Mindy McAdams pointed out, 'illustrated how news sources are not restricted to what we think of as the traditional news media'. Indeed, she added, the 'man-on-the street interview is now authored by the man on the street and self-published, including his pictures' (cited in Raphael 2001). The significance of these interventions was not lost on full-time journalists, of course, as many of them turned to blogs with interest. Commenting on this sudden recognition of blogs as legitimate news sources, blogger Edward Champion observed:

> . . . overworked journalists, laboring in twelve hour shifts, scrambling for a story amidst pressures, contending with demands from editors and the need to fill copy, did what any overworked journalist would do under the circumstances. They pilfered the leads found through the weblogs and followed up on the stories. In other words, it could be suggested that, while journalism has failed to live up to its initial investigative or objective roles, weblogs offered a polyglot of voices crying from the Babel Tower, demanding a media that actually mattered. (Ed Rants, 16 October 2001)

Just as television newscasts were appropriating so-called 'amateur' video footage to supplement their reports, mainstream news sites instigated a similar type of practice wherever it was technically feasible. Several sites moved quickly to make space for eyewitness accounts and photographs produced by members of the public at one of the scenes. At the same time, bulletin boards, such as one on the MSNBC site, enabled readers to post their experiences of what they had witnessed. Washingtonpost.com, which led with the Pentagon story, placed on its opening page: 'Reporter's Query: How were you affected by today's events? E-mail your story and please include your name and phone number', followed by an email address. Calm, level-headed descriptions were being set alongside deeply emotional outbursts. These first-hand accounts and survivor stories, in the words of reporter Pamela LiCalzi O'Connell, were 'social history in its rawest, tear-stained form' (*The New York Times*, 20 September 2001).

Further innovations to online journalism's contribution to reporting the crisis became apparent as the day unfolded. Several news sites extended their email alert lists so as to notify registered users of breaking events. Some made available a timeline, enabling users to better grasp the sequence of occurrences. On other sites, in contrast, a decision was taken not to impose narrative order on the available information, opting instead to follow a blog-like format and lead with the latest details – in some cases presented in bullet-point form – as they emerged. Quite a few sites introduced 'fact sheets' to help users to better distinguish between claims based in fact and those claims which could be more accurately classified as speculation. Sidebars, where they appeared, sometimes provided links to items from the wire services, as well as to more local information (the closing of airports, roads, schools, government offices and so forth). Moreover, as photographs emailed in from users began to accumulate, some sites organized them into discrete collections. 'At first I thought photo galleries on the Web might be superfluous, given the wall-to-wall television', stated Joe Russin, assistant managing editor at latimes.com. 'But millions of page views can't be wrong. It appears people really wanted to look at these images in their own time, contemplating and absorbing the tragedy in ways that the rush of television could not accommodate' (cited in *Editor and Publisher*, 15 October 2001).

Some journalists entered internet chatrooms, requesting contact from people with eyewitness accounts or those willing to discuss efforts to reach relatives in New York City or at the Pentagon. Many such journalists worked for newspapers producing an extra edition that afternoon, and so they wanted to supplement news items with local takes or angles on the events (Runett 2001). In the first 48 hours after the attacks, according to a study by the Pew Internet and American Life Project (2001), '13% of Internet users "attended" virtual meetings or participated in virtual communities by reading or posting comments in chat rooms, online bulletin boards, or email listservs' (Pew 2001: 3). This percentage represented a significant increase in these activities, as the authors of the report maintained that only 4 per cent of online Americans visit chatrooms on a typical day. Yahoo.com's New York room, according to Tim Blair (2001), 'swelled to 1,600 (about 1,400 more than usual for early morning) as desperate web searchers sought updates'. Meanwhile, the Yahoo club IslamOpenforum, said to have 2700 members, became caught up in an anti-Muslim backlash. One posting after the next vented certain readers' fury as they sought to affix blame for the tragedy.

Particularly pertinent here were the online chats hosted by different news sites. Among the first to set up a chat area was ABCNews.com, where message titles reportedly included: 'Pray for America', 'Why? Oh Why?' and 'Nuke the Middle East' (Wendland 2001). Users were also given the opportunity to discuss issues with invited experts on a diverse number of topics. Question and Answer (Q&A) discussions were held, as were 'roundtable' online discussions. 'Shaken, raw and vulnerable, we all want – no, NEED – our opinions on the matter to be heard', wrote newspaper reporter Winda Benedetti. 'And with the Net', she added, 'there is someone to listen, whether it's in some chat room, bulletin board, or at the receiving end of an endlessly forwarded e-mail'. Describing her hunger for information in the days following the attacks as insatiable, she found the sheer volume of material on the internet to be a comfort of sorts. 'It's as though if I comb through enough Web pages, sift through the right chat rooms, click on the right e-mail, I might somehow find some semblance of an answer to this ugly mess' (*Seattle Post-Intelligencer*, 17 September 2001).

Alternative perspectives

In the months leading up to September 2001, it had been increasingly apparent that online news sites were able to provide users with a depth and immediacy of information unmatched by any other news medium. However, as the discussion to this point demonstrates, few of the major news sites in the US were able to make effective use of this capacity on September 11. For those users unable to access these sites or who wanted to draw upon news sources where different types of perspectives were being heard, international news sites became a necessary alternative.

Interestingly, just as people living around the world were looking to US news sites for breaking developments, vast numbers of users in the US were turning to foreign or international sites than was typical prior to the tragedy. Most of the considerable traffic to the site of al-Jazeera, the satellite news channel, was from the US, even though it was entirely in Arabic at the time (the internet operation is operated from al-Jazeera's base in Doha, Qatar). Amongst the English-language sites, however, BBC News Online received the greatest share of 'hits' from US users looking abroad. The Corporation's new media editor-in-chief, Mike Smartt, later stated:

> People appear to be increasingly turning to the web for their breaking news. It's the biggest story since the second world war. We decided to clear everything off the front page, which we've never done before and concentrate all our journalists on the story. We work hand in hand with the broadcast teams but don't wait for them to report the facts. It works both ways. [...] Most important to us were the audio and video elements. It was among the most dramatic news footage anyone has ever seen. The ability to put all that on the web for people to watch over again set us apart. (cited in *The Guardian*, 17 September 2001)

Nevertheless, BBC News Online experienced difficulties in coping with the traffic to its servers at times, albeit to a lesser extent than several of the major sites in the US. 'Hits' numbered into the millions, a level of demand engendering constant transmission problems. Streamlining the site's contents helped, but it remained a struggle for staff to maintain a presence online. Also in London, Philippa Edward, commercial director at Independent Television News (ITN) New Media, commented: 'More than 30% of our traffic comes from the US, and people were sidestepping US sites to come to us, which was gratifying' (cited in *The Guardian*, 17 September 2001).

US readers were similarly turning to other counties' online newspaper sites as well. In the case of the British newspaper *The Guardian*, for example, its ombudsperson, Ian Mayes (2001a, 2001b), reported that letters sent to the editor almost doubled in the immediate aftermath of the crisis, with well over 600 arriving on both September 13 and 14. The majority of these letters arrived by email, offering prompt responses to the newspaper's coverage. According to Mayes, a large number of the letters (but apparently still a minority) were highly critical of some of the views being expressed. 'The email response', he pointed out, 'has provided a graphic reminder that writers in the *Guardian* no longer address only a generally sympathetic domestic constituency' (Mayes 2001a). This wider audience, it seems, is less likely to share the newspaper's centre-left political orientation than its regular British readership. Some readers expressed their objections to particular articles using strong language, particularly where they felt that they were intrusive, insensitive or anti-American (a few, Mayes noted, went so far as to threaten a given journalist with torture and mutilation). In contrast, many of those readers writing to make appreciative remarks stated that it was the breadth of coverage that attracted them to *The Guardian* website. 'I hope the *Guardian* will continue to provide a forum for different opinions and world views', one British reader wrote, adding: 'It is important to keep channels of communication and understanding open.'

Of particular importance to these readers, Mayes (2001a) maintained, is the space devoted to alternative viewpoints on *The Guardian*'s pages. Especially pertinent here is the inclusion of voices from the Muslim world, a distinctive feature of the news coverage when it is compared with that available in other countries. To support this observation, Mayes (2001b) offered several quotations from letters written by US readers to the website:

> 'I am an American who fears, more than any terrorist, the apparently fierce determination among many Americans to remain ignorant about what lay behind this tragedy ...' (reader from Massachusetts)
>
> 'You have somehow escaped the biases of the American press ...' (reader from Hawaii)
>
> 'You help me sift through the smoke and soot fanned by America's media, their shrill jingoism, and [help me] to preserve my sanity.' (reader from New York)
>
> 'Most of the US media tends to be rather shallow ... word of mouth has a fair number of people who work for the film studios here perusing your site.' (reader from Los Angeles)
>
> 'I live in a very small town [...], surrounded by radical fundamentalism. There is absolutely no one here to talk with about such modern ideas and interpretations.' (reader from Kentucky)

Evidently Mayes has examined a sufficient number of similar emails to deem these responses reasonably representative. He estimates that there are more than half a million regular readers of the *The Guardian* website in the US alone, a number believed to have been significantly enhanced there – as well as in other countries – by the dramatic increase in demand for news and analysis after September 11. It is in relation to this growing international readership that he quotes the *The Guardian's* editor, Alan Rusbridger, as stating: 'Many Arabs and Muslims are astonished at what they read. I love that thought.' Moreover, Rusbridger comments, 'I suppose that once you are aware of this international dimension you can't help but think a little more internationally and be a little less anglocentric' (cited in Mayes 2001b).

Not surprisingly, many of those turning to the internet looked beyond news sites altogether for further background information to help them better understand the imperatives underpinning the day's events. In the first 24 hours following the attacks, the most popular search words at Lycos included: 'World Trade Center', 'Nostradamus', 'New York', 'Osama bin Laden', 'Terrorism', 'Pentagon', 'Afghanistan', 'Camp David', 'FBI', 'Palestinians', and 'Taliban' (*CNET News*, 17 September 2001). As this list of search terms would suggest, at a time of national emergency people turn to government agencies. Such was clearly the case with regard to the Pentagon website, as well as that of the Federal Bureau of Investigation (FBI), which in any case offered little by way of alternative insights into the attacks. Several hours later, the FBI created an online form for people to use if they believed they had an important fact or tip to submit. 'If anyone out there has information to relate', an FBI agent announced at a news conference, 'they can do so via the Web'. Evidently, however, the webpage in question, with its 'Report Terrorist Activity' link, was promptly overloaded and ceased to operate effectively (Langfield 2001b). More detailed news and information appeared on the Pentagon's site the next day, including the streaming of audio files of its briefings to reporters. One explanation for the delay was provided by an official: 'Today there was more clarity as opposed to yesterday, when you literally didn't know what was going to go bang' (cited in *Washington Post*, 13 September 2001). Other government sites, such as that of the Federal Emergency Management Agency (FEMA.gov), as well as www.dc.gov and NYC.gov at the local level, did their best to remain accessible. In most cases, only brief press releases were made available at first, although the number and quality of items improved as the day unfolded.

The search for understanding took some online users into unexpected territory. 'At a moment when the world's need for information has never been greater', wrote Amy Harmon, 'the Internet's role as the ultimate source of unmediated news has been matched only by its notorious ability to breed rumors, conspiracy theories and urban legends' (*The New York Times*, 23 September 2001). Placing to one side this rather problematic notion of 'unmediated news', there was ample evidence as the hours wore on that an extraordinary amount of false information, frequently combined with apocalyptic speculation, was proliferating across the web at speed. Some rumours were hopeful, such as those revolving around claims that many people were being rescued from the ruins, or that one man had survived a fall from the 82nd floor by riding the falling debris. The rumour that an unburned Bible was found in the wreckage of the Pentagon may have been inspirational for some. More harmful rumours included the assertion that Britain had been attacked, or that more than four passenger jets had been hijacked. Further examples of rumours receiving wide public circulation via email and websites included:

> The correlation of the date – 9th month, 11th day – with the national telephone dialling code for emergencies in North America (911) was regarded by some to be non-coincidental.
>
> The alleged symbolic significance of the number 11. That is, the attack occurred on September 11 or 9/11, where 9+1+1=11, and also that 'New York City', 'The Pentagon' and 'Afghanistan' each possess 11 letters. Still others pointed out that the twin towers had resembled the number 11 from a distance.
>
> The claim that a close examination of certain news photographs of the World Trade Center ruins revealed the face of Satan in the smoke billowing up from the wreckage.
>
> The allegation that the Israeli Mossad was behind the attacks. 'In true developing-story fashion', journalist Tim Cavanaugh (2001b) writes, 'this tale grew in the telling, with learned references to advanced intelligence and military precision, and the inevitable early-morning phone call to "3,000 Jews" warning them to stay home from work that day.'
>
> The allegation that filmed footage shown on CNN of Palestinian children in Gaza ostensibly celebrating the attacks was actually shot in 1991 during the Gulf War. The Brazilian university student who posted the allegation to a social theory newsgroup subsequently apologized for this 'uncertain information', while CNN released an official statement reaffirming the verity of the footage.
>
> Much was also made of the fact that typing NYC into a Microsoft Word document, highlighting it, and then changing the font to Wingdings creates: ⚥✿◗. At the same time, the widely circulated claim that Q33NY – which becomes ✈▤▤⚥✿ by the same process – was the flight number of one of the crashed planes was false.
>
> Finally, one of the most persistent hoaxes was the proclaimed foretelling of the tragedy by the 16-century astrologer Nostradamus, namely his 'prediction' of the attack on the World Trade Center: 'the third big war will begin when the big city is burning' after 'two brothers' are 'torn apart by Chaos' (cited in *New York Times*, 23

September 2001). Evidently there was an average of 140,000 daily unique visitors to Nostradamus-repository.org for the week ending September 16, while *Nostradamus: The Complete Prophesies* was the best-selling book on Amazon.com four days after the attacks.

In crisis situations, Stephen O'Leary (2001) argued, the 'social functions of rumor' are virtually identical to those associated with 'real news'. In his view, '[p]eople spread rumors via the Net for the same reason that they read their papers or tune into CNN: they are trying to make sense of their world'. Barbara Mikkelson, who works to debunk urban legends for the popular Snopes.com, argued that many people find such rumours strangely comforting. This type of practice, she maintained, 'puts a sense of control back in an out-of-control world' (cited in Washtech.com, 20 October 2001). These are somewhat benign interpretations of the phenomenon, although they clearly warrant further investigation.

Testing the limits

'I think Internet news sites really came of age during this terrible crisis', argued Howard Kurtz of the *Washington Post*. 'They blanketed the story with all kinds of reporting, analysis and commentary, and provided readers with a chance to weigh in as well' (cited in Raphael 2001). A similar position was adopted by Katz (2001), who contended that the internet, as a news medium, was 'the freest and most diverse' available, offering more accurate information and in-depth conversation than that typically provided by traditional media. '[F]or all the mainstream media phobias about the dangerous or irresponsible Net', he wrote, 'it's seemed increasingly clear in the weeks since the attacks that the Net has become our most serious medium, the only one that offers information consumers breaking news and discussions, alternative points of view'.

Internet traffic research suggests that while the overall number of US internet users dropped in the days immediately following September 11, significantly more users turned to online news sites than was typical in previous periods. Returning to the Pew Internet and American Life Project report mentioned above, it states:

> Overall, 36% of Internet users went online looking for news in the first two days after the attacks. On Tuesday alone, 29% of Internet users – or more than 30 million people – sought news online. That is one-third greater than the normal news-seeking population on a typical day online. (About 22% of Internet users get news online on a typical day.) (Pew Internet and American Life Project 2001: 3)

Between September 11 and 16, according to a study prepared by the internet research company Jupiter Media Metrix, the online news category grew by almost 80 per cent compared to the previous week in the US. Time.com reportedly saw the largest increase, up 653 per cent, in unique visitor traffic compared to the average for the previous three weeks. Fox News.com's traffic 'spiked' at 437 per cent above average for the week (*Editor and Publisher*, 25 September 2001). To help put these types of figures in context, some 17.2 million people reportedly visited CNN.com in the first four days after the attacks (*ZD Net UK*, 24 September 2001). Further findings from Jupiter indicated that more than 50 million US internet users went to news sites during the month of September, more than half of everyone who went online in the country. CNN.com was the most frequently accessed news site (24.8 million people), followed by MSNBC.com. Of the newspaper sites, *The New York Times* received the most (10.6 million) visitors, with Washingtonpost.com coming next (see *CNET News*, 12 October 2001). 'The [online] coverage grew to the impact of the incident and the ongoing stories in Afghanistan', Neilsen/NetRatings analyst T.S. Kelly argued. 'This is an indication that the Net is growing up a bit, going from infancy to adolescence and finding a proper role in the media' (cited in *USA Today*, 16 October 2001).

Not everyone was quite so enthusiastic about the state of online journalism, of course. Responding to those commentators who maintain that the internet 'came of age' during the crisis, Tim Cavanaugh (2001b) took an oppositional stance. 'If anything', he wrote, 'the World Trade Center assault is the story where the Internet showed its age, generating little more than sound and fury from a largely depleted bag of tricks' (see also Cavanaugh 2001a). Angry about what he regarded as the failure of online news to live up to its potential, he criticized the way television was able to 're-assert its status as the world's foremost news source'. Particularly vexing, in his view, was the amount of propaganda and disinformation in circulation across the web and the apparent inability of some online journalists to correct for such biases accordingly. Still other commentators maintained that it was too early to say how online journalism would develop. 'There's plenty of journalism *on* the Internet', argued Jay Rosen, but '[v]ery little of it is *of* the Internet'. Precisely what 'interactive journalism' actually entails, he said, is still unclear. 'We don't know yet what the Net makes possible because we're still asking how the journalism we've known and loved translates to the new medium – or doesn't' (cited in Outing 2001b).

This process of translation, most commentators seemed to be agreeing at the time, was fraught with difficulties. 'What the [news] sites are doing well is offering a diversity of features on all sorts of topics', argued Amy Langfield (2001c), but they 'are failing to do that within the first few hours as news breaks'. That is to say, one of the main advantages of online journalism – namely its capacity to provide news at speed – has not been fully realized.

'As long as the major Web sites continue to rely on the same wire coverage for breaking news', she added, 'viewers will stick with their TV when they need to know something fast about a developing story'. In the early hours of September 11, this over-dependency on wire service coverage for breaking news was particularly problematic. Only as the day progressed were some news sites able to supplement wire copy with their own reporting, and crucially tap into news leads, information and perspectives appearing elsewhere on the web so as to enhance its investigative depth. Far more successful, in relative terms, were efforts to enhance interactive formats. From one news site to the next, it was clear that readers wanted to express their observations in the online forums being provided. Such *ad hoc* forums represented a far more inclusionary space for diverse viewpoints than was typical for 'letters to the editor' pages in mainstream newspapers, let alone the use of 'vox pops' or 'streeters' in television news. 'As the story of the terrorist attacks evolved and the public demanded more information from more sources, the Internet became the perfect medium for this thing', argued Kourosh Karimkhany, senior producer for Yahoo News. 'This medium will lead to a renaissance in the craft of journalism' (cited in Lasica 2001b).

It is this latter issue, namely the potential capacity of online news sites to provide readers with the means to hear voices beyond the broad parameters of establishment consensus, which has proved to be a central concern for the September 11 coverage. At a time of what he terms an 'understandable patriotic frenzy', Katz (2001) contended that on the internet voices of dissent, including those of peace activists, first surfaced. The internet, he wrote, has 'become a bulwark against the one dimensional view of events and the world that characterize Big Media. All points of view appeared, and instantly.' Basic to the internet, he maintained, is a structure that is 'architecturally and viscerally interactive', thereby ensuring that feedback and individual opinions are 'an integral part of Net information dispersal, its core'. Such a structure stands in sharp contrast with television news, he suggested, as in his view the latter 'arguably transmits powerful images too often and for too long, creating an emotional, almost hysterical climate around big stories even when there's no news to report'. Katz thus appeared to be one of an increasing number of commentators calling for reinvigorated types of online coverage, and with them new vocabularies for news narrative. Online journalism would have to be pushed even further, they were insisting, so as to make full use of the internet as a communication resource (see Outing 2001a; Raphael 2001).

Few would dispute that the tragic events of September 11 demonstrated several significant ways in which the internet has become a vital communications resource. As 'spikes' in traffic to news sites subsided, it became apparent that daily usage levels were remaining at a higher level than they were prior to September 11. It is somewhat ironic, then, that just as user figures were improving, some news organizations faced renewed pressures to trim the financial expenditure on their sites. 'At a time when Internet journalism was being pooh-poohed by a lot of people on the heels of the Internet crash', argued Sreenath Sreenivasan, 'this has shown in many ways the necessity and importance of giving resources and attention to the Web and to Web journalism' (cited in Raphael 2001). The extent to which this would happen was a matter of considerable speculation. In the meantime, J.D. Lasica (2001a) pointed out, 'how we define our journalistic mission – how we perceive ourselves and our role in this new medium – will shape how we cover the still-unfolding drama of the biggest story of our lives'.

5 Sensational scandals: the new(s) values of blogs

The rapid ascendancy of the 'new journalism' exemplified by the weblog can be usefully contextualized in relation to widespread post-September 11 dissatisfaction with older, more traditional types of reporting. Voices challenging the preoccupations of mainstream media – often dubbed somewhat derisorily as 'MSM' by some, or 'Big Media' by others – were being heard from across the political spectrum, and from within every corner of the emergent blogosphere. Whilst war raged first in Afghanistan and then Iraq, a number of 'milestones' in blogging were taking place in the United States that appear, with the benefit of hindsight, to have been decisively shaped by this discontent with the familiar priorities of market-driven news organizations. Taken together, these developments shook the reportorial foundations of newspaper and broadcast media to their foundations, the consequences of which continue to reverberate around the globe today.

'Old' and 'new' journalism

Writing in February 2002, Jeremy Wagstaff of the *Wall Street Journal* described how he could foresee a future where '[t]he editor that determines the content of our daily read may not be a salaried Webmaster or a war-weathered newspaper editor, but a bleary-eyed blogger in his undershirt willing to put in the surfing time on our behalf'. Weblogs, in his judgement, represented 'a milestone in the short history of the Internet' (*Far Eastern Economic Review*, 7 February 2002). It almost goes without saying, of course, that for every assertion that blogs were deserving of recognition as a 'milestone', someone else would counter that they constituted little more than a 'passing fad' that mattered little to the world of journalism.

One advocate prompted to weigh into the debate by Wagstaff's prophecy was British journalist Andrew Sullivan. Speaking as a blogger, albeit in his role as a columnist for a Sunday newspaper, he proposed that 'blogs could well be a milestone in the long history of journalism' (*The Sunday Times*, 24 February 2002; see also Sullivan 2002). An experienced journalist who began blogging in 1999 as a sideline to his work for publications such as *The New Republic*, he proceeded to outline his belief that 'peer-to-peer journalism' was flourishing because individual writers were being empowered at the same time that the cost of entry into publishing was being virtually eliminated. Pointing to the success of his own blog – which evidently attracted 800,000 separate visits from 220,000 people in January of 2002 – he expresses his conviction that the 'blog revolution has only begun to transform the media world', a transformation he warmly welcomed. Leading bloggers, he believes, are rapidly catching up to more traditional media with respect to their audiences and reach. Indeed, he writes, 'if the goal of opinion journalism is not ultimately money but influence and readers, the blogs are already breathing down the old media's neck'. It follows, in turn, that the rapid evolution of this 'genuinely new' genre of writing necessarily signals a sharp departure from familiar types of journalism. Free from the influence of wealthy proprietors – or the restraints imposed by editors – blogging promises to ensure that 'the universe of permissible opinions will expand, unconstrained by the prejudices, tastes or interests of the old media elite'. Consequently, while Sullivan cautions that it may be too early to tell whether blogs herald the end of the current 'monopoly on media power' exercised by mainstream news organizations, there is little doubt in his mind that 'blogging is the first journalistic model that actually harnesses rather than merely exploits the true democratic nature of the web'.

In noting that blogs had recently become 'the topic du jour' for media commentators following web trends, Scott Rosenberg (2002) assumes a different tack. Much of the mainstream blog coverage, he argues, has revolved around certain high-profile political bloggers – 'led by the indefatigable Andrew Sullivan' – when other types of blogs are equally deserving of attention in journalistic terms. Speaking as managing editor of Salon.com, but also as someone who 'has been writing about blogs since before Sullivan had one', Rosenberg strives to add nuance to some of the broader generalizations about blogging being circulated. In the course of showing how certain blogs depart from the model typically adopted by political blogs, he highlights various alternatives – not least those blogs with the capacity to break news stories in their own right. 'Journalistic traditionalists', he concedes, 'might turn up their noses and say, "Sure, but who wants to read them?"' In reply, though, he suggests that the answer is: 'It doesn't matter.' It may be the case, Rosenberg maintains, that a 'blogger with 100 dedicated and passionate readers may consider the endeavor a success even if it's not a road to media mogulhood'. For this reason, he adds, certain longstanding assumptions need to be reconsidered. 'I think too many of us in the media profession have labored so long in the trenches that we've internalized the numbers game of our business', he writes, and thus tend to 'measure the worth of a publication by the size of its audience'. This when bloggers themselves may very well be revelling in the opportunity to report about what fascinates them and a few like-minded individuals, as opposed to being made to focus on only those topics likely to attract the interests of a 'mass' audience.

In the course of discerning certain advantages that 'amateur' bloggers may enjoy over the 'professional' journalist, Rosenberg moves to distance himself from the partisan 'ideologues' attempting to characterize the current debate about blogging as a 'duel to the death between old and new journalism'. This is not to deny, he readily acknowledges, that many 'bloggers see themselves as a Web-borne vanguard, striking blows for truth-telling authenticity against the media-monopoly empire'. Just as it is the case that many 'newsroom journalists see bloggers as wannabe amateurs badly in need of some skills and some editors'. Nevertheless, to define the debate in this way is simply not fair. More to the point, he writes, it is 'stupidly reductive', being 'an inevitable byproduct' of the 'traditional media's insistent habit of framing all change in terms of a "who wins and who loses?" calculus'. For Rosenberg, then, the 'rise of blogs does not equal the death of professional journalism', no matter how many times such a zero-sum relationship is espoused. 'Weblogs', he observes:

> would barely be able to get by without the informational fodder provided by the mainstream media. Meanwhile, time-strapped reporters and editors in downsized, resource-hungry newsrooms are increasingly turning to blogs for story tips and pointers. No one has enough time to read everything on the Web; blogs offer a smart reader the chance to piggyback on someone else's reading time. Good journalists would be fools *not* to feed off blogs.' (Rosenberg 2002)

In order to further complicate the otherwise simple binaries indicative of easy caricatures, Rosenberg endeavours to show how blogs 'expand the media universe'. A 'media life-form that is native to the Web', they 'add something new to our mix, something valuable, something that couldn't have existed before the Web'. In journalistic terms, then, blogs complement the reporting of the mainstream news organization. 'If the pros are criticized as being cautious, impersonal, corporate and herdlike', he maintains, 'the bloggers are the opposite in, well, *almost* every respect: They're reckless, confessional, funky – and herdlike.'

Wherein lies the motivation – the 'fire-in-the-belly', to use Rosenberg's phrase – of the blogging movement, then? In his view, it is less a matter of partisan left or right politics than of 'a more free-floating anger at the professional media's penchant for making mistakes and not owning up to them'. He detects a certain righteous frustration in some blogs, the subtext of which may be expressed as: *'I know this subject better than the reporters – and they're wrong! And I can say so on my Web site and no one can stop me!'* (italics in original). This is the primary reason, in Rosenberg's view, why blogs are poised to become the lazy reporter's worst nightmare. Blogs represent 'an endless parade of experts in every conceivable subject they might write about, all equipped with Internet-style megaphones ready to pounce on errors'. The presence of the blogger – real or imagined – necessarily shapes the craft of the journalist. 'At worst', he remarks, 'it should keep them on their toes and give them an incentive not to slip up, and at best, it should give them a chance to do their job better.' What may be the stuff of nightmares for some reporters, it follows, is an extraordinarily rich resource for others to tap. The blogger, in contrast with the professional journalist, can 'air hunches and speculations without the filter of an editorial bureaucracy (or the legal vulnerabilities of a corporate parent). They trade links and argue nuances, fling insults and shower acclaim.' At its best, Rosenberg believes, this editorial process – conducted between and among bloggers themselves – creates a dynamic exchange of information and ideas. And, in so doing, it secures the basis for an improved quality of journalism: 'we all benefit', he concludes, 'from a more efficient means for seeing the world through someone else's eyes'.

The coming months would witness a diverse array of attempts to redraw the boundaries between 'old' and 'new' journalism. It soon became apparent that the emergent debate was unlikely to be resolved any time soon, with certain points of tension around the relative 'authority' or 'credibility' of blogs proving to be particularly contentious. One of the more curious inflections of this debate took the form of a friendly wager between Dave Winer, creator of UserLand Software and the blog Scripting News, and Martin Nisenholtz, chief executive of New York Times Digital. The two agreed that the sum involved – $1000 (US) to be donated to charity – would be awarded on the basis of their different responses to the question: 'Which will be more authoritative in 2007, weblogs or the *New York Times*?' The criteria to be used when determining the eventual winner of the bet were spelled out in *Wired* magazine (May 2002) as follows:

> For this bet, five searches on Google (which ranks a page's relevance by the number of other URLs that link to it) will determine the outcome. If a blog outranks *nytimes.com* in three or more searches, Winer prevails. If not, the victory goes to Nisenholtz. And what happens if news organizations appropriate the emergent format to bolster their own authority? If *The New York Times* runs a blog that tops a Google search by 2007, Nisenholtz claims the triumph.

Similarly worth quoting are their respective position statements. Winer argued in the same edition of *Wired*:

> We're returning to what I call amateur journalism: created for the love of writing, without expectation of financial compensation. This process is fed by the changing economics of the publishing industry,

which is employing fewer writers and editors. The Web has taught us to expect more information, not less, and that's the sea change the *Times* faces: how to remain relevant to a population that can do for themselves what the big publications won't. The 'dumb it down' philosophy forces all stories through too narrow a channel to serve the diverse world we live in. When the *Times* covers my industry, for instance, it seems to know three stories – Microsoft is evil, Java (or whatever the topic du jour) is the future, and Apple is dead. All other stories are cast as one of those three. Bored readers are looking for alternatives, but because the paper is limited in its number of writers, it can't branch out to cover other angles. My bet says the tide has turned: Informed people will look to amateurs they trust for information they want.

Nisenholtz outlined his opposing view as follows:

Readers need a source of information that is unbiased, accurate, and coherent. News organizations like [*The New York*] *Times* can provide that far more consistently than private parties can. Besides, the weblog phenomenon does not represent anything fundamentally new in the news media: *The New York Times* has been publishing individual points of view on the Op Ed page for 100 years. In any case, *nytimes.com* and weblogs are not mutually exclusive. We would like to extend our ability to act as a host for all sorts of opinions, and weblog technology might well be useful in doing so. After all, in countries whose citizens don't enjoy First Amendment protection, weblogs are run by people who'd be considered professional journalists in the US. In its six years online, *nytimes.com* has been a center of innovation, and it'll continue to be, incorporating weblogs and whatever else will enable our reporters and editors to present authoritative coverage of the most important events of the day, immediately and accurately.

Who will win the bet is readily apparent today, but in 2002 both stances must have looked sufficiently risky to be worthwhile. Interestingly, when interviewed by a newspaper prior to the official announcement of the wager, Winer had stated: 'I think it's a sucker bet. There are half a million Web logs now, and in five years there'll be a lot more' (*Washington Post*, 14 April 2002). Meanwhile, *Wired* magazine hinted to its readers which way it thought the bet might go, observing at the time of the announcement: 'While they don't always hew to traditional news values of accuracy and objectivity, blogs do at their best convey an authenticity and immediacy the big outlets can't summon.'

Shortly thereafter a provocative intervention by *Newsweek* helped to push the debate in a different direction. 'Will the Blogs Kill Old Media?' was the rather pointed title of Steven Levy's article in the 20 May 2002 edition of the magazine. 'Hard-core bloggers, with a giddy fever not heard of since the Internet bubble popped', he writes, 'are even predicting that the Blogosphere is on a trajectory to eclipse the death-star-like dome of Big Media'. Such predictions, *Star Wars* imagery aside, lacked credibility in Levy's opinion. Echoing Winer above, he argues that blogs 'are a terrific addition to the media universe', but then proceeds to insist that 'they pose no threat to the established order'. In this sense, then, he comes down firmly on Nisenholtz's side of the wager. 'What makes blogs attractive – their immediacy, their personality and, these days, their hipness – just about ensures that Old Media, instead of being toppled by them, will successfully co-opt them', Levy writes. Indeed, he suggests that this process of cooptation is already underway, pointing out that several of the most popular blogs are written by journalists otherwise employed by major news organizations. 'I love tech writer Dan Gillmor's site', he remarks, 'but would his boss, Knight Ridder, host it if the company really believed that blogs were stilettos in the ribs of Old Media?'

Interestingly, this view was reaffirmed by William Safire in his column in *The New York Times* a couple of months later. Responding to the question posed by *Newsweek*, he similarly answered in the negative: 'gossips like an old-fashioned party line', he wrote, 'but most information seekers and opinion junkies will go for reliable old media in zingy new digital clothes' (*The New York Times*, 28 July 2002). For some commentators, such as Rachel Leibrock, the fact that a columnist of Safire's stature was writing about blogs represented a sure sign that they were now 'firmly ensconced on the pop culture landscape' (*Sacramento Bee*, 8 August 2002). No one knew at the time, of course, that by the end of the year, bloggers would set in motion a chain of events that would signal a tectonic shift in journalism's landscape too.

'The Internet's First Scalp'

The first tremors were felt in the days following an event that initially failed to cross the threshold of newsworthiness in the eyes of most mainstream news organizations. Widely heralded as a 'watershed moment' for the world of blogging – or 'The Internet's First Scalp' in the boast of a *New York Post* headline – the incident is worthy of close attention here for the way it succeeded in underscoring the rapidly growing legitimacy of blogs as news sources.

The event in question took place at US Senator Strom Thurmond's 100th-birthday party, which was held on the afternoon of 5 December 2002 in Washington, DC. Thurmond, a South Carolina senator set to retire, had formerly been a staunch segregationist, and a fierce opponent of civil rights measures. When running as a States' Rights Party (or 'Dixiecrat') candidate for president in 1948, for example, he made a wide range of deeply offensive statements during the campaign. 'On the question of social intermingling of the races, our people draw the line', he told a crowd of people in Jackson, Mississippi. 'And all the laws of Washington and all the bayonets of the Army cannot force the Negro into our homes, our schools, our churches, and our places of recreation and amusement' (*The New York Times*, 13 December 2002.) Amongst the many guests in attendance at Thurmond's birthday celebration that December was Senator Trent Lott of Mississippi, who spoke in praise of his fellow Republican. 'I want to say this about my state', he declared from the podium. 'When Strom Thurmond ran for President we voted for him. We're proud of it. And if the rest of the country had followed our lead we wouldn't have had all these problems over all these years, either.' This comment, with its plainly racist subtext, was made in the presence of numerous journalists, evidently only one of whom felt compelled to report it – a young 'off-air reporter' for ABC News named Ed O'Keefe – whatever they may have thought privately.

Rather tellingly in retrospect, O'Keefe was unable to convince his ABC News colleagues that Lott's remarks constituted a news story deserving of their attention. A brief mention of the comment was made on the network's 4:30 am 'World News This Morning' broadcast for 6 December, but was then dropped altogether. Very little by way of reportage ensued elsewhere in the mainstream media either for the next few days – where news items did appear, virtually all of them were genial accounts of the birthday celebration. All of the main national television newscasts kept their distance from the inflammatory statement. This was despite the fact that pictures of the event were available (they had been broadcast live on the C-SPAN network) and, moreover, that Lott at the time was set to resume his role as Senate Majority Leader, so was a figure of national prominence. There were a few exceptions to the general rule of indifference, including a brief exchange about the incident on NBC's Sunday morning television show 'Meet the Press', for example, but as media writer Howard Kurtz commented five days after the event 'the establishment press is largely yawning' (*Washington Post*, 10 December 2002).

And that is where the matter may have ended, were it not for ABC-News.com's political news digest, The Note, a blog in the form of a daily compendium of news and analysis. Founded the previous January by Mark Halperin, political director of ABC News, with its origins traceable back to an internal staff email list, it was rapidly finding its place as the most influential 'tip sheet' in Washington. What its readership lacked in numbers – its daily hit count being relatively tiny – it more than made up for by its extraordinarily powerful impact on the political establishment. On 6 December,

Halperin – together with Elizabeth Wilner and Marc Ambinder – posted an entry which drew critical attention to what Lott had said at the birthday party. Drawing on ABC News's producer Ed O'Keefe's quotation of the remarks, they also cited the angry response of Wade Henderson of the Leadership Conference on Civil Rights, who had told ABC News: 'This was an offensive and blatant attempt to rewrite the history of the last 50 years', amongst other points. The Note's entry is then rounded out with Halperin *et al.*'s observation that 'there is no mention of Lott's comments in the Louisiana papers we checked'. They continued, suggesting that it was interesting 'how advocacy by, say, National Right To Life makes the front page in Louisiana, while liberal interest groups can't break through. A measure of the political climate in Louisiana, perhaps.'

What happened next is succinctly described by David Grann (2004) in the *New Yorker* magazine:

> Within hours, Talking Points Memo, a liberal blog written by Joshua Micah Marshall, and Tapped, a blog put out by the left-leaning magazine *The American Prospect*, picked up the story. Crediting The Note, Tapped wrote, 'What about the *national* media? . . . Trent Lott, soon to be the Senate's majority leader, is caught on tape reminiscing fondly about a segregationist presidential campaign, and we hear nothing (although, since The Note is read widely, that might change).' Indeed, it soon did. That night, James Carville, the Democratic strategist, criticized Lott's comments on [CNN's] 'Crossfire.' Tom Edsall, a Washington *Post* reporter, also spotted Lott's remarks in The Note. 'I saw it in cold print, and it really stood out,' he said. 'That's when I got the sense that this deserved significant coverage.' Meanwhile, more and more bloggers began to quote Lott's statement, while decrying the 'old,' print-based media for its silence. The Drudge Report, which had helped establish the Internet as a new form of political grapevine during the Monica Lewinsky affair, also started to promote the story. As the scandal spread to all the major newspapers and cable channels, The Note collected items from these other outlets, which it posted on its site, thereby spreading the story further. (Grann 2004)

The mainstream media, making up ground for having been 'caught off-guard', were stirred into action following the incoming Senate leader's various attempts to offer a public apology, none of which satisfied critics. President George W. Bush, while expressing his strong disapproval of Lott's initial remarks (most sharply in a speech on 12 December), steadfastly refused to call on him to step down. His public criticism nevertheless contributed to the burgeoning interest in the story in newspapers such as the *Washington Post* and *The New York Times*. 'Most political strategists and reporters told me that that is the real power of The Note', remarked Grann (2004). '[A] single item on its site can metastasize until it is picked up by more traditional media.'

Meanwhile, members of the blogging community – where several of the more vociferous voices involved, to the surprise of some, were conservatives themselves – were busy driving the story forward. 'If Lott didn't see the storm coming', *Time* magazine pointed out, 'it was in part because it was so slow in building'. Newspapers 'did not make note of his comments until days after he had made them', reporters Dan Goodgame and Karen Tumulty stated, but 'the stillness was broken by the hum of Internet "bloggers" who were posting their outrage and compiling rap sheets of Lott's earlier comments' (*Time*, 16 December 2002). Indeed, many of the bloggers gathering evidence from other speeches made by Lott were able to show that his remarks on this occasion were entirely consistent with his views over the years. Arianna Huffington (2002) of Arianna Online similarly highlights this point in her account of how bloggers succeeded in moving the story 'out of the shadows and into the political spotlight', crediting them for being 'instrumental in helping connect the dots of the Majority Leader's long history of racist stances'. *New York Times* columnist Paul Krugman observed how remarkable it was that Lott had escaped such criticism before. 'How many readers', he asked, 'ever heard about the flap, several years ago, over Mr. Lott's association with the racist Council of Conservative Citizens?' In Krugman's view, this scandal was even worse than his remarks this time around, 'but it just got buried'. And, he adds, 'without the indefatigable efforts of Mr. Marshall and a few other Internet writers, Mr. Lott's recent celebration of segregation would probably have been buried as well' (*The New York Times*, 13 December 2002).

In the aftermath of Lott's announcement on 20 December that he would step down as Majority Leader – two weeks after The Note posted its story – blogs were being defined as news in mainstream media accounts. 'There's nothing more exciting than watching a new medium mature before your eyes', wrote John Podhoretz in the *New York Post*. 'That's what's been happening over the past week in the so-called blogosphere – the cyberworld of personal op-ed pages on the Internet' (*New York Post*, 13 December 2002). In citing examples of how the 'blogosphere had gone ballistic' in pursuit of the story, he characterizes the coverage as a 'key moment in media history'. This view finds its echo in Oliver Burkeman's report for *The Guardian* newspaper. The controversy, he writes, proved to be 'a defining moment for the vibrant online culture of weblogs – nimble, constantly updated, opinion-driven internet journals, freed from many of the constraints of the established media' (*The Guardian*, 21 December 2002). Consistently singled out for praise was the way in which blogs gave the story momentum, that is, kept it alive when the major news organizations, caught up in the whirlwind of the 24-hour news cycle (where Lott's remarks quickly became yesterday's news), would have allowed it to wither on the vine. And also the way in which blogs provided a historical context for Lott's claims, namely by linking them with a wide range of his earlier pronouncements of a similarly repulsive nature, proved invaluable. Conservative blogger Andrew Sullivan reaffirmed this point in his blog, The Daily Dish, at the time, inviting his readers to compare the blogs' coverage with *The New York Times* to make up their own minds. 'We can't replace the big media', he wrote. 'But we can light fires and keep them going. That matters' (12 December 2002).

Not everyone was prepared to accept the view that bloggers led the way on this story, of course, let alone that mainstream journalists should swallow their pride and admit that blogs played a necessary role. Describing her fascination with the way this story was 'morphing not just daily but hourly', Staci D. Kramer (2002) looks to credit the 'opinion bloggers, including journalists and their amateur counterparts, upped the ante, latching on to the comments and using the instant distribution system known as the Web'. Nevertheless, she emphasizes, the role of the blogs needs to be seen as one part of a larger combination of media outlets – including print and broadcast – necessary to make the incident public. 'The one media item that probably turned Lott into a "walking piñata" – my favorite anonymous quote so far – was the C-SPAN footage of him actually making the comments.' Others concurred, pointing out that it was O'Keefe, the ABC reporter in attendance at the party, who actually broke the story on television news, even if it didn't spark a reaction at first. Meanwhile, Janice Castro, an online media researcher at Northwestern University, sought to give due credit to National Public Radio 'for beating the drum'. In her view, 'it's an exaggeration to say that the blogs made anything happen. I do think though that they have magnified the impact of influential commentators and columnists' (cited in *Christian Science Monitor*, 17 December 2002). Still, explanations for the mainstream media's collective shrug of indifference to the story initially were thin on the ground.

'It's safe to assume that, before he flushed his reputation down the toilet, Trent Lott had absolutely no idea what a blog was', commented Noah Shactman in *Wired* magazine; 'He may have a clue now' (*Wired*, 23 December 2002). Yes, indeed. And the same would be true for many of those following the story, including journalists. The extent to which this event signals an epistemological break of sorts, that is, a juncture where blogging began to rewrite the (largely unspoken) rules of journalism, has been a matter of much debate. It was a victory of *vox populi*, argued Huffington (2002) in her blog, a 'democratic uprising' that 'showed the power of the internet when it is truly free of the dependence on access, and the need to play nice with the powers that be'. This point about access was similarly addressed by Glenn Reynolds, who pursued the story in his InstaPundit blog. 'The hinterlands are full of bloggers who don't care whether Trent Lott is nice to them or not', he wrote. 'That makes them different from the Washington press' (cited in *Washington*

Post, 16 December 2002). Meanwhile, other bloggers were modest about what had been achieved in journalistic terms, refusing to take part in what they regarded as 'blog hyperbole'. In any case, it is striking to note the way in which these events figure in differing accounts of blogging's short history. For advocates, it was the decisive turn when blogging, ripe with promise, finally began to receive the recognition it deserved; whereas critics tend to be dismissive of its significance, insisting that the story would have eventually broken anyway. Either way, the Lott incident has become an important touchstone. 'And the lesson of all this?', asked John Naughton in retrospect. 'Bloggers and hacks need one another. Sad, but true' (*The Observer*, 14 March 2004).

Truth, objectivity and fairness

Over the course of 2003, the year in which 'blog' entered the *Oxford English Dictionary*, the contested status of blogging's relationship to journalism proved increasingly controversial. The immediate aftermath of Trent Lott's departure had witnessed an astonishing array of disputes criss-crossing the blogosphere over the extent to which blogs deserved credit – or condemnation – for having ignited the political firestorm. Regardless of the differing viewpoints adopted, however, there appeared to be something resembling a consensus that blogs were recasting certain longstanding assumptions about what constituted journalism, and who could claim the right to be a journalist, so clearly highlighted on September 11.

Some of the fiercest criticisms of bloggers came from mainstream journalists, not surprisingly. In the words of Tom Regan (2003), associate editor of the website for a daily newspaper, 'many journalists tend to regard bloggers as a sort of mutant breed, viewing them with skepticism and suspicion'. Journalists often hide their fear of the threat posed by bloggers to mainstream news organizations, he suggests, behind masks of professional indifference. Not all of them respond this way, of course. 'Suggest to an old-school journalist that Weblogs have anything to do with journalism', J.D. Lasica (2003) comments, 'and you'll be met with howls of derision'. Even when care is taken to acknowledge that few bloggers consider themselves to be journalists in the first place, so-called 'proper' reporters are often quick to pounce. Amongst the typical sorts of criticisms voiced is the claim that bloggers are too lazy to edit, let alone double-check, their copy. Few make any pretence of objectivity. To be accurate is vitally important, critics point out, and too many bloggers damage their credibility by making mistakes, thereby undermining the public's trust. 'Blogging is not journalism', technology consultant Bill Thompson averred in a commentary item for BBC News Online. 'Often it is as far from journalism as it is possible to get, with unsubstantiated rumour, prejudice and gossip masquerading as informed opinion.' Any information posted in a blog, he believes, will have to be properly verified elsewhere – 'often the much-maligned mainstream media', he adds.

Anyone championing the virtues of blogging would likely bristle at the assertion that blogs require the validation of mainstream journalism, not least because of widespread alarm about the deterioration of its own standards. Indeed, some point to what they perceive to be a widening credibility gap between what the media report and what their audiences are prepared to believe, insisting that it is high time journalists climbed down from their lofty perch and reacquainted themselves with their publics. News organizations, they suggest, need to become web-savvy, that is, they have to come to grips with the importance of establishing new forms of dialogue beyond journalistic circles. Blogs were now propelling this process forward, but it had been underway for some time – a key stage being when newspaper reporters began publishing their email addresses at the end of stories, an initiative further enhanced when public forums began to appear on newspaper websites. Former newspaper reporter turned blogger Paul Grabowicz (2003) extends this point, suggesting that 'if we're going to reconnect with readers, we need to drop grandiose claims of being aloof, objective observers and be more transparent about how we do our jobs' (2003: 75). Too often it is the case, he maintains, that the press's relationship with blogs is characterized as 'the imperious giant under siege by hostile outsiders'. Reporters, in his view, 'need to break out of this us vs. them cycle and be part of the community if we're going to regain the public trust that is essential to journalism' (2003: 76).

This 'us vs them cycle' continues to play itself out in a wide variety of contexts. 'When only news organizations could afford publishing technology', Sheila Lennon (2003) recalls, 'all journalism was "top down": We publish, you read (or view or listen). But the Web offers everyone low-cost access to a vast readership' (2003: 77). It is the rare advocate of blogging who believes that it holds the promise of supplanting conventional reporting altogether, of course, let alone knocking mainstream news organizations out of business. Lasica (2003), for example, does not dispute that 'a vast majority of readers' will turn to traditional media sources when a major news event breaks. Nevertheless, he argues, such a story is likely to see 'the Weblog community [adding] depth, analysis, alternative perspectives, foreign views, and occasionally first-person accounts that contravene reports in the mainstream press'. Other voices are similarly sanguine about blogging's prospects in this regard. 'By widening the disclosure circle through information sharing', blogger and newspaper columnist Paul Andrews (2003) observes, 'Weblogs have contributed to the truth-finding process'. Pointing to the pressure brought to bear on the Bush administration by blogs – leading to retractions in official statements (such as the State of the Union claim concerning African-supplied uranium to Iraq), as well as to resignations (Richard Perle's decision to resign as Chair of the Defense Policy Board, for example) – he credits them with providing important catalysts to journalism. Still, even though blogs can be ahead of news reporting, he argues, at best they are a valuable adjunct to quality journalism, and by no means a substitute.

Amongst the guiding tenets of journalism, which blogging is seen to threaten, at least in the eyes of critics, none has provoked greater concern than that of 'objectivity'. Few would deny that blogs are inherently subjective, in line with their authors' perspectives or predispositions; indeed, for many bloggers, a non-biased blog would be pointless, even if it was possible to achieve. Accordingly, the usually tacit, unspoken rules of mainstream reporting will more likely than not be rendered problematic by bloggers providing alternative accounts, facts or interpretations. That is to say, the 'objective' reporter's decisions about how best to write a particular story – everything from judging which source is credible to which adjective seems appropriate – will be recognized as being 'subjective' to the extent that they are rendered transparent via the bloggers' scrutiny. Some mainstream news organizations welcome this attention, while others do not. Either way, the intensity of this fact-checking can be astonishing, and it cuts both ways. 'My audience is never shy about letting me know when I get something wrong', newspaper columnist and blogger Dan Gillmor (2003) comments. In light of his experiences – for better and otherwise – he has adopted what he calls a new guiding principle in his reporting in either medium. In essence, he states: 'My readers know more than I do, sometimes individually on specific topics, but always collectively' (2003: 79). Electing to define this dynamic as an opportunity, as opposed to a threat, he proceeds to argue that 'when we ask our readers for help and knowledge they are willing to share it – and, through that sharing, we all benefit' (2003: 79). What counts as objectivity, it follows, necessarily takes on a more nuanced inflection as differing viewpoints multiply accordingly.

Still, the strictures of objective reporting were also being interpreted by some news organizations as grounds for prohibiting the use of blogs as news sources in their own right. It is worth noting in this context, by way of example, that *New York Times* columnist Paul Krugman was one of the very few in the major news outlets during the Trent Lott affair to actually quote a blogger, in this case freelance writer Joshua Marshall. Moreover, in crediting him as the person who 'more than anyone else, is responsible for making Trent Lott's offensive remarks the issue they deserve to be', Krugman also cited the name of Marshall's blog, talkingpointsmemo.com, describing it as 'must reading for the politically curious' (*The New York Times*, 13 December 2002). Given the left-of-centre orientation of the blog in question, this endorsement is all the more unusual. In any case, journalists were fast learning that they ignored blogs as sources of information at their peril, even if they were slow to acknowledge them formally in their reports, and even then often grudgingly so. In contrast, bloggers themselves were calling attention to the shortcomings of ostensibly objective journalism, seeing in blogs a more viable alternative. 'While people from journalism backgrounds tend to say they aspire to the high ideals of truth, fairness, and accuracy', Matt Haughey of Metafilter.com argues, 'I don't think the output of most newspapers comes close to that.' When reading a blog that features reportage or fact-checking, he remarks, 'I can determine myself if the author is being factual because they'll reveal their sources in links, and I can read up on them to determine how impartial they are being' (cited in Raynsford 2003).

Further questions about objectivity surfaced in disputes about whether journalism and blogging could coincide in the same news organization. By mid-2003, several full-time journalists engaging in part-time blogging had been forced to cease and desist by their editors. Amongst them was Steve Olafson (2003), who was fired from his day job at the *Houston Chronicle* for writing his blog, The Brazosport News, without his editor's permission. A daily newspaper reporter for 26 years, he had considered his evenings spent blogging – using the *nom de plume* of Banjo Jones – to be exhilarating. 'Forget the inverted pyramid, forget space constraints, and forget five W's and the H', he commented. 'All the pomposity, hot air, and ridiculousness you see and hear are fair game in a Weblog, but not necessarily in a daily newspaper' (2003: 91). Despite his efforts to maintain a clear distinction between his respective commitments, in the view of managers Olafson's blogging had compromised his ability to be an impartial *Chronicle* reporter. Other journalist bloggers finding themselves in trouble were Kevin Sites at CNN, who was told to abandon KevinSites.net so as to concentrate on generating stories for the network; Joshua Kucera, whose editors assumed a similar stance at *Time* magazine; and Denis Horgan at the *Hartford Courant*, who was told that his blog would be suspended because it constituted a conflict of interest. Brian Toolan (2003), editor of the *Courant*, made clear what he considered to be at stake with Horgan's blogging. 'Journalists should operate in ways that don't display bias or predispositions', he wrote. 'These are ethical considerations, not legal ones, but they are central to the conduct of journalism and must be zealously maintained' (2003: 93). Horgan, who had worked at the *Courant* for 22 years at the time, was moved to the Travel section so as to ensure that his views on public issues would not 'interfere' with the newspaper's coverage of them.

Slowly but surely, however, major news organizations were creating spaces for blogs. As they gradually became more mainstream – with sites such as MSNBC in the US or Guardian Unlimited in Britain helping to lead the way – new questions were being posed about how best to align them with other, more traditional forms of reporting. Bloggers engaged in 'random acts of journalism', to use Lasica's (2003) telling phrase, would necessarily have to situate themselves in relation to professional expectations of the craft.

Speaking as someone with 19 years' experience in newspaper newsrooms, he argues that all anyone seeking to be an online journalist really needs is 'a computer, Internet connection, and an ability to perform some of the tricks of the trade: report what you observe, analyze events in a meaningful way, but most of all, just be honest and tell the truth'. At the same time, for news outlets looking to incorporate a blog onto their pages, the importance of preserving the subjective qualities of the blogger's contribution – where the absence of editors and deadlines is regarded as a virtue, as is the commitment to 'wearing our ideology on our sleeve' – would pose a daunting set of challenges. The personal voice of the blog, some feared, risked being lost beneath the impersonal constraints of objective detachment indicative of profit-led news organizations. Even those speaking with proselytizing fervour about the revolutionary potential of blogs as a new form of journalism conceded that there were challenges to overcome in smoothing the way for news organizations to make the most of them without compromising their integrity in the process.

Politics by other means

Rapidly becoming ensconced as journalism's Next Big Thing, blogs were increasingly moving into the realm of breaking news as the year unfolded. Blogging, Matt Welch (2003) wrote in the *Columbia Journalism Review* around this time, 'has begun to deliver on some of the wild promises about the Internet that were heard in the 1990s. Never before have so many passionate outsiders – hundreds of thousands, at minimum – stormed the ramparts of professional journalism.' In effect, he proceeds to suggest, some of the 'outsiders' focusing on news and current events are transforming into 'insiders' in interesting ways. Not only are blogs introducing valuable sources of information in their own right, they were also compelling the people behind them to act like journalists: 'choosing stories, judging the credibility of sources, writing headlines, taking pictures, developing prose styles, dealing with readers, building audience, weighing libel considerations, and occasionally conducting informed investigations on their own.' If certain 'lazy columnist and defensive gatekeepers' felt that the 'hounds from a mediocre hell have been unleashed', more open-minded journalists, he feels, will welcome the ways in which blogs can bring 'a collective intelligence to bear on a question'.

This 'collective intelligence', it needs to be acknowledged, is frequently politicized – often passionately so – along fiercely partisan lines. Few would dispute that the blogosphere has been sharply skewed to the political right from the outset, a primary reason being that conservative bloggers – alongside their libertarian associates – were much quicker to exploit the medium than their opposite numbers on the political left. Their motivation was derived, in the main, by the desire to counter what they regarded to be a 'liberal bias' in mainstream news reporting (however bizarre such a perception may be in the opinion of liberals). Typical in this regard is Andrew Sullivan, who – as noted above – has been one of the more prominent conservative bloggers since the early days. In his view, it is not an accident that 'a good plurality' of US bloggers are situated on the right end of the political spectrum. 'With a couple of exceptions', he contends, 'the established newspaper market in America is dominated by left-liberal editors and reporters. What the web has done is allowed talented writers to bypass this coterie and write directly to an audience' (*The Sunday Times*, 24 February 2002). This sort of criticism, namely that the mainstream news organizations bend the news to conform to a liberal political agenda, is a longstanding feature of public life in the US. It has been given greater saliency by talk radio programmes – with certain obnoxious 'shock jocks' such as Rush Limbaugh leading the way – skewing sharply to the right, but a vast number of bloggers scramble to occupy the same ideological terrain. 'Liberal media bias', in Sullivan's words, 'is a favorite topic in Blogland'.

Arguably *The New York Times*, of all the mainstream media in the US, has attracted the greatest scorn from right-wing bloggers (with CBS News and CNN, respectively, feeling almost as much heat). A case in point occurred when the 'liberal scalp' belonging to the newspaper's executive editor, Howell Raines, was claimed by the blogosphere in June 2003. Initially it had appeared that both he and managing editor Gerald Boyd would endure the fallout from the Jayson Blair scandal, the star reporter having resigned from the newspaper the previous month following allegations that he had committed repeated 'acts of journalistic fraud'. However, the onslaught of criticisms directed at Raines by political blogs, with those of Andrew Sullivan and Glenn Harlan Reynolds proving particularly influential, was such that his chances of weathering the storm were badly undermined. 'The *New York Times* used to be so powerful that anybody who was a professional journalist was leery of taking it on', Sullivan was quoted as saying in *The Sunday Times*. 'For the first time you could have sustained criticism of the paper and people working for it began to send us the latest dope.' Moreover, he adds, the blogs involved 'created a narrative which was "Howell Raines's reign of terror" and that defined the way in which the Jayson Blair affair was interpreted' (*The Sunday Times*, 8 June 2003). Arguably the most serious blow of all, however, was delivered from James Romenesko's *Media News*, a blog which became a forum for emailed memos and descriptions of staff meetings leaked by disgruntled colleagues at the newspaper anxious to give voice to their misgivings about Raines's tenure. Dismayed by the extent of disaffection exhibited on this and other blogs, publisher Arthur Sulzberger evidently felt compelled to accept Raines's resignation. 'My heart is breaking', is what he reportedly said as he ushered Raines out the door.

Conservative bloggers took enormous delight – and the credit – for mobilizing the attacks which toppled Raines. In the immediate aftermath of the events in question, a certain mythology arose about the 'legions of *Times* bashers' which celebrated the events as yet another demonstration of the growing power of blogs. However, alternative interpretations were also on offer at the time. Sounding a sceptical note, for example, is Mark Glaser (2003), writing in the *Online Journalism Review*. 'Certainly bloggers kept the turmoil roasting on high heat', he observes, 'but the blogosphere has flambéed *The Times* for errors in fact and judgement for years'. In his appraisal of the facts, and drawing on interviews with some of the participants, he concludes that boasts such as Sullivan's ('First Lott. Then Raines. And you ain't seen nothing yet') are overstated. Sifting through differing accounts of the brouhaha, he points out that Romenesko himself 'says he has no evidence that bloggers took down Raines', and that *New York Times* colleagues – he names several – 'concurred that there was no sniping from staffers' on Romenesko's site (the status of which as a blog also being a matter of dispute). 'I agree that the Internet provided a remarkable window for the outside world to watch (and speculate on) what was happening at *The Times*', reporter David Firestone, employed by the newspaper, told Glaser. 'I disagree with the blogger triumphalism we're seeing that suggests that the Web helped bring down *The Times* management.' Disagreements about the significance of the onslaught of blogger criticism – or, alternatively, to the relative impact of internal criticisms of Raines made public via the web – would continue to simmer for some time (other voices cite further incidents of damage done to the newspaper's reputation, such as reporter Rick Bragg's over-reliance on material from a freelance journalist, as tipping the scales in the direction of resignations). In any case, though, the editor himself was considered to be a deserving target in the opinion of many of the right-wing bloggers involved simply because he was perceived to be a 'liberal southerner' who was hostile to the war in Iraq.

Incurring the wrath of right-wing bloggers were a wide assortment of targets originating outside of the country as well, with the US-led invasion of Iraq being a particularly heated point of contention. A favourite one is Britain's centre-left *Guardian* newspaper, which has been consistently vilified by them over the years. British blogger James Crabtree, writing in the *New Statesman* magazine, suggests that 'in a country with no recognisable left of its own, bloggers have made [*The Guardian*] the pantomime villain of the right' (*New Statesman*, 30 September 2002). Somewhat ironically, in so doing the number of 'hits' on the *Guardian* website originating from within the US has increased exponentially. Interestingly, *The Guardian*'s site, titled Guardian Unlimited, has long been a leading exponent of blogging as a way to round out its news and features provision. Lloyd Shepherd, the site's chief producer, believed that blogs had a role to play, but were not to be confused with journalism: 'Blogging is not structured in the way journalism is. People are putting their views out in a relatively unprocessed manner.' Two factors, in his view, were important in this context: 'the personalisation of the voice of the blogger and the lack of the subbing workflow you would expect to see for any print or online publication' (cited in Raynsford 2003). This question of personalization – the 'voice' of *The Guardian*, so to speak – was being answered, in the opinion of right-wing bloggers, in the form of a decidedly liberal slant to its news reporting. Allegations of a similar sort were being made about the only other British 'quality' newspaper not safely positioned to the right of the political spectrum, *The Independent*. Especially vexing for right-wing bloggers is the newspaper's foreign correspondent Robert Fisk, who has seen his surname turned into a verb (Fisking) by those bloggers intent on seizing upon any and all perceived inconsistencies in 'liberal propaganda' passing as journalism. Much to their chagrin, Fisk's reporting has consistently withstood their criticism on points of fact, if not on matters of interpretation from their preferred ideological stance.

Concerns about the emergent tensions between journalism and blogging took on an even greater intensity in the months leading up to the 2004 US election campaign. For every critic denouncing blogs as 'soapboxes for the self-absorbed', a diverse array of others were providing upbeat appraisals of their potential to empower voters in the workings of their democracy as never before. The 'boys (and girls) on the bus', newspaper reporter Kathy Kiely pointed out, were being 'joined by a new class of political arbiters: the geeks on their laptops' (*USA Today*, 30 December 2003). During the primaries, Howard Dean of Vermont astonished seasoned commentators by mounting a bold campaign for the nomination of the Democratic Party. Often described as 'the Internet's own candidate' in press accounts, Dean's strategists sought to harness the power of new media from the outset – blogs were used extensively, such as Meetup.com for supporters to self-organize, together with fund-raising efforts revolving around political e-commerce. Despite his remarkable achievements in generating 'grassroots buzz' and record-level fund-raising alike, however, Dean eventually stepped aside in favour of Massachusetts Governor John Kerry, who would go on to win the Party's presidential nomination.

Kerry himself was reportedly well attuned to the nuances of the blogosphere, according to Peter Daou (2005), recognizing as he did that this was going to be – in Daou's words – 'the first general election with blogs as a nascent political force'. Daou speaks from a unique perspective, having been assigned with the responsibility for leading the Kerry campaign's strategy for reaching out to bloggers. He spent what he describes as 'a turbulent 2004 bunkered in John Kerry's D.C. war room, at the nexus of blogs, media, and the Washington political establishment'. Doing his best to improvise as he went along, he recalls that his principal challenge was to 'bring the energy, ideas, and attitude of the netroots into the heart of the campaign, and provide tools, information and support to the online community'. As he quickly discovered, however, he faced two major obstacles. The first was the way in which the 'prodigious fundraising capabilities of the Internet sucked up all the online oxygen', thereby thwarting many of his efforts to realize the web's potential as a research or communications tool. The second, more serious, obstacle was the unwillingness of Democratic strategists to heed what he regarded to be a logical prediction, namely that 'the party that dominated the Internet would win the election'. The new political reality being actively shaped by bloggers meant, in his judgement, that 'if the Kerry campaign truly internalized the confrontational disposition of the netroots, Kerry would win, just as I knew that if Bush channeled the fire of the rightwing blogs, Kerry could lose'. The ensuing struggle within the campaign between the old guard and the new one curtailed the possible advantages that might have been otherwise gained by a more blogger-savvy approach.

Given the array of political skirmishes transpiring in cyberspace, both of the major political parties were struggling to stay on top of developments unfolding at remarkable speed. Rapid-response teams cut through the froth of internet attacks without hesitation. 'Clearly the Internet is accelerating the pace at which politics move', remarked Jim Jordan of the Kerry campaign. 'And increasingly it seems to allow the mainstream media to rationalise editorial decisions that wouldn't have been made in the past' (*The New York Times*, 22 February 2004). A case in point, transpiring during the primaries, revolved around the Drudge Report, a right-wing blog-like website devoted to a colourful mix of news, gossip and scandal. To quote from self-congratulatory headlines cited on its site on 12 February: 'A bomb-shell was dropped on Senator Kerry today', KTBS-TV of Shreveport, Louisiana reported, one of several local television newscasts around the US to break the 'news'. Others included 'Scandalous rumblings tonight inside John Kerry's campaign' (WBTV-TV Charlotte, NC) and 'There's a report on the Internet from Internet gossip columnist Matt Drudge that John Kerry, the front runner, has had a problem with an intern in the past, perhaps an affair' (KABC-TV Los Angeles, CA). Drudge's decision to go public with the claim that several major news organizations were actively pursuing a rumour that candidate John Kerry may have had an extramarital affair was a bold one, in the view of some, and reckless in the opinion of others. In claiming that the unsubstantiated allegation – together with the account of the 'frantic behind-the-scenes drama surrounding a woman [Alexandra Polier] who recently fled the country, reportedly at the prodding of Kerry!' – represented an exclusive, Drudge dared to go where other news organizations feared to tread. In contrast with the Monica Lewinsky story, journalist Jim Ruttenberg pointed out, 'the Kerry rumor had no accompanying criminal investigation, which could justify coverage by itself'. For this reason, he adds, 'newsrooms across the country found themselves in a state of paralysis – caught between ignoring a story millions already knew about or validating a charge without independent confirmation' (*The New York Times*, 22 February 2004).

Some decided to ignore the story, others reported it when Kerry denied the charge, still others buried it deep in their campaign coverage while they waited to see what would happen. None of the news organizations initially involved – which included ABC News, *Time*, the *Washington Post* and AP – pursued it after both Kerry and Polier issued denials. 'It had been looked into', George Stephanopoulos of ABC News (and former Clinton aide) confirmed. 'But according to our investigative people, there was nothing behind it.' Over at *Time* magazine, the verdict was the same. 'I thought it was absurd', stated political columnist Joe Klein. 'There are a whole bunch of things we're looking into all the time. And there's an important word here: Drudge.' Interestingly, both of these quotations appear in a piece written by Polier (2004) in *New York* magazine, where she describes her own efforts to get to the bottom of the story in question, albeit after the damage had been done. She writes:

> It was becoming clearer: No single person had to have engineered this. First came a rumor about Kerry, then a small-time blogger wrote about it, and his posting was read by journalists. They started looking into it, a detail that was picked up by Drudge – who, post-Monica, is taken seriously by other sites like Wonkette, which no political reporter can ignore. I was getting a better education in 21st-century reporting than I had gotten at Columbia J-school. (Polier 2004)

Mark Glaser (2004a) identifies the 'small-time blogger' in question as Stephen VanDyke. Writing under the pseudonym 'Son of Liberty' on WatchBlog.com on 6 February, he stated that 'Rumor has it that John Kerry (D) is going to be outed by *Time* magazine next week for having an affair with a 20-year-old woman who remains unknown'. Evidently he insisted during an email interview with Glaser that his posting was actually a rumination on the effect of political rumours on the campaign, and so had been taken out of context. 'If a blog entry is claiming a fact and they can't back it up with other sources, or don't link to any sources', VanDyke nonetheless cautioned, 'take it with about a pound of salt' (cited in Glaser 2004a). Regrettably, during the full-fledged election campaign over the autumn months, this sort of advice – however self-serving in the case of VanDyke – was rarely heeded.

Both the Democratic and Republican campaign sites featured links to blogs – 'Bloggers for Bush' in the case of the Republicans. The Democrats took the lead in recognizing their potential, courtesy in part of lessons learned during Dean's courting of netizens, during their National Convention held at the Fleet Center in Boston during July 2004. Convention organizers arranged for a number of bloggers to receive press credentials to cover the event. Efforts to include bloggers in this way, strategist Joe Trippi pointed out beforehand, would 'help pull in a lot of younger voters and a lot of younger people. They'll have their reporters, for lack of a better way of putting it' (cited in *Boston Globe*, 10 May 2004; see also Trippi 2004). That said, however, the accommodations provided for bloggers proved somewhat sparse, as Matthew Klam (2004) recalls. 'I spent the day at the Fleet Center', he writes, 'up in the nosebleed seats, Section 320, where 35 of them, the lucky ones who had been credentialed, could fight for any of the 15 bar stools they had been provided, along with some makeshift plywood desks built along the railing'. Bloggers, it seemed, were being kept at a safe distance from their newspaper and broadcast rivals. Their struggle for acceptance continued in the face of opposition throughout the campaign months. 'The explosion of blogs', George Packer (2004) opined in *Mother Jones*' magazine, 'has blown a needed hole in the sealed rooms of the major editorial pages and the Sunday talk shows'. Nevertheless, despite affirming the value of their impact on political reporting, he proceeds to contend that they are 'atomized, fragmentary, and of the instant. They lack the continuity, reach, and depth to turn an election into a story.' Certain bloggers begged to differ, of course. Speaking as someone thoroughly enjoying the experience of blogging the election, Mark E. Madsen (2004) of Extended Phenotype argued that bloggers were engaging in the political process itself. 'What bloggers have done in this election is use a simple technology to provide a deliberative, discussion-oriented addition (not just alternative) to the one-way "broadcast" media that dominate the landscape of democracy.'

This commitment to playing a complementary role is similarly taken up by Rachel Smolkin (2004), writing in the *American Journalism Review*. Political blogs, in her estimation, make a contribution to the 'cacophony of 24/7 information sources' to a significant extent. 'While cable news endlessly repeats political headlines', she writes, 'Weblogs chatter over inside information that mesmerizes the junkies'. Not surprisingly, then, 'Big Journalism' is now 'borrowing elements of blogs, experimenting with them and sometimes even co-opting the bloggers themselves'. Pointing to a range of examples, she notes: 'Even the *New York Times* has launched an edited campaign blog of sorts, Times on the Trail, which is breezier than the paper but more straitlaced than most blogs.' For some commentators, the principal contribution blogs were making to the campaign coverage was to curb the influence of more familiar forms of 'horse-race' election reporting, and with it the 'pack-mentality' of journalists pursuing the same story. To the extent that they called into question traditional conventions, they arguably encouraged a more self-reflexive journalism to emerge – a fraught process, needless to say, which caused a certain degree of resentment. At stake, in part, was 'a battle for turf', suggests Mark Glaser (2004b). Bloggers operating as political pundits, he notes, 'can't help but make editorial writers a bit nervous as the new kids on the cyber-block invade their ink-stained territory'. The contours of this territory were thrown into sharp relief by an extraordinary event – characterized by some as a 'tipping point' in bloggers' wider acceptance – involving CBS News two months before election day.

Checks, balances and memogate

Regardless of whether or not it constitutes a 'tipping point', any appraisal of blogging's significance for the 2004 US election would necessarily acknowledge the importance of the celebrated clash between bloggers and CBS News in the crisis dubbed 'Memogate' by some, 'Rathergate' by others, in September of that year. 'It's an important moment', remarked Jonathan Klein, former executive vice president of CBS News, 'because you couldn't have a starker contrast between the multiple layers of checks and balances, and a guy sitting in his living room in his pajamas writing what he thinks'. One of the purportedly pajama-clad individuals on this occasion was Scott Johnson, a Minneapolis lawyer and one of three bloggers behind the conservative Power Line. He recalled what happened to Brit Hume of Fox News as follows:

> [. . .] I read in *The Boston Globe* early in the week that the Kerry campaign was rolling out a theme called 'Operation Fortunate Son,' to run a kind of round three of attacks on President Bush's Air National Guard service. So I started following the stories related to that in *The Globe*. *The Globe* had one on Wednesday [7 September], which I linked to and wrote about on Power Line. And then on Thursday, I read *The Globe* story about the '60 Minutes' report that had been on the television the night before. I hadn't seen it. But I followed *The Globe* story to the '60 Minutes' site. Read the story and looked at the memos on the '60 Minutes' site.
> And it struck me that the memos were an incredibly convenient fit with the announced Kerry campaign theme of last week. And I wrote a little bit about that on our site. But before I posted it, I looked at the e-mail that we had received that morning. And we had, in fact, received an e-mail from a reader who suggested that that document bore the earmarks of a computer-generated word processing rather than a typewritten document. And I posted that together with the links to the CBS story in *The Boston Globe* story. (from transcript of 'Special Report with Brit Hume', Fox News, 14 September 2004)

Evidently, following the 7:50 am post, Johnson left for work, wondering whether it might have been a mistake to have gone with the story. In the event that it proved to be problematic, however, he was confident that the blog's readers would be quick to 'set us right'. He then proceeds to add to the account:

Well, by the time I got to work, we had 50 e-mails from experts of all kind around the country, supplying additional information. And we kept updating our post with that information through the day.

Asked by Hume to respond to Klein's remarks about 'checks and balances', he states:

You know, Charles Johnson of Little Green Footballs re-created that critical August 18 memo in a few minutes on the default settings of his Microsoft Word processing system after he read the post on our site. He posted that on his site so we could all take a look. By 10:30, those documents looked like a joke. And yet, now here's CBS, five days later still in the middle of a Watergate-style stonewall. It's just incredible.

Johnson then concludes by drawing what he perceives to be a clear distinction between CBS News's actions and those of his blog, insisting that whenever the latter makes an error in judgement or fact, 'we instantaneously post corrections' so as to ensure that their readers continue to regard it as an 'honest broker of information'.

Stepping back from Johnson's account, this sequence of events can be placed in a larger context. On 7 September, the day prior to CBS's Wednesday evening 'Sixty Minutes II' broadcast, Joshua Micah Marshall had posted on his left of centre blog Talking Points Memo (which, as noted above, played a crucial role in the Trent Lott affair) news that the programme was set to present 'documents that shed light on Bush's guard service or lack thereof'. Blogs of all political descriptions were promptly stirred into action in anticipation of the broadcast, especially those on the political right which have long criticized what they perceive to be a 'liberal bias' in CBS's reporting, and an anti-Republican figure in Rather, since the days of Richard Nixon. The documents in question were memos ostensibly written in 1972 and 1973 by Bush's then commander, Colonel Jerry B. Killan (who died in 1984). Nineteen minutes into the broadcast, the first post calling into question the integrity of the memos appeared on the right-wing blog FreeRepublic.com. Four hours later, the documents under scrutiny were decried as a hoax again, this time in a pseudonymous message posted by 'Buckhead' (later to be identified as a longstanding Republican activist) to the same blog. 'I am saying these documents are forgeries, run through a copier for 15 generations to make them look old', Buckhead declared. 'This should be pursued aggressively.'

And so it was from an astonishing array of perspectives – facilitated, to a large extent, by Johnson's decision to link to Buckhead's allegation on his blog Power Line. In the ensuing mêlée, a key point of contention, as noted above, revolved around whether a 1970s typewriter had been used to prepare the documents, or a personal computer with word-processing software. In the eyes of some – including an IBM typewriter repairperson – the proportional spacing in the memos was suspect, as was the typeface of the 'superscripts' – where a raised 'th' appeared after some numbers. Wading into the swirling controversy was the Drudge Report, which linked to Johnson's blog, thereby helping to launch the story on to the national news agenda (the *Washington Post*'s story that day had also drawn attention to the memos, but it would be the next day's edition that zeroed in on the controversy: 'after doubts about the documents began circulating on the Internet yesterday morning').

The verdict from other bloggers, needless to say, was euphoric. The 'in-surrectionary pajama people', Andrew Sullivan wrote in *Time* magazine, 'successfully scaled one more citadel of the mainstream media, CBS News. One of the biggest, baddest media stars, Dan Rather, is now clinging, white-knuckled, to his job. Not bad for a bunch of slackers in their nightclothes' (*Time*, 27 September 2004). Rhetorical excesses aside, he makes the important point that it was the readers – as opposed to the bloggers themselves – who deserved the credit for discovering the clues about the alleged forgery. CBS News's select group of experts called upon to authenticate the evidence were no match for the hundreds recruited within hours to engage in discussion and debate over the precise characteristics of the memos. As a result, Sullivan adds, 'the facts were flushed out more effectively and swiftly than the old media could ever have hoped. The collective mind also turns out to be a corrective one.' Amongst those hesitating to award accolades to the blogs for breaking a story, however, were those who insisted that CBS News's television rivals would have double-checked the claims being made as a matter of course (CBS, to its credit, had made the documents publicly available by posting them online). Still, above dispute was the awesome speed in which the story unravelled under the pressure brought to bear by the blogs. Others drew attention to their function as an 'early warning system' of sorts for the mainstream media. 'In fairness to blogs', stated Christopher Isham at ABC News, 'I think [they were] the first thing that tipped us off that there might have been a problem – because they were on it right away' (cited in *Christian Science Monitor*, 22 September 2004). Few mainstream news organizations, Victor Keegan observed in *The Guardian* at the time, have 'embraced the blogging revolution as an essential part of the future rather than an irritant in the background'. As a result, he predicted, the 'CBS saga may prove to be the wake-up call they needed' (*The Guardian*, 22 September 2004).

Rather, aged 73, announced on 23 November that he would be retiring from the anchor's chair in March 2005, a year earlier than initially planned.

His decision was immediately hailed as yet another 'slaying of Goliath' triumph by some conservative bloggers who believed that they sparked it, while others were content to claim credit for hastening along the inevitable. An independent investigation into the affair, commissioned by CBS, released a highly critical report on 10 January 2005. Network executives responded by announcing that four employees would be leaving: three having been asked to resign, while Mary Mapes, the story's producer, was dismissed. 'Already under duress from years of budget cuts, poor ratings and reduced influence', the *New York Times* reported, 'CBS news suffered a crushing blow to its credibility yesterday because of a broadcast that has now been labeled as both factually discredited and unprofessionally produced' (*The New York Times*, 11 January 2005). Meanwhile, James Pinkerton's tally of the outcome in *Newsday* was 'Blogs 1, CBS 0'. Describing the turn of events as an 'historic shift in media power relationships', he credited the 'so-called pajama gang' for having generated a 'blogstorm' that succeeded in 'burying CBS under questions it couldn't answer'. Despite his obvious delight in seeing the 'Tiffany Network' effectively 'nailed', however, he sounded a note of caution: 'Now, everyone in the journalistic establishment, including this writer, is on notice: The people are not only paying attention, but also providing powerful feedback, whether we like it or not' (*Newsday*, 11 January 2005). Left unresolved by the independent inquiry were questions regarding the actual authorship of the memos. Various theories continued to circulate, as Corey Pein (2005) pointed out in the *Columbia Journalism Review*: 'The Kerry campaign created the documents. CBS's source forged them. Karl Rove [of the Bush administration] planted them. They were real. Some of them were real. They were recreations of real documents.' In essence, and despite the best expert advice, 'copies cannot be authenticated either way with absolute certainty'.

In the wake of the crisis, Rather's journalistic reputation – along with that of his network – had suffered serious damage. Mapes (2005), who had worked at CBS News for 15 years before being fired, published a rejoinder to critics in *Vanity Fair* magazine. The main blogs involved, she argued, were 'hard-core, politically angry, hyperconservative sites loaded with vitriol about Dan Rather and CBS'. Taking issue with the allegations made about typewriters from the 1970s, she referred to analysts who recognized that 'in the process of downloading, scanning, faxing, and photo-copying, some computers, copiers, and faxes changed spacing and altered the appearance and detail of fonts'. Suffice it to say, in standing by the main thrust of her programme's report, she expresses her exasperation about the way the media focused on CBS at the expense of the National Guard story. The unsubstantiated claims of bloggers, in her view, went virtually unchallenged by mainstream journalists. Evidence to support her point is easily found. Arguably typical in this regard among right-wing commentators was George F. Will (2005), who wrote in his syndicated column: 'The [television] networks were very interested in charges pertaining to a Vietnam-era story about George W. Bush's alleged dereliction of National Guard duties – until bloggers, another manifestation of new, small and nimble media, shredded it.' Such an assertion is patently ridiculous, of course, given the wealth of evidence about Bush's activities at the time. To date, no one has decisively refuted the principal claims made in the Sixty Minutes II report. Nevertheless, the coverage of 'Memogate' effectively froze the story of Bush's Guard years during the election, as Pein observes, while those 'who kept asking questions found themselves counted among the journalistic fringe'. It was less a case of victory for democracy, in his view, than a case of mob rule. Mapes herself remains steadfast. 'If I was an idiot', she maintains, 'it was for believing in a free press that is able to do its job without fear or favor'.

6 Online reporting of the war in Iraq: bearing witness

'Day 20 of America's war for the "liberation" of Iraq', British journalist Robert Fisk reported, 'was another day of fire, pain and death'. His article, published in the 9 April 2003 edition of *The Independent*, continued:

> It started with an attack by two A-10 jets that danced in the air like acrobats, tipping on one wing, sliding down the sky to turn on another, and spraying burning phosphorus to mislead heat-seeking missiles before turning their cannons on a government ministry and plastering it with depleted uranium shells. The day ended in blood-streaked hospital corridors and with three foreign correspondents dead and five wounded. (*The Independent*, 9 April 2003)

Fisk, well known for his incisive writing style, was clearly aiming to ensure that his eyewitness description of the unfolding events in Baghdad resonated with his readers. His report appeared beneath the newspaper's lead story, 'The US advance, street by street', on the front page. In contrast with it, however, Fisk's report provided the kind of personal insight that ordinarily falls outside of the conventionalized strictures of ostensibly objective, hard news reporting. Indeed, his commitment to sustaining a reporter-centred narrative – 'The A-10s passed my bedroom window, so close I could see the cockpit Perspex, with their trail of stars dripping from their wingtips, a magical, dangerous performance fit for any air show, however infernal its intent' – presumably would have been particularly valued by many of *The Independent*'s readers, even though the events in question had transpired the day before.[1]

The issue of immediacy is important here. It is altogether likely, of course, that most of these same readers would have been aware of much more recent developments in Baghdad than those described in their newspaper, courtesy of the electronic media. Television, as one would expect, was taking the lead in reporting the battle for control of the city as it unfolded on 9 April. While fighting continued in some areas, images of a statue of Saddam Hussein in Firdous Square being pulled from its plinth by a US armoured personnel carrier (the bronze head promptly, if only momentarily, draped by a US flag) featured in television newscasts around the globe. In visual terms, the fallen statue promptly assumed a charged symbolic status in some news reports, being implicitly held to represent the collapse of the regime's authority, the power of Saddam broken and removed. This television coverage, it would be later claimed by some commentators, effectively demonstrated the immediacy of real-time reporting and its benefits. No war, they argued, had been better recorded, the sheer volume of words and images offering an unprecedented degree of detail in near-instantaneous time. Citing factors such as improvements in news technologies, as well as the use of reports from 'embedded' correspondents, they insisted that many of the criticisms first levelled at 24-hour news in the 1991 Gulf War had been laid to rest.

Meanwhile, observations of a different sort were being made time and again on different internet websites in response to the day's television reporting (well before newspaper reports covering the events in Firdous Square had gone to press). Across chatrooms, bulletin boards, discussion forums, weblogs and the like, internet users gave voice to their points of view about what these events meant to them. Some rejoiced, while others, in sharp contrast, demanded to know what was really happening on the ground in Baghdad. For some, the toppling of the statue appeared to have been almost choreographed for the benefit of the cameras. Awkward questions were posed on various sites about whether it was a spontaneous act (or one organized for the benefit of US television schedules?), the composition of the 'crowd' of onlookers (was their number made to appear more substantial by the camera angles chosen?) and the extent to which these 'jubilant' people were actually 'celebrating', amongst other concerns. Many of those writing online posts vented their anger at what they regarded to be the pro-war, even jingoistic stance of mainstream news reports, singling out Fox News for particular criticism due to its perceived over-reliance on official 'propaganda' and 'spin'. Regardless of differing political perspectives, however, many users simply wanted much more by way of context, critique and explanation than television news was providing that day, and were too impatient to wait for the next day's newspapers.

Accordingly, news sites – whether 'official' ones associated with established news organizations, or 'unofficial' ones such as personal blogs – were proving to be indispensable resources. Already at the time the online reporting of the war in Iraq was being lauded – as well as being assailed – for having a formative influence on the perceptions of different publics. 'In terms of coverage', Dean Wright, editor-in-chief of MSNBC.com, had observed a month before, 'this may well become known as the internet war, in the same way that World War II was a radio war and Vietnam was a television war' (cited in Hewitt 2003). While it may be too early to tell whether this will actually prove to be the case for certain, this chapter aims to contribute to an evaluative assessment. Attention will focus throughout on the ways in which online reporting has provided alternative spaces for acts of witnessing, a process which will be shown to be uneven, contingent and frequently the site of intense resistance.

Media divisions

The differences between mainstream US and European news coverage of the build-up to war – not least with regard to the competing, and frequently contradictory, official justifications in circulation – had been stark. The contrast was readily acknowledged by some US journalists, who offered critical insights. 'Given how timid most US news organizations have been in challenging the White House position on Iraq', observed Deborah Branscom of *Newsweek*, 'I'm not surprised if Americans are turning to foreign news services for a perspective on the conflict that goes beyond freedom fries' (cited in Kahney 2003). For *New York Times* columnist Paul Krugman, there were two possible explanations for what he termed the 'great trans-Atlantic media divide', as follows:

> One is that European media have a pervasive anti-American bias that leads them to distort the news, even in countries like the U.K. where the leaders of both major parties are pro-Bush and support an attack on Iraq. The other is that some U.S. media outlets – operating in an environment in which anyone who questions the administration's foreign policy is accused of being unpatriotic – have taken it as their assignment to sell the war, not to present a mix of information that might call the justification for war into question. (*The New York Times*, 18 February 2003)

It was Krugman's contention that these differences were particularly pronounced with regard to television news, especially where CNN and Fox News (and their associated websites) are concerned. In his view, the cable newscasts appeared to be 'reporting about a different planet than the one covered by foreign media'. Here he provided a telling example, referring to the previous Saturday's (15 February) antiwar rallies:

> What would someone watching cable news have seen? On Saturday, news anchors on Fox described the demonstrators in New York as 'the usual protesters' or 'serial protesters.' CNN wasn't quite so dismissive, but on Sunday morning the headline on the network's Web site read 'Antiwar rallies delight Iraq,' and the accompanying picture showed marchers in Baghdad, not London or New York. (*The New York Times*, 18 February 2003)

Contrasting this kind of news coverage with that offered in other countries, Krugman expressed his lack of surprise that many viewers seem somewhat confused about the factors underpinning the impending conflict.

'For months', he wrote, 'both major U.S. cable news networks have acted as if the decision to invade Iraq has already been made, and have in effect seen it as their job to prepare the American public for the coming war'.

For those members of the public concerned enough about the impending crisis in Iraq to look beyond the confines of the US-centric reporting on offer, international news sources became a vital resource. Evidence garnered from some internet track-monitoring companies suggests that in the days leading up to President George W. Bush's formal declaration of war, there was a dramatic increase in the numbers of US users turning to British and other international news sites. *The Guardian's* online edition for news and information was a case in point. Speaking in February, Jon Dennis, deputy news editor of the site, stated: 'We have noticed an upsurge in traffic from America, primarily because we are receiving more emails from US visitors thanking us for reporting on worldwide news in a way that is unavailable in the US media' (cited Journalism.co.uk, 21 February 2003). US users, according to Dennis, were drawn to the 'breadth of opinion' available on the *Guardian's* site. 'As a journalist', he commented, 'I find it quite strange that there's not more criticism of the Bush administration in the American media'. In his view, it is 'as though the whole US is in shock [from September 11, 2001]. It's hard for [the news media] to be dispassionate about it. It seems as though they're not thinking as clearly as they should be' (cited in Kahney 2003; see also Chapter 4). Consequently, he suggested, it is not surprising that so many people in the US are turning to sites like that of *The Guardian*, given its ongoing commitment to reporting 'across the political spectrum rather than from just one perspective'. Both pro- and anti-war positions are presented, he added, with readers encouraged to debate the issues via the site's talk boards, as well as through various interactive features, such as live interviews with experts.

From the moment news of the first attacks launching so-called 'Operation Iraqi Freedom' on 19 March 2003 was reported, internet traffic to online news services surged dramatically. More people than ever, according to companies monitoring internet traffic such as Hitwise, Nielsen Net Ratings, and the like, were surfing the internet for news and information. In Britain that day, the level of traffic to *The Guardian* newspaper's website soared by nearly 30 per cent to around 4.5 million impressions. According to Hitwise research, *The Guardian's* site was the leading online newspaper service with a 7.26 per cent share of the market, followed by *FT.com* (5.17 per cent), *The Sun* (3.05 per cent), *The Times* (2.86 per cent), *The Daily Telegraph* (2.24 per cent) and the *The Independent* (1.51 per cent). Of the non-print sites, BBC News Online was ranked highest with a 4.69 per cent share. Evidently, traffic to this site was up by 30 to 40 per cent for the day, a level of demand which appeared to have caused the service to repeatedly 'crash' in the early hours. Over the course of the days to follow, people going online during workday hours (not least those deskbound in offices unable to access television or radio) appeared to be largely responsible for the surge in traffic to news sites. Many were seeking out alternative news sources, as well as wanting particular types of perspectives about the factors underpinning the conflict. 'These figures show the desire of British surfers to get a real range of informed opinion on the war', argued Tom Ewing, a Nielsen Net Ratings analyst. 'This shows where the internet comes into its own when fast-moving news stories are involved' (cited by *BBC Online*, 15 April 2003; see also *The Guardian*, 20 March 2003).

In the US, Yahoo.com reported that in the first hour following President George W. Bush's announcement that the conflict had started, traffic levels to its site were three times higher. The volume of traffic to its news section jumped 600 per cent the next day (Thursday, 20 March) and again the day after. The sites associated with different television networks proved particularly popular. On the Thursday, CNN.com evidently secured the highest figures for all news sites with 9 million visitors, followed by MSNBC with 6.8 million (about half of the visitors for both sites were accessing them from their workplaces). Other news sites witnessing a significant rise in demand that day included Foxnews.com (77 per cent increase), Washingtonpost.com (29 per cent increase) and USAToday.com (17 per cent). 'Without a doubt', stated Daniel E. Hess of ComScore, 'people are glued to their Web browsers for virtually minute-by-minute updates of the war as it unfolds' (cited in *Washington Post*, 22 March 2003; see also *The New York Times*, 23 March 2003). 'The new war in Iraq has made world news sources far more important', online writer Stephen Gilliard argued. 'While not all news sources are reliable, there is such a gap between the way Americans see the world and the way other people do that it is invaluable to use these resources' (cited in Kahney 2003).

For many internet commentators, the US-led attack on Iraq represented the 'coming of age' of the internet as a news medium. Regularly singled out for attention was the role of high-speed, broadband internet access, not least its capacity to enable news sites to offer users live video and audio reports, multimedia slideshows, animated graphics, interactive maps, and so forth. The rapid rise in the number of users availing themselves of the technology – over 70 million people in the US at the time – meant that providers could further enhance existing types of digital reportage accordingly (*The New York Times*, 24 March 2003). Moreover, other commentators pointed to the ways in which online news was consolidating its position as a primary news source. Research conducted during the first six days of the war by the Pew Internet and American Life Project (2003) indicated that 56 per cent of online users in the US had turned to news sites for reports about the conflict. 'More than half the people who are online are getting their news online – that's never happened before', Lee Rainie, the project's director, maintained. 'It's another milestone moment for online news' (cited in Weaver 2003).

Framing realities

'The Battle of Iraq', an ebullient President George W. Bush declared to the world, 'is one victory in a war on terror that began on September the 11, 2001, and still goes on'. Speaking before cheering officers and sailors aboard the aircraft carrier *USS Abraham Lincoln*, he stated: 'The liberation of Iraq is a crucial advance in the campaign against terror', before adding that 'we will continue to hunt down the enemy before he can strike' (cited in *The Guardian*, 1 May 2003).

This discursive alignment of the tragic events of September 11 with the war in Iraq was very much in keeping with official definitions of the crisis, definitions which sought to secure popular support for pre-emptive military action. Findings from a number of different polls carried out in the US in the weeks prior to the onset of 'Operation Iraqi Freedom' suggested that a large segment of the public remained seriously misinformed about the key issues at stake. Abi Berman, writing in *Editor and Publisher*, provided this overview of the polling results:

> In a Jan. 7 Knight Ridder/Princeton Research poll, 44% of respondents said they thought 'most' or 'some' of the Sept. 11, 2001, hijackers were Iraqi citizens. Only 17% of those polled offered the correct answer: none. [...] In the same sample, 41% said that Iraq already possessed nuclear weapons, which not even the Bush administration claimed. Despite being far off base in crucial areas, 66% of respondents claimed to have a 'good understanding' of the arguments for and against going to war with Iraq. [...] Then, a Pew Research Center/Council on Foreign Relations survey released Feb. 20 found that nearly two-thirds of those polled believed that U.N. weapons inspectors had 'found proof that Iraq is trying to hide weapons of mass destruction.' Neither Hans Blix nor Mohamed El-Baradei ever said they found proof of this. The same survey found that 57% of those polled believed Saddam Hussein helped terrorists involved with the 9/11 attacks [...] A March 7–9 New York Times/CBS News Poll showed that 45% of interviewees agreed that 'Saddam Hussein was personally involved in the Sept. 11 terrorist attacks,' and a March 14–15 CNN/*USA Today*/Gallup poll found this apparently mistaken notion holding firm at 51%. (*Editor and Publisher*, 26 March 2003)

Several of these polls were conducted, as Berman acknowledges, after members of the Bush administration had abandoned explicit references to the assertion that Saddam Hussein had provided assistance to those responsible for the September 11 attacks. Still, the alleged connection continued to form an implicit presupposition in a wide array of official pronouncements in addition to Bush's victory speech cited above. To the extent that it was re-produced as an unspoken, seemingly 'common sensical' assumption in news reports, certain journalists became complicit – intentionally or not – in up-holding a rationale for the conflict without an adequate basis in fact.

It is precisely this type of acquiescence on the part of some journalists where the dictates of official sources are concerned that throws into such sharp relief the limitations of much mainstream reporting. 'We are seeing this increased need for alternative news sources', argued Catriona Stuart of the Independent Media Center (IMC) in New York, 'because many more people are feeling generally disillusioned with our government, our corporate lea-dership and the mainstream media which favors these interests'. Her collea-gue, Jeanne Strole, added: 'More and more Americans are waking up to the fact that the US corporate-mainstream media has been bought and paid for' (cited in *Asia Times*, 7 March 2003). There can be little doubt, critics argued, that there is a corresponding link between public distrust of mainstream media and the increased popularity of international news sites. Much of what passes for journalism in the US, in Mediachannel.org editor Danny Schech-ter's (2003) assessment, 'is seen as nothing but propaganda by people in other countries and by an increasing number of Americans, who are turning to international Web sites to find the kind of news they can no longer get here'.

Online journalism, at its best, brings to bear alternative perspectives, context and ideological diversity to its reporting, providing users with the means to hear voices from around the globe. News accounts that are overly reliant upon official truth-claims are likely to be revealed as such when compared and contrasted with reports from elsewhere available online, pos-ing acute difficulties for those engaged in information management. 'After all', as *Guardian* journalist Owen Gibson observes, 'when you can see op-posing views at the click of a mouse, controlling the nation's perception of a conflict becomes a lot more difficult' (*The Guardian*, 17 February 2003). From the vantage point of most UK and US users, no site in the region attracted more intense interest during the Iraq war than that associated with the al-Jazeera satellite television network.[2] Indeed, at the outbreak of hostilities in Iraq, aljazeera.net was widely recognized as receiving the most 'hits' of any Arabic site in the world.

Of critical significance here was al-Jazeera's commitment to pushing back the boundaries of Western definitions of 'objective' journalism so as to help give voice to contrary definitions of the world. In the case of the conflict in Iraq, this meant those of the Iraqi people themselves – victims, in the eyes of the network, both of Saddam Hussein's regime and the invasion of US and UK forces to destroy it. By including in its reports what were frequently horrific images of civilian casualties, al-Jazeera re-inflected Western notions of 'balanced' reporting. It was precisely these images, in the view of Faisal Bodi, a senior editor for the site, that made al-Jazeera 'the most sought-after news resource in the world'. In his words:

> I do not mean to brag – people are turning to us simply because the western media coverage has been so poor. For although Doha is just a 15-minute drive from central command, the view of events from here could not be more different. Of all the major global networks, al-Jazeera has been alone in proceeding from the premise that this war should be viewed as an illegal enterprise. It has broadcast the horror of the bombing campaign, the blown-out brains, the blood-spattered pavements, the screaming infants and the corpses. Its team of on-the-ground, unembedded correspondents has provided a corrective to the official line that the campaign is, barring occasional resistance, going to plan. (*The Guardian*, 28 March 2003; see also Iskandar and El-Nawawy 2004)

At no time was this difference in news values cast in sharper relief than on 23 March, the night al-Jazeera broadcast footage of US casualties, as well as Iraqi television's interviews with five US prisoners of war. Al-Jazeera's decision to air the interviews was promptly denounced by US Defence Secretary, Donald Rumsfeld, who alleged that it was a violation of the Geneva Convention protecting prisoners of war. In reply, the network's London bureau chief, Yosri Fouda, argued that Western news reports were being constrained to the extent that they failed to provide accurate coverage. Regarding the Geneva Convention, he insisted that a double standard was being invoked. 'We and other broadcasters were not criticised for showing pictures of Iraqi dead and captured', he stated, 'or those famous pictures from Guantanamo Bay' (cited in *BBC News Online*, 29 March 2003).

The more heated the ensuing furore became, of course, the more news headlines it generated around the world. The very images deemed by Western news organizations to be too disturbing to screen were being actively sought out by vast numbers of people via online news sites. According to figures compiled by popular search engines, such as Google, Lycos and AltaVista, the term 'al-Jazeera' was quickly becoming one of the most searched-for topics on the web. Figures for the week in question indicated that the term 'al-Jazeera' (and variant spellings) was the term that showed the greatest increase on Google, while Lycos reported that it was the top search term, with three times more searches than 'sex' (a perennial favourite with web surfers). For Karl Gregory of AltaVista, the popularity of al-Jazeera's online sites was clear evidence of 'people branching out beyond their normal sources of news' (*BBC News Online*, 1 April 2003). The decision taken at al-Jazeera to broadcast the images, as well as to display them online, was justified by its spokesperson,

Jihad Ali Ballout, as being consistent with its journalistic ethos of reporting the war as it was being fought on the ground. In his words: 'We didn't make the pictures – the pictures are there. It's a facet of the war. Our duty is to show the war from all angles' (cited in *The Guardian*, 24 March 2003).

In the opinion of others, however, the network and its site had become mouthpieces for Iraqi propaganda. Citing the images in question, some military officials began ignoring questions from al-Jazeera's reporters at briefings. At the same time, two of the network's financial reporters were evicted from the floor of the New York Stock Exchange, their press credentials having been revoked (Nasdaq would follow suit, citing 'al-Jazeera's recent conduct during the war' as the reason). It was in cyberspace, however, that the backlash registered most decisively as various pro-war individuals and groups made clear their intent to make al-Jazeera a target of retaliation by hacking into the site until it crashed, rendering it inoperable for several days. In effect, its domain was effectively 'hijacked', such that user traffic was re-directed to a pro-war webpage featuring a US flag, together with the messages 'Let Freedom Ring' and 'God bless our troops' signed by a self-proclaimed 'Patriot'. Further attacks continued apace, one of which succeeded in di-verting users to a pornography site. Communications manager Ballout de-scribed the actions as 'a frontal, vicious attack on freedom of the press' (cited in *BBC News Online*, 27 March 2003).

The emergence of warblogs

Across the webscape in the weeks following the September 11 attacks, a new type of blog began to emerge, described by its proponents as a 'warblog'. Taking as their focus the proclaimed 'War on Terror', these blogs devoted particular attention to the perceived shortcomings of the mainstream news media with regard to their responsibility to inform the public about possible risks, threats and dangers. Warbloggers were divided, as one might expect, between those who favoured US and UK military intervention in the Middle East, and those who did not. In both cases, however, an emphasis was placed on documenting sufficient evidence to demonstrate the basis for their dis-satisfaction with what they deemed to be the apparent biases of the main-stream news coverage of the ensuing conflict in Afghanistan, and later in Iraq. For pro-war bloggers, a 'liberal bias' was detectable in much mainstream war reporting, leading them to call into question the patriotism of well-known journalists and news organizations. In sharp contrast, bloggers opposed to the war were equally convinced that mainstream reports were over-reliant on sources from the Bush administration and the Pentagon, and as such were failing to provide fair and balanced coverage. Many were able to show, with little difficulty, how voices of dissent were being routinely marginalized, when they were even acknowledged at all. For warbloggers of either persuasion, then, it was desperately important to seek out alternative sources of information from across the web in order to buttress their preferred perspective.

In the meantime, as this debate raged in the blogosphere, several warbloggers were actively crafting stories from war zones within Iraq. While it is difficult to generalize, a good number of them seemed motivated to share their eyewitness experiences of the conflict so as to counterbalance more traditional forms of war reporting. The work of CNN correspondent Kevin Sites was a case in point. In addition to filing his television reports, Sites wrote 'behind the scenes' features for CNN.com, all the while maintaining a multimedia blog. Published on his own site, Sites' blog provided his personal commentary about the events he was witnessing from one day to the next, along with various photographs and audio reports that he prepared. Evidently in light of the media attention Sites' blog received, however, CNN asked him to suspend it on Friday, 21 March 2003. A spokesperson for the network stated at the time that covering war 'is a full-time job and we've asked Kevin to concentrate only on that for the time being' (cited in *Washington Post*, 23 March 2003). Sites agreed to stop blogging, later explaining that 'CNN was signing my checks at the time and sent me to Iraq. Although I felt the blog was a separate and independent journalistic enterprise, they did not.' Reactions from other bloggers were swift. CNN's response, according to Steven Levy (2003) of *Newsweek*, 'was seen in the Blogosphere as one more sign that the media dinosaurs are determined to stamp out this subversive new form of reporting'.[3]

In contrast, MSNBC's support for blogging meant that three warblogs were focused on war coverage at the height of the conflict. 'Weblogs are journalism', argued Joan Connell, one of the site's executive producers. 'They can be used to great effect in reporting an unfolding story and keeping readers informed'. Nevertheless, while she does not share CNN's stance that blogs lack a sufficiently 'structured approach to presenting the news', she does believe that there is a necessary role for an editor in the process. In her words: 'Unlike many Weblogs, whose posts go from the mind of the writer straight into the "blogosphere", MSNBC's Weblogs are edited. Our editors scrutinize our Weblogs for accuracy, fairness and balance, just as they would any news story' (cited in Mernit 2003). Not all bloggers on the front lines were associated with a major news organization, however. Many worked as a 'sojo' or 'solo journalist', writing and editing their own copy for both online and print or broadcast media. Being almost constantly on the move entailed relying on mobile technologies, such as a notebook computer and digital camera, or even a videophone and mini-satellite dish. Still, for these bloggers, their relative freedom of movement enabled them to pursue the stories which mattered most to them – and the readers of their warblog. Herein lay the popularity of the warblogs amongst users, which in the opinion of journalist Bryony Gordon was hardly surprising: 'if a television reporter's movements aren't subject to Iraqi restrictions, then his [or her] report is likely to be monitored by the Allied Forces. Devoid of such regulations, the internet is thriving' (*The Daily Telegraph*, 2 April 2003).

Freelancer Christopher Allbritton had announced his intention to be the web's first independent war correspondent in the months leading up to the invasion. His blog, titled Back to Iraq. 2.0 at the time, called upon readers to help contribute to the financial support necessary to fund his travel and expenses in Iraqi Kurdistan. 'It's a marketplace of ideas', he maintained, 'and those who are awarded credibility by their readers will prosper' (cited in Warner 2003). Support was such that his expenses were met by some 320 donors, allowing him to file daily stories from the country using a borrowed notebook computer and a rented satellite phone. As his blog's daily readership grew to upwards of 25,000, he became accustomed to receiving emails which posed questions and suggested story leads, while others provided useful links to online materials. 'My reporting created a connection between the readers and me', Allbritton (2003) later observed, 'and they trusted me to bring them an unfettered view of what I was seeing and hearing'. This involvement on the part of his readers in shaping his reporting worked to improve its quality, in his view, each one of them effectively serving as an editor. 'One of the great things about the blogosphere', he maintained, 'is that there's built-in fact-checking. Given that so many people will 'swarm' over posts, 'generally the truth of the matter will come out' (cited in Glaser 2003b).[4]

This sense of disjuncture between conventional modes of war reporting and warblogs can be summarized as a set of structural oppositions, which include tensions such as the following identified by Matheson and Allan (2006):

authorised	unauthorised
polished	raw
objective	subjective
second-hand	first-hand
dependent	independent
packaged	behind the scenes
distanced	connective
top-down	interactive
lecture	conversation

Precisely what counts as truth in a war zone, of course, is very much in the eye of the beholder. Above dispute, in the view of many commentators, was that some of the best eyewitness reporting being conducted was that attributed to the warblog of 'Salam Pax' (a playful pseudonym derived from the Arabic and

Latin words for peace), a 29-year-old architect living in middle-class suburban Baghdad. Indeed, of the various English-language warblogs posted by Iraqis, none attracted a greater following than Salam's *Where is Raed?* (dear_raed.-blogspot.com), which had begun to appear in September 2002. His motivation for blogging was later explained as a desire to keep in touch with his friend Raed, who had moved to study in Jordan. In the months leading up to the initial 'decapitation attack', to use his turn of phrase, the blog contained material ranging from personal – and frequently humorous – descriptions of everyday life, to angry criticisms of the events around him. It was to his astonishment, however, that he discovered that the international blogging community had attracted such intense attention to his site. As word about *Where is Raed?* spread via other blogs, email, online discussion groups, and mainstream news media accounts, it began to regularly top the lists of popular blogs as the conflict unfolded. For Salam, this attention brought with it the danger that he would be identified – a risk likely to lead to his arrest, possibly followed by a death sentence. At the same time, speculation over the identity of the Baghdad Blogger – and whether or not *Dear Raed* was actually authentic – was intensifying. Some critics claimed that it was an elaborate hoax, others insisted it was the work of Iraqi officials, while still others maintained that a sinister CIA disinformation campaign was behind it. Salam responded to sceptics on 21 March, writing: 'please stop sending emails asking if I were for real, don't belive [sic] it? then don't read it'. Moreover, he added, 'I am not anybody's propaganda ploy, well except my own' (cited in *BBC News Online*, 25 March 2003).

Enraged by both Saddam Hussein's Baathist dictatorship and George W. Bush's motivations for the invasion, Salam documented life on the ground in Baghdad before and after the bombs began to drop. This was 'embedded' reporting of a very different order, effectively demonstrating the potential of blogging as an alternative means of war reporting. His warblog entry for 23 March, 8:30 pm, was typically vivid:

> Today's (and last night's) shock attacks didn't come from airplanes but rather from the airwaves. The images al-Jazeera are broadcasting are beyond any description. [...] This war is starting to show its ugly face to the world. [...] People (and I bet 'allied forces') were expecting things to be much easier. There are no waving masses of people welcoming the Americans, nor are they surrendering by the thousands. People are doing what all of us are doing – sitting in their homes hoping that a bomb doesn't fall on them and keeping their doors shut.
>
> Salam Pax, dear_raed.blogspot.com

Salam's posts offered readers a stronger sense of immediacy, an emotional feel for life on the ground, than more traditional news sites. For John Allemang, 'what makes his diary so affecting is the way it achieves an easy intimacy that eludes the one-size-fits-all coverage of Baghdad's besieged residents' (*The Globe and Mail*, 29 March 2003). As Salam himself would later reflect, 'I was telling everybody who was reading the web log where the bombs fell, what happened [. . .] what the streets looked like.' While acknowledging that the risks involved meant that he considered his actions to be somewhat 'foolish' in retrospect, nevertheless he added: 'it felt for me important. It is just somebody should be telling this because journalists weren't' (cited in transcript, CNN International, 3 October 2003).

Any bold declaration that online journalism will abolish once and for all what social theorist Raymond Williams (1958) once memorably called the 'culture of distance' will invite a more considered response, once it is situated in relation to the sorts of developments discussed above. As has been made apparent, however, these emergent forms of journalism have the capacity to bring to bear alternative perspectives, contexts and ideological diversity to war reporting, providing users with the means to connect with distant voices otherwise being marginalized, if not silenced altogether, from across the globe. In the words of US journalist Paul Andrews (2003), 'media coverage of the war that most Americans saw was so jingoistic and administration-friendly as to proscribe any sense of impartiality or balance', hence the importance of the insights provided by the likes of Salam Pax. This 'pseudonymous blogger's reports from Iraq', Andrews believed, 'took on more credibility than established media institutions'. This point is echoed by Toby Dodge (2003), who argued that Salam managed to post far more perceptive dispatches than those written by 'the crowds of well-resourced international journalists sitting in the air-conditioned comfort of five star hotels'. Communicating to the world using a personal computer with unreliable internet access, he reported 'the traumas and more importantly the opinions of Iraqis as they faced the uncertainty of violent regime change'.

In the aftermath of the invasion, the number of warblogs appearing in occupied Iraq has multiplied at a remarkable rate. Such blogs provide web users from around the globe with viewpoints about what life is like for ordinary Iraqis, viewpoints otherwise likely to be routinely ignored, or trivialized, in their country's mainstream news media. The blog 'Baghdadee' has as its tagline 'An opportunity to hear from witnesses inside Iraq'. 'A Family in Baghdad' posts the online 'diaries' of mother Faiza and sons Raed, Khaled and Majid. This excerpt, written by Faiza, is indicative of its content:

> Wednesday, 21st, May 2003
> Electricity is on at the hours : 6–8 p.m., 2–4 a.m., the Americans are spreading news about achievements they have accomplished . . . but on actual grounds we see nothing . . . we don't know whether they

are truthful or not ... The schools are open, they are teaching whatever, the importance being for the children to finish their school year. Some schools were destroyed during the war, so, they merged the students with others from another school, and made the school day in two shifts, morning and afternoon [...] (*afamilyinbaghdad.blogspot.com/*)

'Baghdad Burning', posted under the name 'Riverbend' (a 'Girl Blog from Iraq'), posted this entry on 7 August 2004:

300+ dead in a matter of days in Najaf and Al Sadir City. Of course, they are all being called 'insurgents'. The woman on tv wrapped in the abaya, lying sprawled in the middle of the street must have been one of them too. Several explosions rocked Baghdad today – some government employees were told not to go to work tomorrow.

So is this a part of the reconstruction effort promised to the Shi'a in the south of the country? Najaf is considered the holiest city in Iraq. It is visited by Shi'a from all over the world, and yet, during the last two days, it has seen a rain of bombs and shells from none other than the 'saviors' of the oppressed Shi'a – the Americans. So is this the 'Sunni Triangle' too? It's déjà vu – corpses in the streets, people mourning their dead and dying and buildings up in flames. The images flash by on the television screen and it's Falluja all over again. Twenty years from now who will be blamed for the mass graves being dug today? [...] (riverbendblog.blogspot.com/)

Words from blogs such as these ones speak for themselves, their importance for users looking beyond the narrow ideological parameters of much Western news coverage all too apparent.

The suffering of others

At no time is this more apparent, of course, than when questions are raised about the horrific consequences for Iraq's innocent civilians caught up in the invasion and its aftermath. 'We don't do body counts', a statement made by General Tommy Franks (recently retired) of US Central Command, is the tagline of a unique website dedicated to providing information about the number of civilian casualties. Operating with the help of about 20 academics and peace activists, the UK-based Iraq Body Count maintains a running tally of the civilians reported to have been killed in incidents associated with the military intervention.

In compiling their figures from thousands of news items, the site's project team is careful to follow a strict methodological framework. Specifically, casualty figures are calculated using a thorough survey of online news reports and eyewitness accounts (where sources report differing figures, a minimum and maximum number is provided), a procedure which is independently reviewed and cross-checked by other members of the team in every instance. This approach, as the authors readily acknowledge, provides the basis for what can only be an estimate. In their words:

> We are not a news organization ourselves and like everyone else can only base our information on what has been reported so far. What we are attempting to provide is a *credible compilation* of civilian deaths that have been reported by recognized sources. Our maximum therefore refers to *reported deaths* – which can only be a sample of true deaths unless one assumes that every civilian death has been reported. It is likely that many if not most civilian casualties will go unreported by the media. That is the sad nature of war. (emphasis in the original; www.iraqbodycount.net)

The project's figures for Iraqi civilian deaths, at the time of writing, were a minimum of 28,535 and a maximum of 32,153. 'By requiring that two independent agencies publish a report before we are willing to add it to the count', the authors add, 'we are premising our own count on the self-correcting nature of the increasingly inter-connected international media network'.[5] In the absence of alternative statistics from US military officials – where evidently no effort has been made to compile them – the project's site has become one of the most widely cited sources of information for journalists around the globe.[6]

Nevertheless, for individuals seeking to place a human face on these sorts of statistics, it is more than likely that they will have to look beyond the narrow confines of mainstream news reporting. It is interesting to note in this context the results of a Pew Internet and American Life Project study (2004) which suggested that more than 30 million internet users in the US have seen graphic war images online, approximately 28 per cent of whom having actively sought them out.[7] Indeed, according to the report's nationwide telephone survey conducted between 14 May and 17 June 2004, internet users are much more inclined than non-users to approve of the display of disturbing war-related images on the internet. Given that events transpiring during this period included the murder and dismemberment of US contract workers in Fallujah, images taken in the Abu Ghraib prison of Iraqi prisoners being tortured, and the capture (and subsequent beheading) of US civilian Nicholas Berg, it is perhaps not surprising that access to such imagery provoked mixed responses from users. 'Millions of Internet users want to be able to view the graphic war images and they see the Internet as an alternative source of news and information from traditional media', stated Deborah Fallows, co-author of the Pew report. 'But many who do venture outside the traditional and familiar standards of the mainstream news organizations to look at the images online end up feeling very uncomfortable.'

The report's findings underscore the extent to which it is difficult to generalize about how internet users in the US relate to online news coverage of the conflict. Evidently, the men surveyed were more likely to approve of graphic and disturbing war-related imagery being made available online than the women surveyed. 'Of the 16 percent of women who have seen the war images online', the report states, 'only 36 percent say they felt they made a good decision in doing so; 52 percent said they wish they hadn't seen them, and 3 percent said both' (Pew Internet and American Life Project 2004: 3). Apparently some 68 per cent of the men surveyed believed it was a good decision to search the internet for extreme images not covered in the traditional media. At the same time, younger users (those 18 to 29 years of age) were more inclined to approve of the use of this imagery than older users. Further findings assert that those users situated at the higher end of the socioeconomic scale, along with those with higher than average educational obtainment, were more favourably predisposed than others. Political partisanship, it seems, was also a factor. Supporters of the Democratic Party were more inclined to approve of the use of such imagery on the internet (52 per cent of them) than Republicans (42 per cent). Although no correlation is drawn with respondents' views on the war itself, one can speculate that it is likely that self-described Democrats are presumably more inclined to see in such imagery vindication for an anti-war position than Republican users.

Across the webscape, news sites are calling into question the military's preferred definitions of the conflict, not least by challenging the 'sanitized' representations prevailing in newspapers and television newscasts. 'While so much is made of the 1,000 US military fatalities', observed online journalist Linda S. Heard on the occasion of the third anniversary of the September 11 attacks, 'an eerie silence surrounds the tally of Iraqi casualties since the invasion'. Pointing out that while the deaths of the September 11 victims had been widely commemorated in public events, 'the deaths of Afghan and Iraqi civilians went unnoticed. When this inequality is publicly remarked upon, US politicians either sidestep the question or glibly parrot prepared answers' (*Gulf News Online*, 14 September 2004).[8] This relative silence is in sharp contrast, as discussed above, to the determined efforts made by internet users to see such types of imagery for themselves. Clearly al-Jazeera, along with various war-blogs, go some distance in challenging the normative limits imposed by mainstream media's definitions of 'balance', 'public decency' or 'good taste'.

Images of the horrific consequences of warfare, it almost goes without saying, are as upsetting as they are necessary.[9]

Journalists under fire

It is similarly disturbing to note the number of journalists whose lives have been claimed by the Iraq conflict. The Committee to Protect Journalists (CPJ) made headlines in January 2006 by presenting data which showed that 60 journalists had been killed on duty in Iraq since the March 2003 invasion, making it the most deadly of conflicts for reporters in the Committee's 24-year history (*Editor and Publisher*, 3 January 2006).

It was this very issue which propelled CNN's chief news executive Eason Jordan into a swirling 'blogstorm' that would sweep away his post. Speaking at a World Economic Forum conference in Davos, Switzerland, on 27 January 2005, he had shared his views about the reasons why so many journalists had been killed in Iraq. According to several witnesses at the event, he stated his belief that US military forces had deliberately 'targeted' several of the journalists in question, and was responsible for the death of 12 of them. Responding to challenges from his audience to be more specific about the intentional nature of the attacks, however, Jordan denied that he had intended to make such an assertion, maintaining instead that he had simply misspoken. He then clarified what he meant to say. One of the other people taking part in the panel discussion, Richard Sambrook of the BBC's World Service, would later recall:

> Eason's comments were a reaction to a statement that journalists killed in Iraq amounted to 'collateral damage'. His point was that many of these journalists (and indeed civilians) killed in Iraq were not accidental victims – as suggested by the term 'collateral damage' – but had been 'targeted', for example by snipers.
>
> He clarified this comment to say he did not believe they were targeted *because* they were journalists, although there are others in the media community who do hold that view (personally, I don't). They had been deliberately killed as individuals – perhaps because they were mistaken for insurgents, we don't know. However the distinction he was seeking to make is that being shot by a sniper, or fired at directly is very different from being, for example, accidentally killed by an explosion.
>
> Some in the audience, and [US Congressman] Barney Frank on the panel, took him to mean US troops had deliberately set out to kill journalists. That is not what he meant or, in my view, said; and he clarified his comment a number of times to ensure people did not

misunderstand him. However, they seem to have done so. [...] (emphasis in original; cited by Jay Rosen, Press Think, 7 February 2005)

The organizers of the conference, who soon found themselves under growing pressure to confirm precisely what Jordan had or had not said, steadfastly refused to release a transcript or videotape of the panel discussion. They insisted that the session, like most of the forum events, was meant to be off-the-record. Participants had been encouraged to speak freely without fear that their remarks would end up in the public domain.

The spark that would ignite the storm occurred when one of the Forum's participants decided to blog his account of the lively incident, thereby effectively placing Jordan's 'off-the-record' remarks squarely on the virtual record of the blogosphere. The blogger in question was not a journalist, but Rony Abovitz, chief technological officer for Z-Cat Incorporated. He had been asked to post his impressions as a first-time attendee in the Forum's blog. 'If true', he wrote about Jordan's alleged claim, 'it would make Abu Ghraib look like a walk in the park'. In the days to follow, both the *Wall Street Journal* and Fox News picked up the story, but neither gave it prominent play. Instead, that role in the unfolding drama fell to nationally syndicated conservative talk-radio show host (and blogger) Hugh Hewitt, whose comments on cable television on 1 February roused a number of viewers into action. The storm was gathering. Meanwhile, Abovitz, having chosen to disregard the journalistic rules about non-disclosure (journalists 'protect their own', he surmised), later claimed to be astonished to discover that his first ever blog entry touched off a furore. Returning to his Florida home from Switzerland – he explained to a radio interviewer afterwards – he found waiting for him 'a whole slew of messages from my office, from our corporate counsel and CNN and Jordan had been calling'. Colleagues in his company, he added, were 'just totally freaked out. I was actually pretty freaked out too that CNN and these people had been calling my office' (cited in Garfield 2005). What had transpired in the interim, not surprisingly in retrospect, was that several bloggers had mobilized in passionate pursuit of the story.

Right-wing bloggers, in particular, were incensed. Their respective reasons for declaring cyberwar against Jordan may have differed, of course, but together they were determined to push the story from the shadows out into the bright light of open debate. Most of these blogs were sharply pro-war in their politics, with a number of them enraged by what they regarded as yet another instance of 'liberal bias' in the mainstream media (the near-absence of news coverage about Jordan's remarks being seen as evidence of complicity). The intense rivalry between CNN and their network of choice, Fox News, similarly provided fervent motivation. Invoking a degree of co-ordination to these disparate efforts was Easongate.com, a hastily built site launched on 5 February. Founded by computer software analyst Bill Roggio, working together with a small group of fellow pro-Republican bloggers, the site strove to define the essence of what was at stake. 'This is a story about citizens being outraged and demanding accountability by those in the MSM', its homepage later declared. 'This is a story about citizens coming together to defend those who are defending us.' Their objectives had quickly snapped into focus. 'During the week that Roggio's site was active', Garance Franke-Ruta (2005) observes, 'it launched a petition, turned readers into letter writers to CNN, worked the phones urging contacts in the military and government to call CNN, and generally acted as a clearinghouse for information on Jordan.' In no time it was poised to commence with 'a wholesale assault' on CNN's finances – evidently a sales representative had helped to set up a database of the network's advertiser contacts – in order to advance its campaign.

Even with storm clouds gathering, most of the major news organizations remained hesitant to become involved (two key exceptions being the *Washington Post* and *The New York Times*). All of that changed at a stroke on 11 February when Jordan abruptly quit his post. Explaining his actions in a memo to staff, he wrote: 'After 23 years at CNN, I have decided to resign in an effort to prevent CNN from being unfairly tarnished by the controversy over conflicting accounts of my recent remarks regarding the alarming number of journalists killed in Iraq.' Maintaining that he had devoted his professional life to 'helping make CNN the most trusted and respected news outlet in the world', he stated that he would never have intentionally compromised his work or that of his colleagues. However, having first reiterated that he had 'never stated, believed, or suspected that U.S. military forces intended to kill people they knew to be journalists', he nevertheless conceded that his comments in the Forum panel discussion 'were not as clear as they should have been'. It had not been his intention, he insisted, 'to imply U.S. forces acted with ill intent when U.S. forces accidentally killed journalists, and I apologize to anyone who thought I said or believed otherwise' (CNN, 11 February 2005). While Jordan was hardly the first journalist to draw attention to the number of journalists killed by the US military – notorious incidents, including its April 2003 bombing of the Palestine hotel in Baghdad, where journalists were known to be staying, as well as two attacks on al-Jazeera's offices – he would be the first one to 'resign' for expressing his opinion about it. 'None of this does Mr Jordan credit', a *Wall Street Journal* editorial commented. 'Yet the worse that can reasonably be said about his performance is that he made an indefensible remark from which he ineptly tried to climb down at first prompting. This may have been dumb but it wasn't a journalistic felony' (*Wall Street Journal*, 14 February 2005).

Jordan's announcement that he was stepping down astonished colleagues – CNN's own report of the incident said it sent 'shock waves' through the television network. It also posed pressing problems for the major news organizations who had kept silent about the burgeoning controversy. As Edward Morrissey observed in the *Weekly Standard*, 'almost no national news outlet had ever covered the story, which put them in the uncomfortable position of announcing the resignation of a major news executive over a two-week scandal about which they had not bothered to report' (*Weekly Standard*, 17 February 2005). Suddenly, there was no shortage of sources willing to spin their preferred angle on events. Others elsewhere were expressing their dismay, including David Gergen of *US News and World Report*, who had served as the moderator of the panel discussion in Davos. In conveying his sadness about the resignation, he suggested that it was 'too high a price to pay' for someone who had contributed so much over 20 years. 'And he's brought down over a single mistake because people beat up on him in the blogosphere?', he asked. 'They went after him because he is a symbol of a network seen as too liberal by some. They saw blood in the water' (cited in Kurtz 2005). Gergen's apparent incredulity was understandable for those bloggers sympathetic to Jordan's plight. Outraged by what they saw as a partisan attack on the executive for the simple purpose of damaging CNN, they gave voice to their scorn. 'The salivating morons who make up the lynch mob prevail', Steve Lovelady, managing editor of the *Columbia Journalism Review*, lamented. 'This convinces me more than ever that Eason Jordan is guilty of one thing, and one thing only – caring for the reporters he sent into battle, and haunted by the fact that not all of them came back', he added (*BBC News Online*, 22 February 2005).

Further criticisms directed at the bloggers' vilification of Jordan – one headline in *The New York Times* called them 'New Media Trophy Hunters' – characterized their campaign as a relentless attack on free speech. Other critics were sounding the alarm at how quickly the network had folded under pressure from the 'conservative blogswarm'. Once again the *Wall Street Journal* offered a pertinent observation when its editorial pointed out that 'it does not speak well of CNN that it apparently allowed itself to be stampeded by this Internet and talk-show crew', before reminding the network that amongst its obligations was to 'show the good judgment and sense of proportion that distinguishes professional journalism from the enthusiasms and vendettas of amateurs' (*Wall Street Journal*, 14 February 2005). Columnist Jack Lessenberry, in an item called 'The New McCarthyism' on Metrotimes.com, did not mince his words about CNN's actions:

> [. . .] the cowardly corporate media are so terrorized by the right that they seem to have forgotten what this nation is supposed to stand for. I can't say for sure, but I have a suspicion that if Ted Turner, the mouth of the South, still owned CNN, he would have torn up Jordan's resignation, told him to get back to work, and told the weblog scribblers to go kiss his America's Cup-winning ass. But the news

network he invented is now part of the huge AOL-Time-Warner conglomerate, and money and profits are what it's all about. (Lessenberry, Metrotimes, 16 February 2005)

For others, it was a flagrant abuse of blogpower, designed to intimidate mainstream journalists who dared to stray from the Bush administration's official line on Iraq. Jordan's faith in the longstanding tradition that 'off-the-record' remarks would be respected as such had been violated, engendering a chilly climate of mistrust and suspicion. Conservative bloggers such as Glenn Reynolds of InstaPundit were unrepentant, however, insisting that 'it was the stonewalling, the lame response' that determined Jordan's fate. 'And although there are some people calling it "another scalp for the blogosphere," it was really a case of Jordan taking his own scalp' (cited in Kurtz 2005). Jay Rosen of Press Think, a progressive blog, adopted a similar line of argument. Jordan might have saved his job, he told the BBC, had he made a better effort to respond to calls for more transparency, possibly even giving interviews to bloggers (cited in *BBC News Online*, 23 February 2005). Perhaps the last word belongs to Abovitz, whose blog entry set alight the controversy. 'If you're going to do this open-source journalism, it should have a higher purpose', the neophyte blogger stated shortly after Jordan's departure. 'At times it did seem like an angry mob, and an angry mob using high technology, that's not good' (cited in *The New York Times*, 14 February 2005).

7 Participatory journalism: IndyMedia, OhmyNews and Wikinews

'Once upon a time, before the Internet revolutionalized public discourse', Joan Connell (2003) recalls, 'there was only one sure way for a person to become a pundit: get a job as a journalist and hold forth from the pages of a newspaper, magazine or a broadcast organization'. Thanks to blogs, however, everything has changed. Now, she adds, 'anyone with something to say and access to the right software can be a publisher, a pundit and observer of events great and small'.

Speaking on the occasion of MSNBC.com's launch of Weblog Central, Connell makes clear her passionate advocacy of blogging as a medium rich with promise to transform, even democratize, the media landscape. 'What had once quietly flourished in the grassroots of cyberspace has now burst into the mainstream', she maintains, 'changing the way Internet news and communities are perceived'. It is in thinking through the implications of this for MSNBC in her role as executive producer of Opinions and Communities that she advances the case for Weblog Central as the user's 'gateway to the world of personal news'. Describing the site as a 'perch' from which the user can both observe and, crucially, participate in 'the brave new world of personal news', she argues that it will provide them with the means to be a pundit too. More specifically, she envisions users making the site their daily destination as they look to interact with specific blogs – such as Altercation (Eric Alterman on politics, media and culture), Cosmic Log (science editor Alan Boyle on science and space exploration), Hardball (Chris Matthews on the art of politics), The Juice (Jan Herman on entertainment news with attitude) and Practical Futurist (Michael Rogers on technology) – as well as to a blog about blogs, namely Will Femia's Blogspotting, which 'shines a light on life in the blogosphere'. Moreover, and in keeping with Weblog Central's commitment to conducting experiments with this new narrative form, Connell issues a call to users themselves to become involved. 'We'll count on bloggers and those who know and appreciate online journals', she states, 'to help us spot trends, share tips and make connections'.

At first glance, Weblog Central's rationale for adopting this role of facilitating connections is appealing. Connell credits blogs with democratizing news-gathering and commentary, not least by providing non-journalists with access to the necessary tools and platforms. Attention is similarly drawn to the value of the blog format as 'a vehicle for breaking news', thereby re-affirming their proclaimed status as a form of journalism. She also expresses the conviction that blogs represent 'the next generation of online commu-nities, making human encounters in cyberspace more coherent and more civil'. These laudable aims, in practice, will entail a number of additional resources, including links to sites offering proprietary and open-source soft-ware so that users can start their own blog, and a continually updated list of blog indices to help users find information along with other like-minded bloggers, among other features. Weblog Central seeks to help users realize the potential of blogs as an emerging form of 'unmediated personal and public expression'. In so doing, it represents a significant intervention for efforts to take grassroots initiatives into the mainstream with the aim of enriching public dialogue and debate.

Then again, looking at Weblog Central from a different angle, it also represents an attempt to consolidate and extend the corporate hegemony of market-driven journalism. In other words, it is a question of appropriation. At risk of being obscured by laudable proclamations about this brave new world of citizen blogging are the political and economic imperatives shaping its development. In considering Weblog Central's aims and objectives, it is im-portant to recognize that MSNBC.com is owned and operated as part of the NBC News group, which draws its material from its television counterpart, MSNBC (a 24-hour cable news channel), along with NBC News, the *Wa-shington Post* newspaper, and *Newsweek* magazine, among other sources. Weblog Central, it follows, is the online extension of two extraordinarily powerful corporations, namely Microsoft and the General Electric Company (GE). Underpinning this ostensibly grassroots initiative, with its rhetorical appeal to the revolutionary potential of the internet for news reporting, lie the commercial interests of the world's largest software company in Micro-soft, and those of one of the largest multinational conglomerates in GE. The latter's interests span financial services, energy supply, manufacturing (in-cluding nuclear weapons systems), transportation, and beyond. Regardless of the relative sincerity of the individuals' motives behind this initiative, there can be no denying that Weblog Central's ownership effectively curtails its potential for developing forms of journalism capable of transgressing the limits of its corporate ethos.

Alarm bells have long been sounded about the dangers for independent journalism posed by the growing concentration, conglomeration and globa-lization of news media ownership. Some have aptly likened the control over information exercised by these companies as 'the new censorship', especially where the collective interests of public service collide with the private ones of shareholders. News, they warn, is at risk of being transformed into a mere commodity, the value of which is defined by its potential for maximizing profits. The 'bottom-line' pressures engendered by this process encourage journalists, in turn, to internalize a company mindset as being consistent with the ideals of professionalism – even where the ensuing news coverage is so often demonstrably superficial, if not misleading, as a result (see also Allan 2004a, 2005). 'I'm absolutely certain that the journalism industry's' modern structure has fostered a dangerous conservatism – from a business sense more than a political sense, though both are apparent – that threatens our future', argues journalist Dan Gillmor (2004) in his book *We the Media*. 'Our resistance to change', he adds, 'some of it caused by financial concerns, has wounded the journalism we practice and has made us nearly blind to tomorrow's realities' (2004: xv).

In light of these sorts of issues, it is hardly surprising that the language of 'crisis' is recurrently being used to describe journalism today – and why so many people look to the less-travelled corners of the web in the hope that genuinely alternative types of non-corporate journalism will emerge, develop and flourish. In the course of this chapter's discussion, several distinctive initiatives to recast mainstream reporting will be examined, each of them representing 'bottom-up' projects intended to reverse the preoccupations of 'top-down' traditional media. In the first instance, our attention turns to the Independent Media Center (IMC or IndyMedia for short), a grassroots forum of news reporting about social and political issues. The mission statement posted on its homepage describes it as 'a democratic media outlet for the creation of radical, accurate, and passionate tellings of truth', before explaining that it is a collective made up of a diverse range of independent media organizations and hundreds of journalists – professional and amateur alike – committed to social change. 'We work out of a love and inspiration for people who continue to work for a better world', the statement elaborates, 'despite corporate media's distortions and unwillingness to cover the efforts to free humanity'.

Tellings of truth

The origins of IndyMedia may be traced back to what became known as the 'battle of Seattle', when thousands of people took to the streets of the city to protest against the impact of global free trade relations. Free trade, in the opinion of many, was not fair trade, especially where the interests of developing countries were concerned. In the days preceding the World Trade Organization (WTO) meeting in late November 1999, Seattle saw the anti-globalization movement's efforts to mobilize dissenting voices gathering momentum – and a fledgling IndyMedia there to report it.

The internet had been abuzz with discussions about how best to organize a demonstration for days beforehand. Ordinary citizens from all walks of life –

including anti-poverty activists, environmental groups, trade unions, women's groups, Third World advocacy groups, farmers and lobbyists from non-governmental organizations, amongst others – were coming together in Seattle to express their demand that the WTO improve its policies. Surrounding the Paramount Theatre, where the opening ceremonies were scheduled to take place, they effectively disrupted the meeting of the trade ministers from 135 WTO member countries. To their astonishment, heavily armoured riot police moved in, firing CS spray and pepper gas into groups of demonstrators at close range. Violent clashes erupted, with many injuries on both sides. Certain members of an increasingly desperate police force resorted to the indiscriminate use of stun grenades and rubber bullets in a heavy-handed effort to claim back the streets, arresting many innocent people in the process. While the vast majority of protestors remained peaceful – some chanting 'The whole world is watching' in front of television cameras – a small number lit bonfires in the streets, and smashed what were perceived to be iconic symbols of US corporate culture – including shops such as Starbucks, Niketown, and the Gap, and branches of the Bank of America. A state of civil emergency was declared by the city's mayor, a night-time curfew was invoked around the Convention Centre, and reinforcements from National Guardsman and Washington State Patrol troopers arrived to help impose a 50-block 'no protest zone' across the city. By the end of the meeting, little of substance had been achieved by frustrated WTO delegates, and the new round of talks had been postponed. 'History has been made in Seattle', declared Lori Wallach of the Public Citizen's Global Trade Watch, 'as the allegedly irresistible forces of corporate economic globalization were stopped in their tracks by the immovable object of grassroots democracy' (cited in Weissman 1999).

News of the events unfolding on the streets of Seattle made headlines around the world. Much of the mainstream media, predictably enough, remained narrowly focused on the flashpoints of confrontation between police and protestors, offering little by way of insight into the issues at stake or their broader context. Even then, some local news organizations refused to cover protests that were not officially sanctioned by the City of Seattle, thereby dramatically reducing the scope of their reporting. Meanwhile, however, various activist-led media organizations sought to provide their own news coverage of the protests so as to show what was really happening on the ground, as opposed to what the mainstream media were reporting was taking place. To the surprise of some, they were pressing new media technologies, not least the internet, into service to provide alternative forms of coverage. Playing a vital role in this regard was the Independent Media Centre with its all-volunteer team of journalists and alternative media activists – including independent video makers, radio producers and web techies – dispersed across Seattle. 'If the mainstream media are like elephants', observed newspaper reporter Dean Paton (1999), 'then these eclectic independents are like mosquitoes, buzzing their messages through cracks and virtual crannies too small and insignificant for CBS or *The New York Times'*. Moreover, he pointed out that the type of reporting being performed by these individuals – whom he describes as 'part-activist, part-journalist' – represents a 'role model for a kind of democratic reporting made possible by new and emerging technologies'. Indeed, he saw in their presence on the scene a 'prototype for the vast democratic media of the future'.

The relative advantages of 'open source' reporting became ever more pronounced as the protests intensified. 'Don't hate the media; be the media' was quickly proving to be an effective rallying cry for the rapidly fashioned Seattle IMC. Some 400 volunteers, many of them equipped with mobile telephones, digital video cameras and tape recorders, were engaged in do-it-yourself reporting: news consumers were being transformed into producers. Many of them were proud to wear the press badge of Indymedia.org when gathering eyewitness material for the impromptu newsroom, not least disturbing evidence of police brutality that was otherwise being underreported (Seattle's chief of police would later announce his resignation in early December, amid severe criticism of his handling of the crisis). This material – which included breaking news reports, photographs, audio segments and video footage – succeeded in attracting considerable attention from around the world when it was posted on the IMC site. 'Despite having no advertising budget, no brand recognition, no corporate sponsorship, and no celebrity reporters', Jennifer Whitney (2005) points out, 'it received 1.5 million hits in its first week – more than CNN got in the same time'. At the height of the crisis, some 2000 copies of a daily news sheet, called *The Blind Spot*, were produced for distribution on the street (as well as via its website). A radio broadcast was streamed, and a nightly programme prepared for public access television. In assuming this role, IndyMedia served as a 'clearinghouse of information' for both journalists and activists who would otherwise have had great difficulty securing the resources to provide alternative viewpoints than those on offer from official sources. The internet, some commentators were recognizing, was coming into its own as a news source.

IndyMedia's promise to democratize the media struck a profound resonance. Operating on a shoestring budget, with donated equipment in borrowed space in a downtown building (provided by the Low Income Housing Institute), its volunteer workforce had shown what could be achieved. In light of this success of the Seattle intervention, independent media centres began to spring up elsewhere in the US in the months that followed – first in Boston, then in Washington DC – and around the world in places such as London, Canada, Mexico City, Prague, Belgium, France, and Italy (a process which continues to unfold today). IndyMedia's proclaimed self-determination has been at the heart of its operation. Given that its financial basis rests on small contributions from users, it is effectively positioned against the influence of market forces or government control. Its organizational structure is decentralized in that it is composed of autonomous collectives, all of which share the available resources. No attempt has been made, nor would it have been feasible in any case, to simply reproduce the structures of mainstream news organizations. Similarly, no pretence is implied about being an objective recorder of events. Although in broad terms the espoused politics of its contributors are typically oriented to the left, no official mindset is imposed from above nor is there any sort of party line to be adopted from below. An overall sense of unity or shared purpose is made meaningful, to a significant extent, by this commitment to preserving the diversity and flexibility of the local groups involved.

There are currently over 150 independent media centres situated in about 45 countries across six continents. While each local IMC admitted into the network shares the aspirations of the collective, each is also relatively autonomous, defining the details of its mission statement, finances and logistical approach on its own terms. Accordingly, although there is a degree of coordination from the centre with respect to technical decisions and editorial policy, each of the IMCs associated with the network enjoys sufficient freedom to pursue its own agendas. In refusing to be 'a conscious mouthpiece of any particular point of view', IndyMedia itself avoids any direct association with a partisan position or stance while, at the same time, furnishing the conditions for those who seek to post non-corporate news, information or analysis to be heard. Its aim in encouraging people to 'present their own account of what is happening in the world' on its newswires revolves around a desire to empower individuals to effectively 'become the media' themselves. As such, it is intended to be a 'safe place' for dissent to be articulated, given that no formal prohibition is placed on the points of view expressed, other than that they are respectful of the editorial policy. On those occasions when offensive outbursts of hate occur (sexist, racist, homophobic, and so forth), the discussion can be temporarily blighted until the item in question is 'hidden' from sight – even then, in the case of most centres, it will remain viewable behind the main pages. Ever sensitive to questions of censorship, activists seek to ensure as open a dialogue as possible.

Taken together, editorial rules of inclusion – and, more to the point, exclusion – constitute a political statement. Principled commitments to a collaborative, non-hierarchical mode of operation, based on group consensus, can be sorely tested. Various instances of hate speech – as well as certain libellous allegations – have sparked controversy over the years, earning IndyMedia a certain notoriety in the view of some critics (at one time, Google News moved to suspend IMCs from its searches). Lapses in accuracy, unintentional and otherwise, as well as overly zealous opinions – not to mention occasional acts of deliberate vandalism or sabotage – similarly pose serious problems for 'admins' (trusted to hold the passwords) responsible for maintaining the site's journalistic integrity. Advocates contend that this is the price to be paid for upholding the principle of open publishing, where anyone with an internet connection may publish to the newswire simply by clicking on the 'publish' link. Posts are typically anonymous, which poses questions about accountability. Indymedia relies on those who are contributing posts to do so in accordance with its editorial guidelines, namely to be thorough, honest, and accurate in their reporting, on the understanding that the actual post will not be edited by a designated editorial collective. Those posts that violate the guidelines will be promptly cleared from the front page of the newswire. At the same time, IndyMedia does not seek to set an overall news agenda, choosing to depend instead on its reporters – and readers – to determine what should be covered, how and why. Each of these users, it goes without saying, will exhibit their own biases, so the site advises everyone to read its contents with a critical eye (just as they should do with corporate news, it hastens to add). Anyone objecting to the content of what is posted can express their alternative view by using the 'add your own comments' link situated beneath each post. This strategy, while sound in principle, can be ineffectual at times, as reasoned critique is sometimes lost in a flurry of heated rants and diatribes.

The thorny question of whether or not an individual contributor posting a news item qualifies as a 'journalist' is left by IndyMedia for each person involved to decide for themselves. In the early days, much of the news coverage focused on up-to-the-minute reporting of various demonstrations following in the wake of Seattle around the world. What the activists turned DIY reporters lacked in journalistic experience, they typically made up for with enthusiasm and commitment. Gradually, as the network grew and its resources improved, the range of news items expanded to encompass a much wider array of stories, and reporting styles. In the case of New York IndyMedia, for example, the collective teaches people how to become good journalists. 'We've had lots of community reporting workshops', states John Tarleton, which have proved worthwhile. He adds:

> [...] people have come in off the street with little or no experience, but burning with a story they want to tell. Sometimes it takes them several months to write their first story, but they stick it out. We do a lot of skill sharing – people who want to communicate their ideas can get better at it. Anyone who sticks it out for six months or so can be writing regular news stories. The bottom line is that articles have to be well-written, accurate, fairly non-rhetorical, and convey radical ideas through quality writing and research. (cited in Whitney 2005)

There is always the danger, he points out, that good reporting will be discredited by weaker efforts, so certain standards need to be maintained. At the same time, however, questions of quality are unlikely to be answered in strict journalistic terms when for many of the reporters involved what matters most is the message being communicated. Informing their efforts is a keen desire to make available news that can be used to effect social justice, a commitment that will necessarily fashion IndyMedia first and foremost into an alternative, non-commercial resource for citizen power. Activists are mistaken to rely on the mainstream media to communicate their message, Chris Burnett, a founding member of the Los Angeles IMC, observes. 'Inherent in the structure of the mainstream press is the need to sell people's minds to advertisers', he argues. 'It makes absolutely no sense for the mainstream press to cover issues the way activists would like to see them covered' (cited in *LA Weekly*, 21 July 2000).

Indicative of IndyMedia's success, paradoxically, is the degree of pressure being brought to bear upon it by the state. A case in point was the police seizure on 7 October 2004 of two of IMC's computer servers in the UK, thereby disabling some 21 IMC sites worldwide as a result. The servers in question were hosted by the London branch of the US-based Rackspace Managed Hosting company, which felt it had little choice but to comply with the seizure pursuant to a court order, even though it was not clear who was behind the action. The servers were eventually returned on 13 October, although suspicions of Federal Bureau of Investigation (FBI) involvement – possibly intervening on behalf of the Italian and Swiss governments – were unconfirmed. Official silence similarly descended over questions raised about the legality of the seizure, with no effort made to disclose the nature of the specific allegations at stake (evidently Rackspace itself was prohibited from providing information). Although this was not the first occasion when IndyMedia had found itself placed under such pressure, the ensuing controversy garnered mainstream press attention. Condemnations of the action were swift and widely reported. 'We have witnessed an intolerable and intrusive international police operation against a network specialising in independent journalism', declared Aidan White of the International Federation of Journalists (IFJ). 'The way this has been done smacks more of intimidation of legitimate journalistic inquiry than crime-busting' (cited in IFJ statement, 8 October 2004).

Nor would such Kafkaesque situations, tantamount to censorship in the view of IndyMedia, stop there. Bristol IndyMedia had its server seized on 27 June 2005 by British Transport Police apparently concerned about an anonymous post proposing an 'action' against a railway train which, in their view, represented an 'incitement to criminal damage' of property. This type of intervention reaffirmed the view of some observers that the internet was being treated in a manner reminiscent of efforts made centuries ago to silence the printing press. Significantly, what for IndyMedia was considered to be a violation of the rights of the free press was, in the view of the police, a criminal matter involving a server that was 'not journalistic equipment'.

Amongst those alarmed by the dispute was Kurt Opsahl, staff attorney at the digital rights group, the Electronic Frontier Foundation. 'By seizing the server, the UK authorities pulled the plug on the entire Bristol website – our modern printing presses – and took down a host of political journalism', he told the BBC. 'Every news publisher should be wondering, "will I be silenced next?"' (cited in BBC News Online, 30 June 2005).

The people's news source

South Korea is frequently described as 'the most wired country in the world', and as such one of the world's leading 'webocracies'. High-speed broadband connections exist in some 78 per cent of households, which is more than double the current rate in the UK (and several times greater than in the US). It is in this milieu that a new interactive approach to citizen journalism has emerged. Typically described as an 'online newspaper', OhmyNews shares some features with IndyMedia, but is organized in accordance with different imperatives – not least its aim to call upon ordinary people to provide a form of reporting that serves as an alternative to the mainstream, conservative media while, at the same time, striving to ensure that the news site generates a financial profit. 'My goal was to say farewell to 20th-century Korean journalism, with the concept that every citizen is a reporter', declared Oh Yeon Ho, the site's founder. 'The professional news culture has eroded our journalism', he adds, 'and I have always wanted to revitalize it. Since I had no money, I decided to use the Internet, which has made this guerrilla strategy possible' (cited in French 2003). This 'guerrilla strategy', as Oh describes it, has indeed proven to be a remarkably successful, not only financially – rather unusually for an online news organization – but also in journalistic terms within Korean society. OhmyNews – in the words of one British newspaper – has become 'the world's most domestically powerful news site' (*The Guardian*, 24 February 2003).

The shoestring operation behind OhmyNews was set in motion by Oh, a 'lifelong journalistic rabble rouser' (to borrow an apt phrase from *The New York Times*), working with four students who were attending a journalism school where he was employed at the time. Its formal launch on 22 February 2000 at 2:22 pm represented the first major step in the fulfilment of his impassioned belief that all citizens can be paid reporters with the help of the internet. The choice of name, Oh takes care to point out, is not a play on his name. Rather, it was derived from a celebrated comedian's catchphrase, 'Oh my God', popular at the time of the launch, which seemed to capture something of the sense of surprise – 'when you see something that really has news value and you get excited about it' – that Oh was keen to convey. The initial idea for the site occurred to Oh while he was working on his master's degree in journalism in the US in the late 1990s. Major influences on this thinking were the strategies he saw being used by the Christian right to attack what they perceived to be the 'liberal media' in the US (Oh was impressed by the tactics, if not their desired objective), as well as by the experiences he had acquired as a reporter for a monthly progressive magazine, *Mal*, during Korea's years of dictatorship. Like many of his fellow members of the 386 generation (people in their 30s, educated in the 1980s, and born in the 1960s), Oh had long envisioned a day when they would 'overthrow the right-wing media establishment' once and for all. 'My generation, the 386 generation, were in the streets fighting in the 80s against the military dictatorship. Now, 20 years later, we are combat-ready with our internet', he told a BBC interviewer. 'We really want to be part of forming public opinion – and all of us, all of the 386 generation are now deployed with the internet, ready to fight' (cited in BBC News Online, 12 March 2003).

In striving to realize its aim of being 'the people's news source', OhmyNews very quickly established itself as an ambitious challenge to conventional journalism. An initial staff of four (since grown to over 50) were confronted with a range of logistical difficulties in coping with the demands placed upon them by a rapidly growing community of citizen reporters (from an initial 700 to about 35,000 according to a recent calculation by the site). The vast majority of stories appearing on the site – some 80 per cent – are written by ordinary citizens keen to try their hand at journalism. The content for the remaining 20 per cent of the newspaper is prepared by staff journalists, some of whom cover major stories, while others assume responsibility for editing and fact-checking the material sent in by 'amateurs', such as students, office workers, police officers and shopkeepers. 'Reporters are not some exotic species', Oh observes, 'they are everyone who has news stories and shares them with others' (cited in *Financial Times*, 6 November 2004). The site's founding principle is that everyone is invited to participate, once they have registered, by emailing a news or opinion item (or blending of both therein) regarding whatever topic interests them, from highly personal musings about everyday life, to a sports report about a local team's triumph, to a fresh angle on the most pressing international issues of the day. As Oh himself elaborates:

> I think citizens like to write their own articles, but simultaneously, they like to be edited by professional reporters [. . .]. OhmyNews is a kind of combination of the merits of the blog and the merits of the newspaper. We know what the netizen wants: at the end of every article we have a comment area, and one issue had 85,000 comments. That story began with a suggestion from a citizen reporter, and citizens commented, so it's a unique way to generate a lot of content [. . .] Our main concept is the citizen reporter. Our second concept is: demolish the news-writing formula. We say: 'Please

communicate in your style: if it is convenient for you, that's fine. Don't just follow the professional reporters.' (cited in Schofield 2004)

The overall editorial policy is fashioned to a significant extent by the emphases discernible in the collective response, which means in a practical sense that diverse publics are shaping the agenda. Citizen reporters are openly encouraged to identify stories that the mainstream media are not pursuing. The site's editors sift through the flow of items arriving each day (about 200 on average) to rank them on the basis of their relative newsworthiness, before making a judgement about where to place them in the hierarchy on the site. Those items deemed to warrant priority are positioned on the top of the most prominent pages, while those considered to be of a more specialized interest are relegated to back pages (distinctions are made between 'basic', 'bonus' and 'special' items). Such decisions determine, in turn, the relative size of the payment awarded to the citizen reporter for his or her story. A highly valued item can earn as much as £12 or so (about $20 US), although a more typical sum would be a small fraction of that amount. Even for those employed as editors by OhmyNews (the majority of whom having been drawn from the ranks of citizen reporters), the sense of reward is greater than the monies involved. 'We are becoming very powerful', Bae Eul-sun, a member of the editorial team, comments. 'The pay is lousy, but it is very satisfying to work here because I really feel like I can change the world little by little' (*The Guardian*, 24 February 2003).

The news site's reputation for investigative reporting is hard-won. Editors interact with citizen reporters on discussion forums, answering questions but also negotiating story ideas, angles and possible sources to approach. 'When the contributors send us stories', Jean K. Min states, 'we often send them back and ask them not to try to imitate the official news writing style but be themselves instead' (cited in *Helsingin Sanomat*, 8 January 2005). Some critics have noted that certain imbalances exist in this regard, not least with respect to gender and age, which impact on the nature of the items. Statistics gathered by the site indicate that about three-quarters of citizen reporters are male, and that the largest age group is made up of people in their 20s. Other critics complain that little pretence is made of objectivity; rather, citizen reporters typically make their personal point of view explicit, thereby inviting a more dynamic relationship with the reader than that derived from dispassionate forms of journalism. In the eyes of critics, this makes OhmyNews appear less professional than it should be, but its advocates consider this departure from the bland strictures of impartiality to be a virtue. In any case, no formal responsibly is assumed by OhmyNews for the accuracy of the content provided by its reporters, who post using their real identities and in accordance with an agreed code of ethics (copyright for what they write is shared between them and the site). To date, only a handful of stories have sparked legal repercussions – four retractions published in the first four years – none of them serious enough to test this policy. The site has also fallen victim to hoaxes (news that Microsoft's Bill Gates had been assassinated was reported using a source that turned out to be a fake CNN news site), and must always guard against public relations or marketing people posing as citizen reporters so as to try to pass off advertisements for a commercial product or service as a legitimate news item. 'We put everything out there', states Oh, 'and people judge the truth for themselves' (cited in AP, 12 May 2003).

OhmyNews's guiding ethos is similarly defined by its commitment to investigative reporting, which partly explains its appeal to South Koreans, who see on its pages an array of stories otherwise being ignored or down-played by the mainstream media. Scoops have been numerous, as the site's reporters have made the most of their contacts, access to information (re-velations concerning secret payments made by the Hyundai group to North Korea, for example, was an OhmyNews exclusive), or presence on the scene to file an eyewitness report. One of the site's formative breaks from its rivals occurred in June 2002. Two schoolgirls were struck down and killed by a US armoured vehicle during a training exercise in a village a short distance from the heavily fortified border with North Korea. OhmyNews's intensive, hard-hitting reporting of the accident, which was otherwise being studiously ig-nored by the country's predominantly conservative press, pushed the story into national prominence. One of the site's readers was sufficiently moved to call for anti-US demonstrations to be organized in response, an idea that ignited several such events in the months to come, all of which received extensive coverage on the site. In this way, its citizen reporters were seen to be tapping into a rising tide of anti-Americanism (even exacerbating it, in the eyes of critics), which would have far-reaching implications for South Korea's political establishment.

OhmyNews's greatest 'moment of glory' to date occurred on election day on 19 December 2002, when Roh Moo-hyun – widely considered to be a distant prospect at the outset – won an extremely close presidential race. Roh, a reformist human rights lawyer, was relatively unknown on the political scene. In the view of the leading newspapers, he was a dangerous leftist un-deserving of their attention. In a sharp departure from this stance, Ohmy-News reported his campaign events in considerable depth. The growing popular support for Roh was propelled even further by the coverage, even-tually to the point that the mainstream media were forced to recognize its significance. OhmyNews's readers were energized, triggering sharp spikes in hits to the site, and also generating an extraordinary e-campaign of emails and mobile telephone text messages aimed at persuading people, especially younger voters, to become involved (the site registered 20 million page views per day during the campaign). Roh's victory astonished the political – and media – establishment, ushering a decisive shift in Korean public life. 'In the past, the conservative papers in Korea could – and did – lead public opinion. They had the monopoly', Oh points out, before crediting OhmyNews for overcoming their hostility to Roh by generating support for his candidacy. In the 'battle between the conservative media and the netizens of Korea', he surmises, 'the netizens won' (cited in BBC News Online, 12 March 2003).

The 'one-way street' of Korean journalism, as Oh characterized it, was rapidly opening up in multiple directions in the aftermath of the election. An ebullient Roh granted OhmyNews his first interview as president-elect, the exclusive being an effective way to express his gratitude for the support given to him by so many of its readers (members of the younger generation being labelled 'wired red devils' in some newspaper accounts). This recognition for its role in galvanizing netizens further enhanced the site's credibility in journalistic terms, sending powerful signals to its conservative-oriented rivals that a sea change in media politics was underway. Oh himself, in acknowledging that the media system is tilted decisively in favour of conservative interests, sees in OhmyNews a means to redress the imbalance. Few deny that the influence of this 'news guerrilla organization' has grown to the point that it cannot be safely ignored by politicians, even though many of them continue to object to its perceived anti-corporate, anti-government and anti-American ideals informing its collective sense of news values. Its creative use of the web as a news medium is seen to be especially effective in engaging the interests of young people, who otherwise are assumed to be disinclined to follow current affairs closely, or at least not mainstream press coverage of them. Commentators frequently point out that OhmyNews's success appears to be at the expense of rival media, given that evidently more than half of the younger generation do not read newspapers on a regular basis. 'Our readers have high loyalty', states Oh, 'because the mainstream media ignores their voices' (cited in *Financial Times*, 6 November 2004). In any case, above dispute is the fact that the number of OhmyNews's users continues to grow while circulation figures for its leading newspaper rivals are in marked decline. Meanwhile, President Roh's charmed relationship with the site has proved to be short-lived. His efforts to improve relations with the Bush administration have seen the site redouble its efforts to challenge the political status quo.

Now firmly ensconced as a household name in Korea, OhmyNews averages about 2 million page views each day, with major stories sending those figures skyrocketing. After a slow start, the site has been financially profitable since the autumn of 2003. It relies on advertising revenue in the main, but also sells content licences (such as to the portal Naver as well as to Yahoo Korea) and receives voluntary donations from supporters. 'Making money is important, but more important is maintaining our identity', Oh states. 'The importance of advertisers must not grow too big' (cited in *Helsingin Sanomat*, 8 January 2005). An additional source of income is a weekly paper-based version of OhmyNews, which first appeared in April 2002. Distributed in the streets for free, it carries advertisements, and also encourages readers to take out paid subscriptions. On its pages the relative share of citizen reporters' stories is reversed, with staff preparing about 90 per cent of the content (here it is also worth noting that the weekly also enables the site to be recognized, in legal terms, as a member of the news media). Profits continue to be modest for OhmyNews overall, but have improved markedly for some of its citizen reporters due to a recent innovation best described as a tipping service. Readers can now express their appreciation of a particular reporter's story by contributing a small fee directly to him or her on the site. OhmyNews receives a small commission as well, which has proven to be surprisingly lucrative on occasion. Meanwhile, the drive for financial security has seen the site's multimedia presence continue to expand, with new initiatives such as OhmyTV and Web radio underway, and an ever greater emphasis being placed on news photographs in recognition that the majority of Korea's young people carry a camera-equipped mobile telephone with them.

OhmyNews's pioneering efforts to reconcile citizen journalism with the dictates of the financial balance-sheet has hardly gone unnoticed, of course. The site, as *Newsweek* magazine has observed, has 'attracted the attention of media giants around the world who wonder: is this Korean start-up the future of journalism?' (*Newsweek*, 18 June 2004). Certainly, Oh and his team took an important step in this direction with the launch of OhmyNews International, an English-language site, in February 2004. It has already gone some distance towards realizing its declared aim of drawing upon 'world citizen reporters' for its content, with some 300 citizen journalists already signed up – and plans for several thousand more to be added over the next few years. A further step toward realizing Oh's ambition to make OhmyNews the 'epicentre of world opinion' will be Japanese and Chinese versions of the site, both of which are in the planning stages. Each country importing its business model enhances the main site's profitability, but he insists that his primary motivation is to see the OhmyNews philosophy, namely 'citizen participatory journalism', spread around the globe. In so doing, it simultaneously extends a political project. 'OhmyNews is a kind of public square in which the reform-minded generation meet and talk with each other and find confidence', Oh contends. 'The message they find here: we are not alone. We can change this society' (cited in *Newsweek*, 18 June 2004). Quite how this type of engagement will impact on different national contexts promises to be fascinating to watch, but there is no reason to believe it will take hold in the same way. Much will depend on the relative openness of the public sphere in question, especially where the exercise of state and corporate control is concerned, and the reach of the informational infrastructure. To build alternative forms of journalism in the name of enhancing democracy, as the experience of OhmyNews demonstrates, is necessarily to contravene the interests of the more traditional elite news organizations.

The politics of neutrality

Wikinews – 'the free news source you can write' according to its main page – represents a similarly bold venture launched under the rippling banner of citizen journalism. The site's principal aim, as detailed in its mission statement, is to 'create a diverse environment where citizen journalists can independently report the news on a wide variety of current events'. Computer programmer Ward Cunningham is widely credited with creating the first wiki-software in 1995. Evidently his 'writeable web page' program acquired the term 'wiki' from the Hawaiian phrase 'wiki wiki' (meaning 'quick') which he had happened to notice was being used by a bus service on the islands during his honeymoon visit. Several years later he was contacted by internet entrepreneur Jimbo Wales, who was curious to know whether the 'wiki' concept could be applied to an online encyclopaedia he was planning to develop. In essence, a wiki is an editable page that enables any user to post an item or, alternatively, edit or correct anyone else's item (or even vote for it to be removed) within a wider social network. Any changes made will be recorded for viewing, and can be easily reversed – or further improved upon – by the next person. What would soon prove to work for Wales's multilingual encyclopaedia, Wikipedia, would be pressed into service to create the nascent news service Wikinews soon after.

Wikinews is an initiative of the non-profit Wikimedia Foundation, its parent organization, based in St Petersburg, Florida. Founded by Wales, the Foundation oversees its extraordinarily popular Wikipedia, launched online in January 2001. Wikipedia operates by drawing upon the energies of dedicated volunteers, being financed on the basis of donations from its community of supporters (no online advertising is allowed to appear). The Wiki commitment to developing free, open content for the public in a manner that is ideologically 'neutral' is intended to overcome the digital divide of information inequality. The Wikipedia project is guided by transparent decision-making, where posted entries are never complete, being open to revision and elaboration by anyone at any time. For better or for worse, there is no 'deference to experts' – everyone enjoys equal status within a larger process of 'collective intelligence'. This collaborative information-gathering has also been extended to several other Wiki initiatives, such as Wiktionary (a dictionary and thesaurus), Wikiquote (a repository of quotations), Wikibooks (with Wikijunior and Wikiversity versions), Wikisource (a library collection of free content source texts), Wikimedia Commons (a resource made up of texts, images, music, sound and video clips to be used on the pages of any Wikimedia project), and Wikispecies (a directory covering animals, plants, fungi, bacteria, and so on). More closely associated with Wikinews are three subprojects: Audio Wikinews (to provide audio files), Wikinews Broadcast (video content) and Wikinews Print edition (a daily pdf version), amongst others. 'Imagine a world in which every single person on the planet is given free access to the sum of all human knowledge. That's what we're doing', states Wales with reference to Wikipedia. In the case of Wikinews, however, a related point is made. 'If the mainstream media can't do good, unbiased journalism', he adds, 'then we'll have to do it for them' (cited in Ulmanu 2005).

Ideas about how best to establish a collaborative system of news-gathering and reporting continue to evolve. Evidently the inspiration for Wikinews can be traced back to a two-sentence proposal contained in an anonymous post to the Meta-Wiki community. Writing under the name 'Fonzy' on 5 January 2003, Daniel Alston stated: 'I thought of another brilliant sister project idea: Wiki + news = Wikews. The point of this project is to have the news on a wide variety of subjects, unbiased and in detail.' Intrigued by this suggestion, Erik Möller (using the name Eloquence) drafted the original project proposal. In the months to follow, the idea gradually took shape – initially in the face of opposition expressed by some Wikipedians – with an eye to creating a rudimentary prototype for testing in 2004. A demonstration wiki was introduced by November, which led to a beta version being made operational on 3 December (a German edition was launched at the same time). This decision to proceed had been taken following an online vote, where it received widespread support. In the words of its mission statement:

> We seek to promote the idea of the *citizen journalist*, because we believe that everyone can make a useful contribution to painting the big picture of what is happening in the world around us. The time has come to create a free news source, by the people and for the people. We invite you to join us in this effort which has the potential to change the world forever.

By March 2005, the English version of Wikinews had reached 1000 pages, a remarkable achievement by any measure, albeit one that is easily overshadowed by the spectacular success of Wikipedia, with its millions of entries in over 200 languages. The wiki ethic at the heart of Wikinews invites a particular type of relationship with its volunteer journalists, or 'wikinewsies' as they are sometimes called, that revolves around their continued good will, reliability and – even though the vast majority of them post anonymously – shared accountability.

Mutual trust and cooperation are the key 'checks and balances' guiding the conduct of Wikinews. Given that it is impossible to determine who has posted a particular entry, or altered someone else's, the site is always vulnerable to those seeking to deliberately compromise its integrity as an alternative news source. 'We live in a universe of new media with phenomenal opportunities for worldwide communications and research', remarked one

individual claiming to have been defamed in a Wikipedia entry, 'but popu-
lated by volunteer vandals with poison-pen intellects' (cited in Seelye 2005).
Of particular import for Wikinews in this regard is the policy to be followed
by users when referring to points of fact. Specifically, all such sources used for
information must be cited, and they must be verifiable, at least in principle,
by someone else. In the case of original reporting, field notes must be presented on the article's discussion (Talk) page. 'In Wikipedia, the writing style
of an encyclopedia is more timeless', Wales explains. 'You can get it right
eventually. It's going to be the same article for many years. With a news story,
the actual story has a limited lifespan. If it's not neutral, you've got to fix it
quickly' (cited in Glasner 2004b). Disputes over points of fact and interpretation are inevitable, of course, as the site's policy guidelines readily
concede: 'None of us are mind-readers, and as nifty as Wikinews is, even this
is not a perfect communication medium.' In encouraging users to be patient
and polite with one another, it also offers specific tips for resolving problems.
Criticisms, as one might expect for a fledgling site, are not in short supply.
Some point to gaps in the coverage – identifying important stories that escaped Wikinews attention – while others highlight the scoops achieved by the
network of volunteer reporters. Still others complain that too large a percentage of the items are rewritten news stories from elsewhere, when what the
site needs is more original reporting (a criticism also directed at IndyMedia, as
noted above).

Easily the most contentious policy adopted by Wikinews is its insistence
that a 'neutral point of view' (NPOV) be upheld by its citizen journalists. For
Wales, NPOV is 'absolute and non-negotiable' for several reasons, the most
important of which is that it is the only way to prevent bias ('If you want to
tell the world what you think', he argues, 'try blogging'; cited in Mandel
2005). The incentive for users to avoid exhibiting bias in their writing is
readily apparent – failure to do so will mean that your words will be promptly
rewritten by someone else. 'The only way it can survive', he points out, 'is if
your writing is acceptable to an extremely wide audience' (cited in Glasner
2004b). In maintaining that news items should be written without bias, the
policy revolves around the belief that it is possible to ensure that differing
views can be represented fairly. Rather than suggesting that a single, 'objective' point of view is advanced, each item should avoid advocating (explicitly
or implicitly) a particular position at the expense of alternative ones. In
Wales's original formulation, the NPOV clause states:

> The neutral point of view attempts to present *ideas* and *facts* in such a
> fashion that both supporters and opponents can agree. Of course,
> 100% agreement is not possible; there are ideologues in the world
> who will not concede to any presentation other than a forceful
> statement of their own point of view. We can only seek a type of

writing that is agreeable to essentially rational people who may differ on particular points.

Given the site's acknowledgement that 'people are inherently biased', an emphasis is placed on encouraging 'intellectual independence' by presenting multiple viewpoints as fairly as possible so that users can make up their own minds about what to accept as true. 'Neutrality subverts dogmatism' is a key philosophical tenet, one to be rendered in practice as: 'presenting conflicting views without asserting them'. In other words, the prevailing understanding of NPOV is that it is not actually a point of view at all, but rather the conviction that 'when one writes neutrally, one is very careful not to state (or imply or insinuate or subtly massage the reader into believing) that *any particular view at all* is correct'. The belief that 'fact' can be separated out from 'opinion' – a longstanding, if in my view highly problematic, principle of impartial journalism – is in this way given a novel re-inflection to the extent that it is made possible by collaborative contributions from across the community of users.

Accordingly, in contrast with IndyMedia's political agenda, on the one hand, and OhmyNews, where users are free to express a subjective opinion, on the other, Wikinews occupies a more traditional journalistic realm. An interesting attempt by a mainstream news organization to test the practicality of its NPOV philosophy was undertaken by the *Los Angeles Times* in June 2005. Latimes.com enjoys a reputation for being more innovative than most when it comes to experimenting with new approaches, such as event-driven blogs, in the pursuit of original content. 'Members of our staff are using the Internet in their daily reporting', stated the site's editor Richard Core, 'and they're seeing for themselves how the pace of news and exchange of information happens' (cited in Colombo 2005). In deciding to introduce a new feature dubbed a 'wikitorial', the newspaper sought to empower its readers to edit or rewrite an editorial each day. The editorial page editor Andrés Martinez, during an interview shortly before the launch, outlined the rationale. 'We'll have some editorials where you can go online and edit an editorial to your satisfaction', he said. 'We are going to do that with selected editorials initially. We don't know how this is going to turn out. It's all about finding new ways to allow readers to interact with us in the age of the Web.' Conceding that it may prove to be a 'complete mess', he nevertheless underscored his commitment to trying something new. 'Wikitorials may be one of those things that within six months will be standard', he argued. 'It's the ultimate in reader participation' (cited in Shepard 2005). The notion, he elaborated in a further interview, 'is that if you have something that is communally built from scratch, you might end up with a comprehensive truth' (cited in Dotinga 2005).

Regrettably Martinez's worst fears were realized less than 48 hours after the first wikitorial went live. The wiki-concept was formally introduced to the newspaper's readers on Friday 17 June with an editorial headlined 'A Wiki for Your Thoughts'. Having first briefly explained the nature of the concept, it proceeds to invite anyone who would like to rewrite the selected editorial for the day – the chosen editorial being about the war in Iraq – to join the 'public beta' by challenging its reasoning, checking its facts or suggesting improvements. 'Plenty of skeptics are predicting embarrassment; like an arthritic old lady who takes to the dance floor, they say, the *Los Angeles Times* is more likely to break a hip than to be hip', the editorial observed wryly. Acknowledging that it may 'lead straight into the dumpster of embarrassing failures', it insisted at the same time that it also held open the promise of generating 'a new form of opinion journalism, reflecting the opinions of everyone who chooses to participate'.

All too quickly, however, the experiment unravelled. Although the site's 'Terms of Service' set down the rules to be followed – including the need to avoid posting anything that is 'disparaging', 'inaccurate', 'unfair' or 'contains gross exaggeration or unsubstantiated claims' – they were roundly ignored by a series of users engaging in 'edit wars' over that morning's wikitorial. The initial plan of situating the original Iraq editorial, titled 'War on Consequences', alongside the collectively rewritten version, was abandoned by the site's monitoring editors (overseen by Wales himself as a voluntary advisor), all of whom were struggling to cope with the conflicting viewpoints expressed by the nearly 1000 registered users. By noon on Saturday, the editorial had been split into two pieces – one in favour of the US presence in Iraq, the other opposed to it – but it was quickly apparent that the wikitorial was becoming too politically charged. Profanities accumulated, but were soon swamped by a deluge of pornographic images posted to the site by 'cyber-creeps' (to use one of the editor's words). By 4:00 am, the decision had been taken to shut down the wikitorial. For users looking to find it in the days to come, they encountered this statement on the page instead:

> Where is the Wikitorial?
> Unfortunately, we have had to remove this feature, at least temporarily, because a few readers were flooding the site with inappropriate material.
> Thanks and apologies to the thousands of people who logged on in the right spirit.

The first attempt at incorporating a Wikinews format by a major newspaper had ended prematurely, but not in despair. 'As long as we can hit a high standard and have no risk of vandalism', stated managing editor Rob Barrett, 'then it is worth having a try at it again' (cited in *The Guardian*, 22 June 2005).

Not surprisingly, the experiment in reader-written news had been watched closely by commentators – as well as by rival news organizations – from around the world. Some were quick to question the *LA Time's* decision to focus on such a controversial editorial topic as the US-led invasion of Iraq, while others wondered aloud why an editorial – as opposed to a news item – had been chosen for the test in the first place. Enthusiastic speculation about other possible applications of the idea, including its potential to facilitate reader involvement in a news organization's investigations (although user statistics show that it is a tiny fraction of the total users who actually involve themselves in the writing and editing), encountered its opposite in the form of scepticism about its viability as a business model. Some considered the wiki format to be irreconcilable, by definition, with the 'brand' of a news organization based on accuracy, amongst other criticisms. Amongst those at least willing to applaud the spirit of the wiki initiative is Jan Schaffer of J-Lab: The Institute for Interactive Journalism. 'There is an enormous capacity for citizens to want to be able to participate in news and information in various ways', she contends, by 'interacting with it, questioning it, truth-squaring it and creating it. And now that they have the tech tools and the tech skills to do that, the appetite has only increased' (transcript, The NewsHour with Jim Lehrer, 16 November 2005).

Above dispute, in any case, is the way in which Wikinews allows its users endless scope to pursue stories that matter to them. No undue influence is exercised by corporate proprietors, nor are market forces brought to bear, when determining what counts as a newsworthy event deserving of coverage. Still, it is worth noting the extent to which the types of news items they produce tend to reproduce, to varying degrees, journalistic features broadly consistent with mainstream reporting. David Speakman, a Wikinews administrator (whose username is Davod) underlines this point. 'I don't think we at Wikinews have tapped the full capabilities of collaborative journalism for original reporting', he stated. 'Many of the writers are new to news, and try to model themselves after what they are familiar with – newspaper reporting' (cited in Glasner 2004b). There can be little doubt, however, that the potential of Wikinews to contribute to the slow dismantling of several of the more restrictive of these conventions is coming into clearer focus as it evolves. 'We invite you to join us in this effort', the site's mission statement declares, 'which has the potential to change the world forever'.

Capitalizing alternatives

In rounding out this chapter's discussion, it is worth returning to MSNBC.com, our point of departure at the outset. In the time since Connell's (2003) comments cited in the introduction above, the site has flourished to the point that it is now widely considered to be at the forefront of online journalism in the commercial sector. MSNBC.com's predominance over its rivals – the site regularly draws 23 million-plus monthly unique visitors, more than ABCNews.com, CBSNews.com and FOXNews.com combined – seems to revolve around advantages gained via its web-centred ethos. 'We are the leader in online news because in the last ten years, we have focused only on being the best online', maintained Charlie Tillinghast, president of MSNBC.com, in the lead-up to the site's tenth anniversary in July 2006. 'Unlike many of our competitors, whose websites have evolved as necessary extensions of their TV brands, we are a distinct online brand whose focus is, and always has been, using the full capability of the Internet to tell stories in new and innovative ways, and we're being recognized as such in the industry' (cited in *Huston Chronicle*, 7 February 2006). Evidence to support Tillinghast's assertions consists of data from monitoring organizations such as Nielsen// Net Ratings and JupiterResearch, which show that it consistently tops the ratings, as well as the various awards its content has garnered over the years.

One such award was conferred by *OMMA Magazine*, which credited MSNBC.com with being the best news and information site in the US: 'Online journalism doesn't get much better or more real-time than here', it declared in its February 2006 issue. In sharp contrast with its commercial rivals, OMMA's Steve Smith (2006) observes, MSNBC.com 'grew up online', and therefore appears to possess a firmer understanding of how the web actually works. 'Its TV-like console design, highly evolved video stream interface, and best-of-breed content partnerships with *Newsweek, The Washington Post, Forbes*, and NBC News, along with other partners and its own original reporting, make it a strong example of online journalism', he writes. Smith similarly points to the ways in which the site has proven its ingenuity, such as with its collection of blogs – examples include a blog by *NBC Nightly News* anchor Brian Williams, as well as Keith Olbermann's and those of reporters in Iraq – and audio streams from reporters in the field. The site's bulletin boards have similarly proven to be popular with users, especially during times of crisis. However, Smith writes, 'what we like most about this brand is its ability to demonstrate how major media can embrace the next generation of the Web'. Of particular importance in this regard, he believes, is how 'the site makes it easy for amateur newshounds to link to stories and even shows how the items, as well as MSNBC cable columns, are playing in the user-generated blogosphere ("Blog Talk" and "Blog Roundup")'. It is this type of convergence, in Smith's view, that explains how the site's 'news brand' attracts 23 million monthly visitors online.

This example of how a major commercial news site capitalizes – in every sense of the word – on the active participation of 'amateur newshounds' underscores yet again how certain 'old media' institutions are looking to the alternative, openly experimental forms of journalism developed by sites such as IndyMedia, OhmyNews and Wikinews for ways to enhance their connectivity with users. Given that their primary motivation is financial, however, what counts as quality reporting will be largely dictated by the business model necessary to ensure long-term profitability. Precisely what such a model will eventually entail is open to question, but the types of cost-cutting strategies associated with bottom-line pressures sharply reduce the scope for innovation and improvement. In the meantime, it is likely that citizen journalism will be increasingly recognized by commercial sites for its attractiveness to users (its pulling power being sold, in turn, to advertisers), as well as for the relatively modest operational costs involved. Both are crucial considerations in the eyes of managers, especially those inclined to consider serious, investigative news-gathering to be too expensive to justify further investment from shareholders. And yet, I would suggest, both similarly promise to curtail the very aims, values and commitments which citizen journalism, at its best, represents.

8 Citizen journalists on the scene: the London bombings and Hurricane Katrina

'I was on Victoria Line at about 9.10 this morning' wrote Matina Zoulia, recalling her experience on an underground train crowded with rush-hour commuters. 'And then the announcement came as we were stuck at King's Cross station that we should all come out.' She described how the passengers took their time, slowly making their way from the halted train. 'As I was going towards the exit there was this smell', she stated. 'Like burning hair. And then the people starting walking out, soot and blood on their faces. And then this woman's face. Half of it covered in blood.'

The morning in question was that of 7 July 2005, when four 'suicide bombers' detonated their explosive devices on three London Underground trains and a bus in the centre of the city, killing themselves and 52 other people, and injuring over 700 others. Responsibility for the attack was promptly claimed by the previously unknown Secret Organization Group of al-Qaeda of Jihad Organization in Europe. A statement posted on an Islamist website declared that the attacks represented 'revenge against the British Zionist Crusader government in retaliation for the massacres Britain is committing in Iraq and Afghanistan', and that the country was now 'burning with fear, terror, and panic'. For Mayor of London Ken Livingstone, it was a 'cowardly attack' that would fail in its attempt to divide Londoners by turning them against one another. In his words:

> This was not a terrorist attack against the mighty and the powerful. It was not aimed at presidents or prime ministers. It was aimed at ordinary working-class Londoners, black and white, Muslim and Christian, Hindu and Jew, young and old. Indiscriminate slaughter irrespective of any consideration for age, class, religion, whatever. That isn't an ideology. It isn't even a perverted faith. It is just an indiscriminate attempt at mass murder.[1]

Londoners, he was convinced, would 'stand together in solidarity alongside those who have been injured and those who have been bereaved'. His reference to 'presidents and prime ministers' pertained to the fact that 7 July was also the first full day of the 31st G8 summit at Gleneagles, Scotland, where Prime Minister Tony Blair and other leaders of the member states were meeting to discuss issues such as global climate change and Africa's economic development (the latter having been the focus of the Live 8 concert held five days before). Livingstone himself was in Singapore, where he had been supporting London's bid to host the 2012 Olympic Games.

News of the explosions that morning had punctured the euphoria surrounding the city's Olympic success, the decision to award the Games having been announced the previous day. Splashed across the front pages of 7 July's early edition newspapers were triumphant stories, complete with photographs of jubilant crowds celebrating the day before in Trafalgar Square. In the immediate aftermath of the blasts, however, the day's initial news agenda was being quickly cast aside, rewritten on the fly by journalists scrambling to cover breaking developments. This chapter, in taking as its initial focus the online reporting of the London bomb attacks, seeks to explore how the component elements of a local news story of instant global significance were drawn together. Singled out for particular attention will be the ways in which ordinary Londoners caught up in the explosions and their aftermath – such as Matine Zoulia, cited above, whose eyewitness account appeared in Guardian Unlimited's news blog – contributed to the mainstream news coverage on the day. Next, the chapter turns to the online reporting of Hurricane Katrina, where it will be similarly shown that citizen news-gathering made vital contributions to the reporting of unfolding events. 'I think Katrina was the highest profile story in which news sites were able to fill in the gaps where government wasn't able to provide information, where people were unable to communicate with each other', observed Manuel Perez, supervising producer of CNN.com. 'A lot of the most compelling info we got was from citizen journalism' (cited in Online News Association, 28 October 2005). In both London and New Orleans, this chapter will argue, the social phenomenon of citizen reporting, especially where mobile technologies were pressed into service, demonstrated its potential to challenge more traditional forms of journalism in new and unexpected ways.

Digital citizens

'In 56 minutes', an Associated Press (AP) reporter observed on 7 July, 'a city fresh from a night of Olympic celebrations was enveloped in eerie, blood-soaked quiet'. Three of the four bombs involved had exploded within a minute of one another at approximately 8:50 am on the London Underground system in the centre of the city. British Transport Police were immediately alerted that there had been an incident on the Metropolitan Line between Liverpool Street and Aldgate stations (some 25 minutes would pass, however, before they were notified of the explosion at the Edgware Road station).

By 9:15 am, the Press Association had broken the story with a report that emergency services had been called to Liverpool Street Station. By 9:19 am, a 'code amber alert' had been declared by Transport for London Officials, who had begun to shut down the network of trains, thereby suspending all services. It appeared at the time that some sort of 'power surge' might be responsible. At 9:26 am, Reuters.co.uk's news flash stated:

> LONDON (Reuters) – London's Liverpool Street station was closed Thursday morning after a 'bang' was heard during the rush hour, transport police said.
>
> The noise could have been power-related, a spokesman said. Officers were attending the scene.

Speculation mounted about the source of disruptions, with a number of different possibilities conjectured. 'It wasn't crystal clear initially what was going on', John Ryley, executive editor of Sky News, later recalled. 'Given the Olympic decision, the G-8 and the world we now live in, it was my hunch it was a terrorist attack' (cited in *The New York Times*, 11 July 2005). At 9:47 am, almost an hour after the first explosions, a fourth bomb detonated on the Number 30 double-decker bus in Tavistock Square. The bus had been travelling between Marble Arch and Hackney Wick, diverted from its ordinary route because of road closures. Several of the passengers on board had been evacuated from the Underground. At 11:10 am, Metropolitan Police Commissioner Sir Ian Blair formally announced to the public that it was a coordinated terror attack, a point reaffirmed by Prime Minister Tony Blair at 12:05 pm. In a televised statement, a visibly shaken Blair condemned the attacks as 'barbaric', appealed for calm, and offered his 'profound condolences to the victims and their families'. It would be 3:00 pm before the first official calculation of the number of people killed was formally announced.

For many Londoners, especially those who were deskbound in their workplaces, the principal source of breaking news about the attacks was the internet. In contrast with the mobile telephone companies, internet service providers were largely unaffected by the blasts, although several news websites came under intense pressure from the volume of traffic directed to them (overall, traffic to news websites was up nearly 50 per cent from the previous day, according to online measurement companies). BBC News was amongst the first to break the news online, thereby attracting considerable attention. It was the most visited of the pertinent news sites (accounting for 28.6 per cent of all news page impressions in the UK), prompting technicians to introduce additional servers to cope. 'We know it will be, without question, our busiest day in history', stated Peter Clifton, editor of BBC News Interactive (cited in the *Independent on Sunday*, 10 July 2005). Other leading sites which saw dramatic increases in their hits were *The Guardian* newspaper's Guardian Unlimited, Sky News, *The Times*, *The Sun* and *The Financial Times*. All of them remained operational despite the pressure – in marked contrast with the crashes experienced on September 11, 2001 – although response times were slower than usual.

In addition to the more typical types of news reportage made available, several sites created spaces for first-hand accounts from eyewitnesses to the attacks. Wherever possible, minute-by-minute updates from their journalists situated – either by accident or design – around the capital were posted. Several BBC reporters, for example, contributed their own observations in blog form, titled: The BBC's 'Reporters' Log: London Explosions'. The first three entries read:

> Jon Brain: Edgware Road : 11:15 BST
> There's been a scene of chaos and confusion all morning here but it's beginning to settle down. The entire area around the tube station has been sealed off and there are dozens of emergency vehicles here.
> We've seen a number of walking wounded emerge from the station, many of them covered with blood and obviously quite distraught. They are being treated at a hotel opposite the tube station.
> The concern now is whether there are still people trapped inside the tube station underground. I've seen a team of paramedics go into the station in the last half hour.
>
> Nick Thatcher: Royal London Hospital : 11:30 BST
> The Royal London Hospital have been receiving casualties all morning. This is a major hospital in East London. There's an air ambulance landing on the roof behind me. There are buses behind me which have come from the Kings Cross area in central London. On board are walking wounded who have been ferried here.
>
> Richard Foster: Liverpool Street: 11:35 BST
> Hounsditch is sealed off and there are police on horseback there. Liverpool Street station is sealed off. The number of people there was in its thousands when I first arrived, but now it has thinned out. The pubs are full round here; people are gathering for news updates and sending texts to let people now they are alright.
> (BBC News, Reporters' Log, 7 July 2005)

Significantly, however, spaces were also created online for ordinary citizens bearing witness. In the case of the BBC News site, a page 'London explosions: your accounts' was posted, which asked: 'Did you witness the terrorist attacks in London? How have the explosions affected you?'

This request for users to send their 'experiences and photos' (together with their telephone number for verification purposes) attracted a vast array of responses. Examples include:

> It was hot, dark and the smoke filled atmosphere made breathing difficult. We could hear loud screams that came from further down the tunnel, although I don't think any of us had any idea of just how bad things were in the front carriages. I suppose that not knowing what was really going on was a blessing in disguise, otherwise I'm sure there would have been mass panic. About 30 minutes later station staff managed to get to us and guided us off the train. It was only when I got home that I realised that this was a terrorist attack, which sent a chill down my spine.
>
> Jahor Gupta, London, UK

> I was onboard one of the trains that was caught by the bomb at Edgware road [...]. Innocent people of all nations and creeds screaming, crying and dying. A huge explosion rocked our train and the one passing us, putting the lights out and filling the tunnel with an acrid, burning smoke. Panic set in with screams and shouts of 'fire' then came the shouts from the bombed carriage. Not strong shouts for help, but desperate pleas.
>
> We realised that it was the train next to us that had been badly damaged, with the bombed carriage stopping directly opposite the carriage we were in, people cover in blood and with tattered, burnt clothing where trying to escape that train and enter our carriage, but we couldn't open the doors – they were calling for help and we couldn't get to them. Passengers with medical experience where found, I found a tool box and we smashed a window, allowing the medical guys to enter the other train, There was nothing left in that carriage, nothing. Blackened shredded walls, roof buckled, heavy tube doors twisted off. We collected warm coats, water, ties for tourniquets anything to help ... but there are no medical supplies to be found on the train, not even a torch. [...] I wish I could have done more. Everyone that helped was great – the train staff, the passengers, the medics, firemen and police – all were brave, calm and professional, but we were all reacting in shock, all going too slowly for the people in real trouble.
>
> Ben Thwaites, Crowthorne, Berkshire, UK

'People were sending us images within minutes of the first problems, before we even knew there was a bomb', said Helen Boaden, BBC director of news. In the hours to follow, the BBC received more than 1000 pictures, 20 pieces of amateur video, 4000 text messages and around 20,000 emails. 'Some of them are just general comments', Boaden added, 'but a lot are first-hand accounts. If people are happy about it – and, if people have contacted us, they usually are – we put our programmes in contact with them' (cited in *Independent on Sunday*, 10 July 2005).

Newspapers-based sites, such as Guardian Unlimited, similarly sought to gather insights from readers to help round out their coverage. A page in its news blog, headlined 'Your eyewitness accounts', stated: 'Tell us your experiences, and send us your photographs, by emailing us at newsblog.london@gmail.com.' The response, by any measure, was extraordinary. Entries included:

> I was on the southbound Piccadilly line, between King's Cross and Russell Square this morning, when the incident occurred. At just after nine, there was an almighty bang and the train came to a sudden stop. The lights in the carriage went out and the air became thick with dust and soot. [...] We left the train within half an hour. I feel very lucky.
>
> John Sandy

> I was in a tube at King's Cross when one of the explosions happened. I was stuck in a smoke-filled, blackened tube that reeked of burning for over 30 minutes. So many people were hysterical. I truly thought I was going to die and was just hoping it would be from smoke inhalation and not fire. I felt genuine fear but kept calm (and quite proud of myself for that).
>
> Eventually people smashed through the windows and we were lifted out all walked up the tunnel to the station. There was chaos outside and I started to walk down Euston Road (my face and clothes were black) towards work and all of a sudden there was another huge bang and people started running up the road in the opposite direction to where I was walking and screaming and crying. I now realise this must have been one of the buses exploding.
>
> Jo Herbert

> The explosion seemed to be at the back of the bus. The roof flew off and went up about 10 metres. It then floated back down. I shouted at the passengers to get off the bus. They went into Tavistock Park nearby. There were obviously people badly injured. A parking attendant said he thought a piece of human flesh had landed on his arm.
>
> Raj Mattoo

Behind the scenes at Guardian Unlimited, technicians were moving quickly to dispense with unnecessary pages and links with the aim of freeing up capacity. Over the course of the day, it attracted the most page impressions for a newspaper site. At its peak between 1 pm and 2 pm, there were 770,000 page views on its site, the equivalent of 213 pages per second. 'A news site has two jobs' stated Simon Waldman, director of digital publishing at the site; 'one to deliver the story accurately and as quickly as possible, and two to make sure that your site stays up. If you're doing that, everything else will slot into place' (cited in Journalism.co.uk, 13 July 2005).

A range of the major news sites also made extensive use of personal blogs or online diaries written by Londoners caught up in the events and their aftermath. Some opened up newsblogs for their readers or viewers to post their stories, while others drew upon different individual's blogs in search of material to accentuate a more personalized dimension to the tragedy. The up-to-the-minute feel of these blogs typically made for compelling reading. While many of these blogs offered little more than information otherwise being presented from television or radio news, albeit typically with some sort of personal reaction by the blogger in question, a small number of bloggers – ordinary citizens from a wide variety of backgrounds – were engaging in news reporting online. These 'citizen journalists' or 'instant reporters', as they were self-described by some, were relaying what they had seen unfold before them. Widely credited with being amongst the first blogs to post eyewitness accounts were Londonist, Skitz, Norm Blog, and London Metroblogger. Justin Howard posted the following entry on his blog, Pfff: a response to anything negative, just four hours after an underground explosion. Titled 'Surviving a Terrorist Attack', it reads:

> Travelling just past Edgware Road Station the train entered a tunnel. We shook like any usual tube train as it rattled down the tracks. It was then I heard a loud bang.
>
> The train left the tracks and started to rumble down the tunnel. It was incapable of stopping and just rolled on. A series of explosions followed as if tube electric motor after motor was exploding. Each explosion shook the train in the air and seems to make it land at a lower point.
>
> I fell to the ground like most people, scrunched up in a ball in minimize injury. At this point I wondered if the train would ever stop, I thought 'please make it stop', but it kept going. In the end I just wished that it didn't hit something and crush. It didn't.
>
> When the train came to a standstill people were screaming, but mainly due to panic as the carriage was rapidly filling with smoke and the smell of burning motors was giving clear clues of fire.

> As little as 5 seconds later we were unable to see and had all hit the ground for the precious air that remaining. We were all literally choking to death.
>
> The carriage however was pretty sealed; no window could open, no door would slide and no hammers seemed to exist to grant exit. If there were instructions on how to act then they were impossible to see in the thick acrid black smoke. (Pfff, 7 July 2005)

Members of London's blogging community were mobilizing to provide whatever news and information they possessed, in the form of typed statements, photographs or video clips, as well as via survivors' diaries, roll-calls of possible victims, emergency-response instructions, safety advice, travel tips, links to maps pinpointing the reported blast locations, and so forth. Many focused on perceived shortcomings in mainstream news reports, offering commentary and critique, while others dwelt on speculation or rumour, some openly conspiratorial in their claims.

Technorati, a blog tracking service, identified more than 1300 posts pertaining to the blasts by 10:15 am. While it is impossible to generalize, there can be little doubt that collectively these blogs – like various chatrooms, public forums and message boards across the internet – gave voice to a full range of human emotions, especially shock, outrage, grief, fear, anger and recrimination. Of particular value was their capacity to articulate the sorts of personal experience which typically fall outside journalistic boundaries. Examples include:

> Picked up a couple more messages – people who know that Edgware Road is my station. One of them was from a friend who I haven't heard from in two years.
> 'Metrocentric', from There Goes the Neighbourhood

> Once the shock had settled, I started to feel immense pride that the LAS, the other emergency services, the hospitals, and all the other support groups and organisations were all doing such an excellent job. To my eyes it seemed that the Major Incident planning was going smoothly, turning chaos into order.
>
> And what you need to remember is that this wasn't *a* major incident, but instead **four** major incidents, all happening at once.
>
> I think everyone involved, from the experts, to the members of public who helped each other, should feel pride that they performed so well in this crisis.
> Tom Reynolds, an Emergency Medical Technician for the London Ambulance Service, from Random Acts Of Reality

Today's attacks must – and they will – strengthen our commitment to defeat this barbaric hateful terrorism. We will not bow – I will never bow – to these despicable terrorists, even if my life depends on it. What happened to London today was an outrageous evil act by shameless criminals who, sadly, call themselves Muslims.
Ahmad, from Iraqi Expat

Call me a coward if you like, but the first instinct was to get as far away from London as possible. And I was not alone. I have NEVER seen so many taxis on the motorway heading west away from the city.
'Chris,' from Metroblogging London

I have to say that this was a strange night to be at work. It was certainly the quietest Friday night I've ever experienced. I picked up a grand total of 23 people travelling through the city late tonight. It would usually be ten times that amount. [. . .] I've been asked several times by members of the public whether I'm scared to drive my train now. I answer that we can't allow ourselves to be beaten. I admit that while I was driving through the city, the events were constantly in the back of my mind, but we can't let these cowardly bastards win.
'DistrictDriver,' a train driver for London Underground, from District Drivers Logbook

The significance of blogging was not lost on mainstream journalists, some of whom welcomed their contribution as a way to further improve the depth and range of their reporting. 'I see our relationship with bloggers and citizen journalists as being complementary on a story like the one we had today', stated Neil McIntosh, assistant editor of Guardian Unlimited. 'Clearly', he added:

we're going to be in there early, and we have people who are prac-tised in getting facts. We'll still be looking a great deal to blogs to almost help us digest what's happening today. It's very com-plementary in that I think the blogs look to us to get immediate news and we maybe look to them to get a little bit of the flavour of how people are reacting outside the four walls of our office. (cited in *The Globe and Mail*, 9 July 2005)

Certainly, McIntosh's editor in chief, Emily Bell, shared his conviction that local people's blogging came in to its own on the day. 'The key thing about blogs', she stated, 'is that they are not like internet or newspaper front pages, where you get the most important thing first. With blogs you get the most recent thing first [which is what you want when] you are following a major story.' Moreover, it is quicker to update the information in a blog than other types of news reporting, she added, and also affords people a place to connect emotionally with the events (cited in *The Guardian*, 8 July 2005).

Moving images

Particularly vexing for reporters during the crisis, especially those in television news, was the issue of access. Unable to gain entry to London Underground stations due to tight security, the aftermath of the explosions was out of sight beyond the reach of their cameras. On the other side of the emergency services' cordons, however, were ordinary Londoners on the scene, some of whom were in possession of mobile telephones equipped with digital cameras. As would quickly become apparent, a considerable number of the most newsworthy images of what was happening were taken not by professionals, but rather by these individuals who happened to be in the wrong place at the right time. The tiny lenses of their mobile telephone cameras captured the perspective of fellow commuters trapped underground, with many of the resultant images resonating with what some aptly described as an eerie, even claustrophobic quality. Video clips taken with cameras were judged by some to be all the more compelling because they were dim, grainy and shaky, but more importantly, because they were documenting an angle to an event as it was actually happening. 'Those pictures captured the horror of what it was like to be trapped underground', Sky News executive editor John Ryley suggested (cited in *Press Gazette*, 14 July 2005). 'We very quickly received a video shot by a viewer on a train near King's Cross through a mobile', he further recalled. 'And we had some heart-rending, grim stories sent by mobile. It's a real example of how news has changed as technology has changed' (cited in *Independent on Sunday*, 10 July 2005).

This remarkable source of reportage, where ordinary citizens were able to bear witness, was made possible by the internet. A number of extraordinary 'phonecam snapshots' of passengers trapped underground were posted on Moblog.co.uk, a photo-sharing website for mobile telephone images. 'Alfie' posting to the site stated: 'This image taken by Adam Stacey. He was on the northern line just past Kings Cross. Train suddenly stopped and filled with smoke. People in carriage smashed tube windows to get out and then were evacuated along the train tunnel. He's suffering from smoke inhalation but fine otherwise' (cited in www.boingboing.net; 7 July 2005). By early evening, the image had been viewed over 36,000 times on the Moblog.co.uk website (cited in *The New York Times*, 8 July 2005). Stacey himself was reportedly astonished by what had happened to the image. 'I sent it to a few people at work like, "Hey, look what happened on the way to work",' he explained. 'I never expected to see my picture all over the news' (cited in Forbes.com, 8

July 2005). Elsewhere, Adam Tinworth, a London magazine editor and free-lance writer, later recollected: 'I was grabbing photos to give people a feel of what it's like to be an ordinary person.' He posted a range of images on the web, including shots of blockaded streets, while he waited in a cafe for his wife to call. 'I started posting pictures simply as displacement activity while I waited to hear if she was OK', he said. 'Eventually I did, but there was so much interest in the photos and descriptions of what was happening that I kept on going, and took my lunch break from work to grab some more' (cited in *National Post*, 8 July 2005).

Handling Tinworth's images online was Flickr.com, also a photo-sharing service that enables people to post directly from a mobile telephone free of charge. More than 300 bombing photos had been posted within eight hours of the attacks. With 'the ability for so many people to take so many photos', Flickr co-founder Caterina Fake stated, 'the real challenge will be to find the most remarkable, the most interesting, the most moving, the most striking' (cited in AP, 7 July 2005). Individual photographs were 'tagged' into groups by words such as 'explosions', 'bombs' and 'London' so as to facilitate efforts to find relevant images. Many of these photographs, some breathtaking in their poignancy, were viewed thousands of times within hours of their posting. 'It's some sense that people feel a real connection with a regular person – a student, or a homemaker – who happens to be caught up in world events ... how it impacts the regular person in the street', Fake remarked (cited in *PC Magazine Online*, 7 July 2005).

It was precisely this angle which journalists and editors at major news sites were also looking for when quickly sifting through the vast array of images emailed to them. 'Within minutes of the first blast', Helen Boaden, BBC director of news, affirmed, 'we had received images from the public and we had 50 images within an hour' (cited by Day and Johnston in *The Guardian*, 8 July 2005). Pete Clifton, a BBC online interactivity editor, elaborated: 'An image of the bus with its roof torn away was sent to us by a reader inside an hour, and it was our main picture on the front page for a large part of the day.' Evidently several hundred such photographs, together with about 30 video clips, were sent to the BBC's dedicated email address (*yourpics@bbc.-co.uk*) as the day unfolded. About 70 images and five clips were used on the BBC's website and in television newscasts. 'London explosions: Your photos' presented still images, while one example of a video clip was an 18-second sequence of a passenger evacuating an underground station, taken with a camera phone video. 'It certainly showed the power of what our users can do', Clifton added, 'when they are close to a terrible event like this' (cited in BBC News Online, 8 July 2005).

Over at the ITV News channel, editor Ben Rayner concurred. 'It's the way forward for instant newsgathering', he reasoned, 'especially when it involves an attack on the public'. ITN received more than a dozen video clips from mobile phones, according to Rayner. The newscast ran a crawl on the bottom of the screen asking viewers to send in their material. Every effort was made to get it on the air as soon as possible, but not before its veracity was established. This view was similarly reaffirmed by John Ryley, the executive editor of Sky News. 'We are very keen to be first', he maintained, 'but we still have to ensure they are authentic'. Nevertheless, according to Ryley, a video clip from the blast between King's Cross and Russell Square stations that was received at 12.40 pm had been broadcast by 1 pm. 'News crews usually get there just after the event', he remarked, 'but these pictures show us the event as it happens' (cited by Day and Johnston in *The Guardian*, 8 July 2005).

'This is the first time mobile phone images have been used in such large numbers to cover an event like this', *Evening Standard* production editor Richard Oliver declared. It shows 'how this technology can transform the news-gathering process. It provides access to eyewitness images at the touch of a button, speeding up our reaction time to major breaking stories.' Local news organizations, in his view, 'are bound to tap into this resource more and more in future' (cited in *National Geographic News*, 11 July 2005). Such was certainly the case with national news organizations. One particularly shocking image of the Number 30 bus at Tavistock Square, for example, which had been received at the website within 45 minutes of the explosion, was used on the front page of both *The Guardian* and *The Daily Mail* newspapers the next day. Some images were quickly put to one side, however. 'We didn't publish some of the graphic stuff from the bus explosion', stated Vicky Taylor at the BBC. 'It was just too harrowing to put up.' Even so, she said, the use of this type of imagery signalled a 'turning point' with respect to how major news organizations report breaking news (cited in *The Australian*, 14 July 2005). 'What you're doing', Taylor observed, 'is gathering material you never could have possibly got unless your reporter happened by chance to be caught up in this' (cited in AP, 7 July 2005). For Sky News associate editor Simon Bucks, it represented 'a democratisation of news coverage, which in the past we would have only got to later' (cited in Agence France Presse, 8 July 2005). Above question, in any case, was the fact that many of the 'amateur photos' taken were superior to those provided by various professional photographic agencies.

Still, there were certain risks for news organizations intent on drawing upon so-called 'amateur' or 'user-generated' digital imagery. One such risk concerns the need to attest to the accuracy of the image in question, given the potential of hoaxes being perpetrated. Steps had to be taken to ensure that it has not been digitally manipulated or 'doctored' so as to enhance its news value, and to attest to its source in a straightforward manner. For example, with regard to the image taken by Adam Stacey mentioned above, Sky News picked it up, crediting it as 'a passenger's camera photo', while the BBC added a caveat when they used it: 'This photo by Adam Stacey is available on the Internet and claims to show people trapped on the underground system' (cited on Poynteronline, 8 July 2005). A further risk is that rights to the image may be owned by someone else, raising potential problems with respect to the legality of permission to use it. While citizens turned photojournalists pro-vided the BBC with their images free of charge, they retained the copyright, enabling them to sell the rights to them to other news organizations (Sky TV, for example, reportedly offered £250 for exclusive rights to an image). Peter Horrocks, current head of BBC television news, believes that trust is the central issue where gathering material from citizen journalists is concerned. For individuals to send their work to the BBC, as opposed to rival news or-ganizations (especially when the latter will offer financial payment), they have to share something of the Corporation's commitment to public service. It is important to bear in mind, he suggests, that some of the individuals involved had taken the photos 'because they thought they were going to be late for work and wanted something to show the boss. Very few of them thought of themselves as journalists, and no-one that we've interviewed thought about the commercial potential', he stated. 'The idea for most of them that there was any commercial motivation is anathema. They trusted the BBC to treat the information respectfully and, where appropriate, to pass it on to the police' (cited in *The Independent*, 26 September 2005).

Cross-cutting concerns raised about the logistics involved when using this kind of imagery are certain ethical considerations. A number of the in-dividuals involved did have pause for thought, some expressing regret, others moved to explain their actions. Tim Bradshaw hesitated before sending his images to flickr.com. 'It seemed kind of wrong', he commented, '[but] the BBC and news Web sites were so overwhelmed it was almost like an alter-native source of news' (cited in *The New York Times*, 8 July 2005). London blogger Justin Howard, cited above, posted this angry comment on the day:

> I was led out of the station and expected to see emergency services. There were none; things were so bad that they couldn't make it. The victims were being triaged at the station entrance by Tube staff and as I could see little more I could do so I got out of the way and left. As I stepped out people with camera phones vied to try and take pictures of the worst victims. In crisis some people are cruel. (Pfff, 7 July 2005)

Pointing to this type of evidence, some critics contend that using the phrase 'citizen journalist' to describe what so many ordinary people were doing on the day is too lofty, preferring the derisive 'snaparazzi' to characterize their actions. In the eyes of others, serious questions need to be posed regarding why such people are moved to share their experiences in the first place. John Naughton, writing in *The Observer* newspaper, expressed his deep misgivings: 'I find it astonishing – not to say macabre – that virtually the first thing a lay person would do after escaping injury in an explosion in which dozens of other human beings are killed or maimed is to film or photograph the scene and then relay it to a broadcasting organisation', he wrote. Naughton refuses to accept the view that such imagery is justifiable on the grounds that it vividly captures the horrors of the event, contending that 'such arguments are merely a retrospective attempt to dignify the kind of ghoulish voyeurism that is enabled by modern communications technology.' Broadcasting organizations, he maintains, should refuse to use this type of 'amateur' material. In recognizing that 'enthusiastic cameraphone ghouls on 7 July' were offered 'the chance of 15 minutes of fame' by picture-messaging to broadcasters, he questions how many of them avoided attending to the pain of others as a result. '[I]f I had to decide between the girl who chose to stay and help the victims and the fiends who vied to take their pictures,' he declared, 'then I have no doubt as to where true humanity lies' (*The Observer*, 17 July 2005).[2]

For many of citizen journalism's advocates, however, the reporting that ordinary individuals engaged in on 7 July was one of the few bright spots on an otherwise tragic day. Its intrinsic value was underscored by Mark Cardwell, AP's director of online newspapers, who stated 'The more access we have to that type of material, the better we can tell stories and convey what has happened' (cited in Newsday.com, 8 July 2005). Still, others emphasized the importance of exercising caution, believing that its advantages should not obscure the ways in which the role of the journalist can be distinguished from individuals performing acts of journalism. 'The detached journalistic professional is still necessary', insisted Roy Greenslade in *The Guardian* newspaper, 'whether to add all-important context to explain the blogs and the thousands of images, or simply to edit the material so that readers and viewers can speedily absorb what has happened' (*The Guardian*, 8 August 2005). At Times Online, news editor Mark Sellman pointed out that several of the tips received in the aftermath of the attacks turned out to be false. 'You're in a very hot point, stuff was coming in but it's not necessarily reliable, and you have to check it out', he stated. 'Someone said a suicide bomber was shot dead in Canary Wharf, and that was an urban myth.' Professional journalists, in his view, necessarily play a crucial role as editors. 'To create an open stream that's not edited is not to offer readers what we're here for. We're editors, and you've got to keep that in mind' (cited in *The Globe and Mail*, 9 July 2005). Simon Waldman, director of digital publishing at Guardian Unlimited, makes the pertinent observation that '[e]verything on the internet is about acquired trust, and news sites earn their spurs with each news story' (cited in Journalism.co.uk, 13 July 2005). Reflecting on the site's use of readers' material on the day, his colleague Emily Bell similarly underscored the importance of relationship between news organizations and citizen reporters. 'It might take only one faked film, one bogus report to weaken the bond of trust', she contended, 'and, conversely, one misedited report or misused image to make individuals wary once again of trusting their material to television or newspapers' (*The Guardian*, 11 July 2005). The role of the trained, experienced journalist was being transformed, most seemed to agree, but remained as vitally important as ever.

In the eye of the storm

'This is not Iraq, this is not Somalia', correspondent Martin Savidge of NBC News told viewers. 'This is home.' Savidge was surveying the catastrophic landscape left behind in the wake of Hurricane Katrina, one of the worst natural disasters in US history that left more than 1300 people dead and tens of thousands homeless.

On Sunday 28 August, with the hurricane gaining strength as it traversed the Gulf of Mexico westward from the Florida Panhandle, New Orleans Mayor Ray Nagin ordered a compulsory evacuation of the city's residents. All routes out of the city – which is situated some six feet below sea level – rapidly became overwhelmed with traffic. Many of those unwilling or unable to comply with the order remained behind, some staying in their homes while others sought shelter in places such as the Superdome sports stadium made available to cope with the emergency. Overnight, as fears grew that the hurricane was possibly intensifying to wind speeds surpassing 140 mph, citizens braced themselves for the worst. Early on Monday morning, the brunt of Katrina hit the Gulf coast, engendering a horrific trail of destruction not only in Louisiana but also in nearby Mississippi and Alabama. Flood waters rose in many areas of New Orleans, with reports emerging that the city's flood defences had been breached. Soon after it was confirmed that the levees were being overwhelmed, engendering a 'catastrophic structural failure' of barriers that should have withheld the storm's force. Meanwhile, network news helicopters circled above, relaying the horrors below. Commenting on the 'endless loops of disaster footage' running throughout the day's television newscasts, Jack Shafer pointed out in Slate.com that broadcasters were sidestepping questions of class and ethnicity in their reporting. 'When disaster strikes', he observed, 'Americans – especially journalists – like to pretend that no matter who gets hit, no matter what race, color, creed, or socioeconomic level they hail from, we're all in it together.' Katrina, as was rapidly becoming apparent, had not wrecked its havoc on all communities equally. 'By failing to acknowledge upfront that black New Orleanians – and perhaps black Mississippians – suffered more from Katrina than whites, the TV talkers may escape potential accusations that they're racist', he remarked. 'But by ignoring race and class, they boot the journalistic opportunity to bring attention to the disenfranchisement of a whole definable segment of the population' (*Slate*, 31 August 2005).

Gradually, as the worst of the storm subsided, the scale of the devastation became apparent. The areas hit hardest were New Orleans and the adjacent Gulf Coast of Mississippi. It was estimated that approximately 80 per cent of New Orleans was submerged. Several hundred people were feared dead, and an estimated 2 million others thought to be without electricity, food or clean water. The majority of those left in harm's way lacked the physical or financial means to evacuate, many of them African Americans living in impoverished conditions in low-lying areas especially vulnerable to flooding. The collapse of the city's communication network meant that local officials were unable to effectively coordinate a response with one another, nor with federal authorities. New Orleans WWL-AM was reportedly the only radio station able to remain on the air, joined by ham radio operators doing their best to relay messages from stranded victims. Station WWOZ-FM only managed to resume webcasting with help from WFMU-FM in Jersey City, NJ, its offices being in a heavily flooded area of New Orleans. In the meantime, its website was transformed into a message board for emergency news and information. New Orleans television station WWL-TV, a CBS affiliate, presented live streaming video of its rolling news broadcasts on its site. Its news blogs provided constantly updated bulletins even as staff abandoned the city's studios as they were flooded. It was the only one of four local television stations to remain on the air, however, a feat made possible by the viability of its transmitter in Gretna. For the other stations, WNOL Channel 38 and WGNO Channel 26 were forced to limit their reporting to what they could make available on the web. WDSU Channel 6 transferred its main operations to two of its fellow network stations outside of the state. Once it became possible to re-establish its own broadcasting provision, it was streamed over the internet. For the majority of individuals caught in the disaster area, however, the lack of electricity meant that this type of information was inaccessible.

City residents able to gain access to the internet found it to be a vital resource. Weather-related sites, not surprisingly, were at the fore. Similarly important were various online forums and discussion boards – such as those provided by some local television stations – provided virtual spaces for people to connect with one another, posing questions and sharing information. Several variants of missing person (lost or found) lists, the latter sometimes dubbed 'I'm Okay' sites, were active. Examples included Katrinacheck-in.org, Find Katrina, Craigslist New Orleans, Hurricane Katrina Survivor Forums, National Next of Kin Registry, Wal-Mart's Hurricane Katrina Message Board, and Yahoo Katrina Message Boards, amongst others. Several news sites performed a complementary role, allowing users to post details about their personal status, such as CNN's Reported Safe List, GulfCoastNews.com's Katrina Survivor-Connector List, the *Sun Herald*'s I'm OK Line, and NOLA.com's Missing; I'm OK lists. Carol Lin, anchor of CNN's 'victims and relief' desk, aired video clips from survivors, and posted information on the network's news site. 'This is the most rewarding work I've ever done', she said. 'It's a situation where it's completely acceptable to step over the traditional journalistic boundaries and make a difference' (cited in *USA Today*, 7 September 2005). Disaster assistance was also provided online by organizations such as the American Red Cross, Habitat for Humanity, Hurricane Housing, and Katrina Help Wiki (started by 20 volunteers from around the world), amongst several others, each acting as a clearinghouse of information. A disaster map wiki site, called Katrina Information Map, was established using the Google Maps' API and markers posted by users, their written entries describing the conditions in their respective neighbourhoods. Several bloggers were similarly stepping in to help. Ernest Svenson, a New Orleans lawyer who evacuated to Houston, recast his blog 'Ernie the Attorney' into an information outlet for the benefit of those looking for missing children, family members and friends. 'People got scattered and are using it as a virtual rally point', he told one newspaper (*Washington Post*, 7 September 2005).

For many news organizations in times of crisis, it is considered a badge of honour to keep operating, regardless of the dangers involved. In the case of the New Orleans *Times-Picayune*, the city's largest daily, going to press meant relying on the internet. Its Tuesday, 30 August edition went online in the form of pdf files posted on its affiliated site NOLA.com. The one-word headline of this electronic edition – 'Catastrophic' – effectively summed up the hurricane's devastation. The newspaper's managing editor for news, Dan Shea, described events in an email to colleagues:

> I stayed with the paper and witnessed the extraordinary death of a city today. We survived the initial assault of Katrina well. While we lost power, I had a bunker prepared where we worked on Internet stories on a generator and prepared a PDF version of the paper. It was hot, dark and smelly but we were initially relieved that the storm seemed to skip east at the last minute. Later Monday, I ventured out in a delivery truck with the *Times-Picayune* editor, and [we] were shocked by the sudden rise in water all over the city. [. . .] Other staffers were caught in it, and some swam for their lives. [. . .] This morning we awoke and found water rising rapidly around our building, and there were people walking up the expressway and fires burning all over the city. We made an instant decision to put 300 journalists, pressmen and support staff into trucks. [We] barely made it to the expressway.

Staffers were on the move to Houma, a town 57 miles away, to re-establish a base in the offices of the Houma *Courier* with working telephones and an email system. 'We haven't slept in days', Shea added, 'but we have air conditioning, and I'm thankful to be at work'. Relying on notebook computers, they set about enhancing the online provision. Needless to say, of course, everyone appreciated how few of the daily's usual readers (circulation ordinarily about 270,000) would gain the benefit of their efforts. 'This is mostly for people who have evacuated the city and are trying to keep up with what's going on', suburban editor Kim Chatelain pointed out. 'Unless you have a generator, you have no idea what we're reporting' (cited in *Washington Post*, 1 September 2005). In the days to come, the ingenuity of the staff would secure a 'magic formula' whereby news was reported via a blog, pdf files and eventually a small print edition, thanks to what managing editor Peter Kovacs aptly described as 'the usual, random, haphazard ways things get done in journalism' (cited in Poynter.prg, 2 September 2005).

In Mississippi, the Biloxi *Sun Herald* struggled to cope with a power cut after the roof covering its generator switch was blown away. While most of the newsroom staff were being evacuated to a newspaper in Columbus (in the hope that the *Sun Herald* could be printed there and then flown back via helicopter), others were busy setting up an emergency blog to keep readers informed about the rapidly changing situation. Elsewhere on the site, a guest book of condolences was opened, together with damage reports, photographs, video clips and eyewitness audio reports provided by staff and users alike. 'Is the Father Ryan House B&B still standing? I looked at the aerial photos and really can't tell', wrote one visitor. Messages posted from survivors were situated alongside others emailed to them from around the world. One picture message pleaded for help in contacting two people temporarily housed in a Red Cross shelter: 'I flew in from South Africa on Thursday and will come and get them ASAP. Please let them know I am in Kansas City. How can we contact them? Please help if you can. We are afraid they will be moved before we can reach them.' The newspaper's site was also the principal point of contact for missing members of staff. One appeal read: 'Power has been restored and the newspaper was printed there Sunday night. It is important for employees to report to work if they're able.' Journalists from neighbouring towns and even from out of state had joined the effort. Night editor Jim Butler summarized the extraordinary commitment demonstrated by colleagues: 'Sloshing through muck and mud in the nastiest of places to get the quote or shoot the picture, giving a stranger their hat, or shoes, or cigarettes, on the job essentially around the clock – not much in the way of vanity or ego shows up' (cited in *The Guardian*, 7 September 2005). By 6 September, the newspaper's doors had once again opened for business, the front-page headline of its print edition reading: 'Inching Back to Normal'.

Communicating crisis

Online news sites, as is now increasingly expected during times of crisis, experienced dramatic surges in hits as users sought out information about the scale of destruction and recovery efforts. The web tracking firm Technorati reported on 30 August that seven of the top ten search terms were related to the hurricane. Evidently sites such as ABC News Digital and MSNBC witnessed triple-digit leaps in their audience figures, while Yahoo News reportedly experienced the 'most-trafficked day in its history' on Monday, 29 August. CNN experienced some 9 million video plays over the course of a single day, its highest record ever. NOLA.com, now working from the *Times-Picayune*'s 'Hurricane Bunker', saw its page views leap several times above its ordinary number, due in large part to the blogs and message boards it was continually updating. These resources became a vital link for people needing to be rescued, the site's editor Jon Donley stated. He described how assistants to the commander of the relief efforts had informed him that they were closely monitoring the site's two blogs (one from the city desk, and one relaying information from a police scanner) for directions to people who were trapped. Lives were being saved because of them. As Donely recalled:

> It was weird because we couldn't figure out where these pleas were coming from. [...] We'd get e-mails from Idaho, there's a guy at this address and he's in the upstairs bedroom of his place in New Orleans. And then we figured out that even in the poorest part of town, people have a cell phone. And it's a text-enabled cell phone. And they were sending out text messages to friends or family, and they were putting it in our forums or sending it in e-mails to us. (cited in Glaser 2005)

Describing a 'paradigm shift in the newsroom', Donely explained how the blogs once regarded with scepticism had suddenly proven to be indispensable in getting the story out. 'We're a place where the community can tell its own story', he added. 'I don't want to overuse the term "citizen journalism", but that's what's going on' (cited in *Editor and Publisher*, 8 September 2005).

The crucial ways in which citizen journalism could augment mainstream news coverage was readily apparent. 'Traditional journalism is the outside looking in', Mitch Gelman, executive vice president of CNN.com, maintained. 'Citizen journalism is the inside looking out. In order to get the complete story, it helps to have both points of view.' Evidently more than 3000 files with hundreds of images and video were emailed to CNN.com over the first three days, according to Gelman, some of which included heart-rending material. 'The text, images and video people have been generating is extraordinary in the manner in which it takes our online audience into the heart and soul of the story', he added (cited in TechWeb News, 1 September 2005). Preparing to cover a major hurricane is anything but straightforward, relying as it does on predictions being made about its possible size, direction and impact. 'Assigning too many people for what might turn out to be a smaller storm is a loss of valuable resources in a time of tightening news budgets', newspaper ombudsperson Richard Chacón pointed out. 'Not having enough reporters and photographers on scene when tragedy breaks leaves readers feeling underserved' (*Boston Globe*, 4 September 2005). In the immediate aftermath of the disaster, eyewitness accounts and imagery posted online by ordinary citizens helped to narrow the information gap in important ways. Several sites associated with national news organizations set aside space on their main pages for 'citizen journalism reporting' (to use MSNBC's tag), thereby signalling a commitment to a different journalistic ethos than might be implied by terms such as 'Tell us your story', 'readers' photos' or 'your opinion'. At MSNBC.com, users accessed almost 50 million video clips in the first week after the storm, evidently a figure three times greater than the previous record (set in the week following the September 11, 2001 attacks). Its searchable database of 'looking for' and 'safe' lists garnered thousands of entries, while a 'Katrina blog' written by reporters in the field similarly attracted wide-ranging comments from users. 'It takes a crisis like this to turn something that has been mostly in the political space, with people trading opinions, into something that has been used for a humanitarian purpose', observed the site's general manager Charlie Tillinghast (*Los Angeles Times*, 10 September 2005).

'If you've got to ride out a hurricane, do it in an Internet data center on the 10th floor of a high rise', remarked Michael Barnett, a blogger calling himself 'The Interdictor' during the height of the storm on Monday. Increasingly concerned about his safety and that of the people sharing the room with him, he continued to update his blog and post digital photos whenever he could manage. 'I am not trying to be an alarmist', he wrote the following morning, 'but until we get a military presence of significance in the city, the roving gangs of thugs own the streets' (interdictor.livejournal.com/). One photo blogger explained that he was connecting through a 'fax line in a closet of a funeral home' (cited in *San Jose Mercury News*, 31 August 2005). Kaye D. Trammell's (2005) decision to 'blog the storm' was made so as to keep loved ones updated about her safety, but within hours her readership for HurricaneUpdate had spread across the world as so-called A-list blogs linked to her site. Her 'humble dispatches', relayed using her handheld wireless BlackBerry device once the electricity was cut (and recharging it using her car battery), helped to keep her calm. For users, she believes, this type of blog helped to put the news coverage into a broader context. 'From "stringers" reporting updates of specific damaged areas to notes of support from around the world', she maintained, 'blogs like mine provided a cathartic release for those seeking information on this crisis'. Moreover, in her view, these blogs were providing an alternative viewpoint on developments, often covering a larger geographical area – and doing so more quickly – than mainstream reporters could manage. 'We on-the-scene citizens don't mean to replace journalism', she added. 'We don't have the resources. But we can provide first-person accounts in our own voices of what is happening.' Its significance, it follows, can be measured in other ways than its immediacy. 'Blogging will not change the world in crisis', Trammell observes, 'but it will make it more human.'

It is difficult to overstate the degree of human despair engendered by the chaos and confusion besetting rescue efforts, a major indictment of the Bush administration's failure to manage the crisis. Angry denunciations of its incompetence were articulated from across the political spectrum. *New York Times* columnist David Brooks, ordinarily an avid supporter of Republican policy, expressed his outrage. 'The first rule of the social fabric – that in times of crisis you protect the vulnerable – was trampled', he wrote. 'Leaving the poor in New Orleans was the moral equivalent of leaving the injured on the battlefield. No wonder confidence in civic institutions is plummeting.' The nation, he added, was ashamed (*The New York Times*, 4 September 2005). Many of the images of the storm and its aftermath were, in a word, ghastly. Some journalists made the connection with the consequences of the South Asian tsunami. 'It's amazingly similar, horrifyingly similar. The scene of whole villages gone is very much the same', CNN anchor Anderson Cooper commented. 'Gulfport, Bay St. Louis, Waveland – it could have been Galle, Sri Lanka. But what makes it different is that this is the U.S. seeing bloated corpses out on the streets for days' (cited in *Hollywood Reporter*, 2 September 2005). News photographs of the city's dead – both professional and citizen-produced – were rapidly becoming iconic symbols of entrenched poverty and neglect. The Federal Emergency Management Agency (FEMA), under intense scrutiny for its agonizingly slow response to the devastation, sought to impose restrictions on photographers, decreeing that no images of the deceased be taken or used as a matter of respect to victims. Enraged critics were quick to respond, arguing that such an order was not about human dignity, but rather about officials trying to manage images so as to mollify public opinion. The blogosphere was electrified, as voices like that of Josh Marshall in his Talking Points Memo intervened:

> Take a moment to note what's happening here: these are the marks of repressive government, which mixes inefficiency with authoritarianism. The crew that couldn't get key aid on the scene in time last week is coming in in force now. And one of the key missions appears to be cutting off public information about what's happening in the city. (Marshall, 7 September 2005)

In the mainstream media, criticisms of FEMA's stance such as that of Rebecca Daugherty of the Reporters Committee for Freedom of the Press received widespread coverage. 'The notion that, when there's very little information from FEMA, that they would even spend the time to be concerned about whether the reporting effort is up to its standards of taste is simply mind-boggling', she argued. 'You cannot report on the disaster and give the public a realistic idea of how horrible it is if you don't see that there are bodies as well' (cited in Reuters, 7 September 2005).

Both Marshall and Daugherty's observations make apparent that concerns about the availability of information – or, more to the point, the lack thereof – were a major point of tension. On 5 September, NBC anchor Brian Williams had written in his 'behind the scenes' blog, The Daily Nightly, that too few details were being made available to members of the public directly affected, let alone reporters. In his words:

> It's one of many running themes of the past week: There were no announcements in the Superdome during the storm, none to direct people after the storm, no official word (via bullhorn, leaflets or any other means) during the week-long, on-foot migration (and eventual stagnation) that defined life in the downtown section of the city for those first few days. One can't help but think that a single-engine plane towing a banner over the city would have been immeasurably helpful in both crowd and rumor control.

In the near-absence of reliable information from official channels, rumour and speculation – much of it marked by racist prejudice – spiralled forth to fill the void. 'Storm victims are raped and beaten; fights erupt with flying fists, knives and guns; fires are breaking out; corpses litter the streets; and police and rescue helicopters are repeatedly fired on', reported the *Washington Times* (2 September 2005). 'People are being raped', Tucker Carlson told MSNBC viewers. 'People are being murdered. People are being shot. Police officers being shot' (cited in *The New York Times*, 19 September 2005). These and related claims proliferated across the 'old' and 'new' media continuum, even though they were rarely aligned with named eyewitness sources, and rarer still with those who could substantiate what was being alleged. In the days to follow, it would become painfully apparent that misinformation had caused serious harm, not least by stigmatizing victims and hindering rescue efforts. News organizations would investigate these assertions, with disturbing results. *The Times-Picayune* report, for example, described inflated body counts, unverified 'rapes', and claims about 'sniper attacks' as being examples of 'scores of myths about the dome and Convention Center treated as fact by evacuees, the media and even some of New Orleans' top officials' (26 September 2005).

For some critics of online reporting, especially where ordinary people are involved, there was little doubt who was to blame. 'The National Guard delayed going into New Orleans for days after the hurricane because they weren't sure whether they would be mounting a relief effort or fighting mobs of armed looters', Les Hinton, executive chair of News International, argued in his post-Katrina assessment. 'But there was no widespread lawlessness, no toxic soup, no confirmed rapes in the Super Dome, and it is unlikely to take six months to pump out New Orleans.' Singled out for criticism in this regard, perhaps not surprisingly in the eyes of a mainstream news executive, was citizen journalism. 'In this case, a lot of bad information came from bloggers and amateur witnesses – all empowered by instant communication' (Society of Editors' Lecture, 16 October 2005). For every critic like Hinton, however, there were far more commentators highlighting the vital contribution made by citizen reporters, often working under acutely difficult circumstances in remote areas to tell their stories. Many were struck by the extent to which mainstream news organizations were relying on citizens to provide them with the information and images necessary to comprehend what was happening as events unfolded. Meanwhile, convergence of a different sort saw network news reporters going online to write blogs rich with insights that could not be relayed in broadcasting terms, while others posted extended interviews and 'Web-only stories' for users. 'It's the first time, really, for all of us in the online industry, when it's all come together', Michael Sims, director of news and operations for CBSnews.com, stated. 'The CBS news television journalists and producers all know that they are working for the Web in addition to working for TV' (cited in *Television Week*, 12 September 2005).

More difficult to discern, but of even greater potential significance, was the degree to which impassioned forms of online reporting inspired in mainstream journalists a renewed commitment to question authority, to speak truth to power. Encouraging signs were appearing post-Katrina, some suggested, that the press was being jostled by its online counterparts to awaken from its post-September 11 slumber. Time would tell, of course, but Susan J. Douglas (2005) was optimistic about the bridges being built between print, electronic and online news in this regard. Describing Katrina as a 'perfect storm journalistically', she maintained that it represented the moment when 'the country's failed war on poverty, its institutional racism and the utter bankruptcy of a "CEO presidency" were all lead stories', and that as such it was 'testimony to what can happen when those at the margins of the mainstream media (and of our country) finally get the podium they deserve'.

Looking ahead

There appears to be little doubt – in the eyes of both advocates and critics alike – that citizen reporting is having a profound impact on the forms, practices and epistemologies of mainstream journalism, from the international level through to the local. 'In a summer marked by London bombings, rising gas prices and record hurricanes, the world is turning to the fastest growing news team – citizen journalists – to get a human perspective through the eyes of those who lived or experienced the news as it unfolds', observed Lewis D'Vorkin, editor-in-chief of AOL News and Sports. Reflecting on the ways in which AOL News had drawn together source material from ordinary people caught up in the aftermath of Katrina, he described the site as 'the people's platform'. The interactive nature of the online news experience, he believes, meant that it could offer 'real-time dialogue' between users joining in to shape the news. In D'Vorkin's words:

> While citizen journalism has existed in forms through letters to the editor, 'man on the street' interviews and call-in radio or television shows, the widespread penetration of the Web has promoted the citizen journalist to a new stature. With new technology tools in hand, individuals are blogging, sharing photos, uploading videos and podcasting to tell their firsthand accounts of breaking news so that others can better understand. What we did is the future of news, except it's happening now. (cited in WebProNews, 6 September 2005)

The significance of participatory journalism, where 'everyday people' are able to 'take charge of their stories', is only now being properly acknowledged, in his view. 'Can't do it in TV, can't do it in newspapers. That personal involvement is what the whole online news space is all about' (cited in *Los Angeles Times*, 10 September 2005).

'It is a gear change', pointed out the BBC's Helen Boaden, especially with respect to the public's contribution to the Corporation's news coverage of the London attacks. 'People are very media-savvy', she argued, and as they 'get used to creating pictures and video on their phones in normal life, they increasingly think of sending it to us when major incidents occur'. Accentuating the positive, she added that it 'shows there is a terrific level of trust between the audience and us, creating a more intimate relationship than in the past. It shows a new closeness forming between BBC news and the public' (cited by Day and Johnston in *The Guardian*, 8 July 2005). Complementary perspectives similarly regarded the coverage of the bombings to be the harbinger of a reportorial breakthrough. 'Today is a great example of how news reporting is changing', proclaimed Tom Regan of the Online News Association, when offering his praise for the vivid eyewitness accounts provided by blog entries sent from mobile phones or computers (cited in Newsday.com, 8 July 2005). Rob O'Neill, writing in *The Age*, declared that 'one of the most amazing developments in the history of media' was the way in which 'victims and witnesses were taking pictures, posting them, sending texts, emailing and phoning in eyewitness accounts to mainstream media organisations and to friends and bloggers around the world'. While this had happened before, he acknowledged, it had never done so 'on the scale or with the effectiveness achieved in London last week. Until then, "citizen journalism" was an idea. It was the future, some people said. After London, it had arrived' (*The Age*, 11 July 2005).

Two months later, in the aftermath of Katrina, similar assessments of the role of the citizen journalist were underway. 'If news organizations don't embrace this, it will embrace *them*, and they'll become less and less relevant', Michael Tippett, founder of NowPublic.com, declared with regard to the hurricane coverage. Echoing O'Neill's point above, he concurs that citizen journalism 'is not the future, it's the present', and as such needs to be reconciled to more traditional ways of reporting. In highlighting the extent to which journalism is being effectively democratized, in his view, he welcomes the 'bare knuckle brawl of news in the marketplace of ideas' transpiring online. Perceptions of the journalist as an impersonal, detached observer, he argues, are being swept away. 'This is the real reality news', Tippett maintains. 'People are uploading videos and publishing blog entries, saying, "Let me tell you about my husband who just died." It's a very powerful thing to have that emotional depth and first-hand experience, rather than the formulaic, distancing approach of the mainstream media' (cited in Lasica 2005).

Precisely how, and to what extent, the emergent principles and priorities held to be indicative of citizen journalism are recasting the familiar features of journalism opens up intriguing questions. Even those who are dismissive of the rhetorical claims being made about its potential – 'We are all reporters now' – should recognize that it is here to stay. In the era of instant communication, when mobile telephone handsets are likely to be camera or video capable, the transfer of communicative power from news organization to citizen is being consolidated. Online news becomes a collaborative endeavour, engendering a heightened sense of locality, yet one that is relayed around the globe in a near-instant. Consequently, as the boundaries between 'local' communities and 'virtual' ones become increasingly blurred, the implications of this emergent social phenomenon for journalism's social responsibilities demand careful analysis and critique.

9   New directions

'News organisations do not own the news any more', the BBC's Director of Global News, Richard Sambrook (2006), has publicly proclaimed. 'They can validate information, analyse it, explain it, and they can help the public find what they need to know.' However, and this is the crucial point in his view, 'they no longer control or decide what the public know. It is a major restructuring of the relationship between public and media.'

The implicit suggestion that there was once a time when news organizations actually did 'own the news' is open to debate, of course, but there is little doubt that Sambrook is on firm ground when he argues that the 'information revolution' now underway 'has the potential to alter the dynamics of public debate, and the interaction between politics, media and the public, beyond recognition'. Vanishing before our eyes is the world where a select number of powerful news organizations could direct the primary flow of information so long as certain regulatory parameters were respected. In its place today, he maintains, is a world where unlimited information is readily available. For the price of a laptop and an internet connection, it will be commoditized and democratized. 'Thanks to the internet, the role of media gatekeeper has gone', he continues. 'Information has broken free and top-down control is slipping inexorably away.' And, at same time, the former gatekeepers – not least the BBC – are discovering that they are being repositioned beneath a bright spotlight, which can be rather uncomfortable at times. 'We are watched and assessed more closely now by those whom we serve', Sambrook (2005) acknowledges. This is the new reality, he adds, and 'we'd better get used to it. Transparency about the news selection and editing process is now as important as the journalism itself in retaining public trust.'

These comments are interesting for the compelling insights they offer, but also because they are indicative of what appears to be a fast-growing consensus amongst senior news executives that radical change must be embraced if their organizations are to survive, let alone prosper, in the digital universe opening up before them. This chapter, in bringing the book's discussion to a close, pinpoints several pressing issues deserving of close attention at this pivotal juncture.

News on demand

'Traditional media is not dead' is the reassuring message Peter Chernin, president and chief operating officer of News Corporation, has sought to share with investors. Challenging the doomsayers, he contends that the 'media industry stands at the dawn of a new golden age', one that is 'fueled on the demand side by ever-more discerning consumers, and on the supply side by fresh thinking, new products and oceans of new content'. Driving the industry forward into the 'networked digital future' – echoes here of Sambrook's observations above – is a 'technology revolution'. As Chernin elaborates:

> The reality is that new technology, far from being a threat, offers media companies the chance to solve an age-old problem. Our businesses were built on our ability to enlighten, entertain and educate – whether through the pages of a novel, the images on a screen, or the facts in a news broadcast. We exist to connect masses of people with compelling content. Yet throughout history, our power to achieve that mass connection has been limited by distribution constraints – prohibitive costs, hard-to-reach locations, sluggish technology, etc. Even as media companies grew and thrived, complete access to a truly global audience was long out of reach.
> (*Wall Street Journal*, 9 February 2006)

Suddenly, it seems, advances in hardware and software are allowing consumers to be reached virtually any where at any time through a number of devices. 'On-demand technology', Chernin suggests, brings with it the promises of allowing consumers to order news programmes 'for immediate viewing with the click of a button, freeing the viewer from the hassle of schedules'. Moreover, consumers will be able to 'personalize' their news 'to suit their own needs and taste – true one-to-one distribution'. And thanks to wireless technology, news updates can be delivered directly to their mobile telephone handsets.[1] News, by this logic, is a form of content that needs to be 'repurposed' so as to comply with the demands of the 'time-shifting' consumer, who interacts and engages with the possibilities created by an explosion of choices otherwise constrained by 'the old analog world'. The 'mass digital conversion' unfolding over the past decade, Chernin believes, 'puts consumers at the very heart of media'. No longer held captive, the 'liberated consumer' is 'bringing about what can and should be the golden age for the so-called old media' (*Wall Street Journal*, 9 February 2006).

Dramatic appeals to a 'new golden age' aside (and with it the view of users as consumers first and foremost, rather than citizens), there is little doubt that rapid growth in broadband penetration is changing 'consumption habits' to a remarkable extent. This is especially so among early adopters – most of whom are young people, who tend not to display the same 'brand loyalty' where their 'news choices' are concerned as previous generations. For companies with extensive holdings in 'old media' resources, time is of the essence if they are to capitalize on the internet's projected growth in an intensely competitive marketplace (as an aside, it is worth noting that the *Wall Street Journal*, where Chernin's comments above appeared, operates one of the very few online news sites that is profitable). Those amongst them emboldened by a desire to anticipate trends are actively experimenting with new forms of connectivity so as to invite more meaningful types of user participation. Digital devices from notebook computers, digital cameras, mobile telephones and the like are as powerful as they are transportable, opening up new possibilities in first-person reporting, fact-checking and 'watch-dogging'. The growing prevalence of RSS (Really Simple Syndication) and associated technologies, employed by sites to syndicate their content, facilitates users' efforts to filter news headlines by organizing a personal 'feed' in accordance with their interests. Beginning with blogs, RSS is now widely incorporated into news sites, and has been instrumental in smoothing the progress of podcasting.

Indeed podcasts – which are essentially radio programmes available to download, either on a computer or portable listening device – allow 'old' media such as newspapers a means to connect with new audiences, and in this way enhance their 'brand' profile. 'Since tablets of stone, news has been delivered in a style we call "push" journalism', the *Daily Telegraph*'s podcast editor Guy Ruddle, remarks. 'That world is over. From now onwards it's "pull". We have to make news available to listeners, viewers, readers in a variety of formats.' The main advantage of podcasting for users, he adds, is that it 'gives you the opportunity to pick up which bits you want and when' (cited in *The Guardian*, 1 February 2006). Newspapers such as the *Telegraph* – which launched its daily podcast of news and features in November 2005 – have seized on the idea as a means to encourage a culture of innovation in the newsroom. Podcasts differ from the relatively widespread practice of streaming audio files in that they are intended to be downloaded and played later at the user's convenience. Print journalists usually do the talking, with some podcasts offering a daily news summary, others discussions about current affairs, or debates about public policy. Some offer weather reports, sports commentary, even letters to the editor, while various experiments with raw feeds direct from events – political debates, for example – are underway. In the main, however, their implementation tends to be seen as a practicable strategy to capture the attention of younger audiences on the move (sometimes dubbed 'the iPod generation'), people who may be otherwise disinclined to turn to a newspaper for their news. 'That is the future that newspapers have to prepare for', David Carr observes. 'Readers no longer care so much who you are, they just want to know what you know' (*The New York Times*, 10 October 2005).

Just as the number of one-way, top-down methods of disseminating news multiply, so do the means available for citizen-led alternatives continue to proliferate. Variations of 'user-generated' reporting are evolving, with blogs at the fore – the term now stretching to accommodate such diverse forms of content as moblogging (mobile blogging, using a telephone or other mobile device), photoblogging (posting photos online), video blogging (vblogging or vlogging of video content) and the audio equivalent, audioblogging (typically in MP3 format). Whether the content in question consists of text, images, media files, or some combination thereof, the blogging phenomenon is now firmly entrenched, and still growing at a remarkable rate. Dave Sifry (2006), founder and chief executive officer of Technorati, stated in his February 2006 report that his site was tracking 27.2 million blogs. Its marshalling of statistics indicates that the blogosphere continues to double in size about every 5.5 months, which means that it is over 60 times bigger than it was three years earlier. Some 75,000 new blogs are created every day, or – put another way – a new blog is created every second of every day. 'It is impossible to read everything that is relevant to an issue', Sifry observes, 'and a new challenge has presented itself – how to find the most interesting and authoritative information' (cited in *The Guardian*, 9 February 2006). RSS helps in this regard, as noted above, but the challenge is formidable, to say the least.

Amongst those routinely engaged in the sifting, of course, are mainstream journalists. 'The little-known secret in newsrooms', political campaigner Joe Trippi (2004) points out, 'is that *right now* reporters are beginning every day by reading the blogs. They're looking for the pulse of the people, for political fallout, for stories they might have missed' (2004: 229; emphasis in original). Given that missing important stories is all too easy, Arianna Huffington (2004) argues, this is the reason 'why we need stories to be covered and recovered and re-recovered and covered again – until they filter up enough to become part of the cultural bloodstream'. Huffington, formerly of Arianna's Blog but now of The Huffington Post, makes plain her belief that 'blogs are the greatest breakthrough in popular journalism since Tom Paine broke onto the scene'. Reporters for major news organizations, she argues, are obsessed with novelty, and as such move too quickly from story to story in a blur. Bloggers, in contrast, are motivated by a passion for enquiry. 'When these folks decide that something matters, they chomp down hard and refuse to let go', she writes. In her view, they are 'the true pit bulls of reporting. The only way to get them off a story is to cut off their heads (and even then you need to pry their jaws open).' It is the nature of this type of journalism, she maintains, that a story – or intriguing aspect therein – otherwise deemed too small or insignificant by 'the big media outlets' is taken up and investigated by bloggers intent on showing why it is newsworthy. 'Big media can't see the

forest for the trees – until it's assembled for them by the bloggers', she contends, adding: 'That's why the blogosphere has become the most vital and
important news source in our country.'

Cultures of dissent

The appeal of blogging as a counterpoint to mainstream reporting is readily
apparent, especially when one sets it against the current tendencies toward
homogeneity and standardization which increasingly characterize market-
driven journalism. And yet, at the same time, some fear that the days when
the blogosphere can be reasonably considered to be a relatively egalitarian
terrain may be rapidly coming to an end. User statistics confirm the obvious,
namely that an emergent hierarchy is forming between a small number of
celebrity bloggers and the vast majority, the latter of whom fall well outside
the sweep of the mainstream media's purview.

'Billmon' (2004) of the blog Whiskey Bar, for example, believes that the
'world of inspired amateurs' is 'rapidly being overshadowed by the blogosphere's potential for niche marketing'. Pointing out that because most of the
advertising revenue is going to a small handful of A-list blogs, namely the
ones attracting media attention, 'the temptation to sell out to the highest
bidder could become irresistible, and the possibility of making it in the
marketplace as an independent blogger increasingly theoretical'. As a result,
he detects in the media's infatuation with blogging 'a distinct odor of the
deathbed'. While the blogosphere has 'a commercially bright future', in his
view, he is becoming increasingly convinced that the end is in sight for 'the
idea of blogging as a grass-roots challenge to the increasingly sanitized
"content" peddled by the Time Warner-Capital Cities-Disney-General Elec-
tric-Viacom-Tribune media oligopoly'. In comparing the current scene with
his experiences as a blogger, he is alarmed by what he perceives to be the
growing commercialization of the 'culture of dissent' that once thrived as an
alternative to corporate-owned media. 'Even as it collectively achieves celebrity status for its anti-establishment views', he writes, 'blogging is already
being domesticated by its success. What began as a spontaneous eruption of
populist creativity is on the verge of being absorbed by the media-industrial
complex it claims to despise'. Typically, it is the case, he points out, that A-list
bloggers are individuals who are 'glib enough and ideologically safe enough
to fit within the conventional media punditocracy' and, as such, are unlikely
to challenge this process of convergence between blogging and the 'increasingly frivolous news agenda' of mainstream media. The small number of such
bloggers being rewarded with media attention means, in turn, that those
bloggers who actively resist pressures to conform – that is, who continue to
strive to speak truth to power – will find it that much more difficult to reach a

broad audience. 'Bloggers aren't the first, and won't be the last, rebellious critics to try to storm the castle', Billmon remarks, 'only to be invited to come inside and make themselves at home'.

These are trenchant criticisms which succeed in throwing into sharp relief the ideological sway of the 'charmed circle of bloggers', a serious point of concern for progressive bloggers committed to democratizing the mainstream media. Criticisms of an altogether different nature are being expressed from angry voices on the political right, however, many of whom are busily assailing blogging as a matter of principle in their passionate defence of the status quo. Signs that the growing 'backlash against blogging' was reaching boiling point appeared in the mainstream media – specifically, as a front-page story, headlined 'ATTACK OF THE BLOGS!', for *Forbes* magazine – in November 2005. 'Web logs,' declared Daniel Lyons, writing in his capacity as a senior member of magazine, 'are the prized platform of an online lynch mob spouting liberty but spewing lies, libel and invective' (*Forbes*, 14 November 2005). Blogs may have started innocently enough years ago, he maintains, but 'suddenly' they are becoming 'the ultimate vehicle for brand-bashing, personal attacks, political extremism and smear campaigns'. This 'new and virulent strain of oratory', Lyons contends, poses a serious danger to everyone concerned about maintaining their reputation: no 'target is too mighty, or too obscure'. Microsoft 'has been hammered by bloggers', he points out, while CBS, CNN and ABC News have similarly felt the wrath of their invective. The experiences of 'dozens of other victims', including 'a right-wing blogger who dared defend a blog-mob scapegoat', constitute evidence for Lyons that such 'online abuse' is growing. Here he quotes Peter Blackshaw, chief marketing officer at Intelliseek, approvingly: 'Bloggers are more of a threat than people realize, and they are only going to get more toxic. This is the new reality', before chastising companies such as Google and Yahoo for their involvement. Such services, with their 'government-sanction impunity', are able to 'serve up vitriolic "content" without bearing any legal responsibility for ensuring it is fair or accurate'. Sometimes, he adds, 'they even sell ads alongside the diatribes'.

It is in distinguishing bloggers from what he calls 'bona fide journalists', however, that Lyons unleashes a particularly memorable salvo: 'if blogging is journalism', he remarks, 'then some of its practitioners seem to have learned the trade from Jayson Blair', the former *New York Times* reporter exposed for fabricating news items and duly fired. 'Many repeat things without bothering to check on whether they are true', he insists, leading him to question the real – as opposed to the proclaimed – motives of the 'blog hordes'. Although 'they have First Amendment protection and posture as patriotic muckrakers in the solemn pursuit of truth', he writes, 'the blog mob isn't democratic at all. They are inclined to crush dissent with the "delete" key.' In acknowledging that individuals on the wrong end of a 'bashing' can seek legal recourse through libel and defamation lawsuits, he cites a comment made by lawyer David Potts in response: 'filing a libel lawsuit, the way you would against a news-paper, is like using 18th-century battlefield tactics to counter guerrilla war-fare'. For Lyons, service providers such as Google, in particular, must take greater responsibility for blog content – 'even the Constitution', he writes, 'doesn't give a citizen the right to unjustly call his neighbor a child molester'.

Thanks, in part, to this type of inflammatory language, Lyons' brief pause to acknowledge that 'attack blogs' make up only 'a sliver of the rapidly ex-panding blogosphere' was almost entirely obscured. In the main, he appeared content to tar all bloggers with the same brush, thereby falling short of the same standards otherwise underlined by his criticisms. Reactions to this in-tervention, as one would expect, reverberated across the blogosphere, with several bloggers regarding the *Forbes* article to be indicative of a growing trend in blog criticism. Many of those weighing into the controversy elected not to mince words, condemning what they saw as 'gross inaccuracies' and 'hy-perbole' in the 'dopey *Forbes* cover piece' with its 'overheated rhetoric'. Bloggers were hardly 'business bogeymen', several insisted, angrily taking issue with Lyons 'damning of all bloggers for the sins of a few'. Some derided the 'headline smear in 90-point type' as a 'cheap publicity ploy', yet one that 'demonstrated the nutty nervousness of the mainstream press'. Others warned that it represented a thinly veiled attack on free speech, with some going so far as to say that were the blogosphere really a 'lawless haven for cyberterrorists', as this example of 'fear mongering' journalism suggested, then *Forbes* itself should be worried about the potential havoc to be wrought by 'the blog hordes'. One of the more restrained responses came from Dan Gillmor in his Bayosphere blog, who characterized the article as 'an alarmist and at times absurd broadside' before asking: 'Do bloggers sometimes go too far?' Of course they do, he wrote, but 'if the best-read bloggers typically did work of the lousy quality shown in the *Forbes* stories, they'd be pilloried – appropriately so'.

Still, elsewhere in the blogosphere, there were those who took issue with the defensive reaction to Lyons' criticisms. 'Stepping back a bit, I get a sense that the blogging world can't take some of its own medicine', wrote Rich Ziade in his blog Basement.org. Likening the article to a blog entry, he added: 'It presented a highly subjective, almost personal perspective on a topic. It's an opinion piece. And love it or hate it, some of its points are valid.' Nicholas G. Carr, in his blog Rough Type, thought it unfortunate that bloggers were not using the piece as an occasion for 'a little bit of soul searching'. While readily acknowledging that Lyons' overstretched when making his points, Carr maintained that these sorts of offences in 'the "citizen journalism" of the blogosphere [are] as commonplace as typos'. In his view, the rush to dismiss the article exposed one of the shortcomings of the blogosphere itself: 'It can dish it out, but it can't take it.' More positively, however, it is also fair to say that while the embers of this debate continued to flare up for some time afterwards, it was possible to discern in the disparate stances of its participants the basis for an enhanced commitment to self-reflexivity. While there remains little prospect of a general agreement about the relative strengths and limitations of blogging being reached, its importance for rethinking journalism's familiar paradigms continues to be above dispute. 'There will always be a number of voices on blogs who react violently to the idea that mainstream media organisations can or even should blog at all', Emily Bell, editor-in-chief of Guardian Unlimited, observes. 'Personally', she writes, 'I think that if we fail to engage our journalists with the possibility of blogging, then we are pretty much consigning ourselves to history' (*The Guardian*, 18 February 2006).

Who needs reporters?

The prospect of journalism being consigned to history's dustbin has been rehearsed in a wide array of contexts over the years, more often than not in accordance with a particular technology-driven 'breakthrough' (the emergence of the telegraph, newsreel, radio, television and internet were each decried as harbingers of the demise of newspaper journalism, for example). In the view of some commentators, however, the possibility that journalism as we know it is swiftly coming to an end has acquired a greater degree of plausibility with the arrival of Google News.

In what seems to some to be a perfectly logical, even inevitable consequence of technological progress, computers are poised to replace human news editors. Or at least such has been the typically apprehensive reaction to Google News since the beta (or test) version went live in September 2002. At the time of the launch, a message situated at the bottom of the screen read: 'This page was generated entirely by computer algorithms without human editors. No humans were harmed or even used in the creation of this page.' A humorous aside, to be sure, but one that nevertheless sent a chill down the spine of some editors, judging from reactions in the blogosphere. In actual fact, though, this claim glosses over the fact that Google News relies on the efforts of thousands of editors and journalists (both of the human variety) to generate its content in the first place. The site enables users to conduct searches on any subject, and then links them to news stories from more than 10,000 news sources (some 4500 in the English language) around the globe. Its main page automatically – that is, without human intervention – arranges the leading news stories gathered, presenting the most relevant news first, and is updated every 15 minutes. Clusters of related links for each story make the reading of multiple reports straightforward. Each 'top story' is clearly time-stamped and sourced, and sorted by robotic 'spiders' into genre categories, such as World, Business, Sci/Tech, Sport, Entertainment and Health. Pages can be filtered – that is, 'customized' for UK users or 'personalized' for US users, for example – on the basis of news from different regions (22 at the time of writing) and languages (currently 10), as well as by the individual user's own interests and preferences.

News objectivity is assured, according to the site's account of its operation, because the algorithms ensure 'news sources are selected without regard to political viewpoint or ideology, enabling you to see how different organizations are reporting the same story'. Moreover, it explains to the user, this 'variety of perspectives and approaches is unique among online news sites, and we consider it essential in helping you stay informed about the issues that matter most to you'. Given that objectivity is very much in the eye of the beholder, though, this principle will be realized in practice to the extent that the user compares and contrasts various renderings of a news event from a sufficiently diverse range of linked sources. The site's capacity to encourage this degree of engagement is certainly one of the chief reasons it has been heralded by some as 'the news junkies' web site of choice'. Further considerations of this proclaimed objectivity similarly need to recognize that Google News neither creates or owns its content, thereby alleviating it of direct responsibility for perceptions of 'bias' that may be levelled against the news organization behind the story. In any case, Google refuses to divulge its precise ranking criteria, beyond a general indication that relevance to search words, timeliness and the reputation of the news source figure into its calculations when collating stories. For the news organizations included in its sweep, it provides them with a much greater audience of users – 'eyeballs' in advertising parlance – than they might otherwise attract on their own (a portion of any advertising revenue generated being shared between them).

'People increasingly want their news on demand', Nikesh Arora (2006), who runs Google's operations in Europe, maintains. 'They want control over their media, instead of being controlled by it. People used to wait to be told what the news was but now they want to find out what their news is.' Google News has no 'hidden agenda', she insists; rather, 'we just want to provide news on demand for everyone'. This conception of 'everyone' has proven problematic, however, with various individuals, groups and even governments bringing legal pressures to bear during disputes regarding types of content over the years. One of the most serious crises has involved the Chinese-language Google News, which since its launch in September 2004 has been mired in controversy with Chinese authorities attempting to block access to the site at various times. 'China is censoring Google News to force Internet users to use the Chinese version of the site which has been purged of the most critical news reports', alleged Reporters Without Borders in November 2004. 'By agreeing to launch a news service that excludes publications disliked by the government, Google has let itself be used by Beijing' (RSF.org,

29 November 2004). Due to these and related concessions since, Google has continued to pay a heavy price in the form of damage to its reputation in order to develop its service out of China. In February 2006, officials from the company, together with those from Yahoo, Microsoft and Cisco Systems, appeared before a Congressional committee to answer charges that it was complicit in Chinese efforts to silence dissidents. Meanwhile, on another front, the Bush administration was seeking to compel Google to release its search data so as to facilitate efforts to enact a law to prosecute website operators involved in pornography, especially where children are concerned. In sharp contrast with rivals Microsoft and Yahoo!, Google refused to comply with the Justice Department's demand for data. So far, anyway.

Censorship of a more subtle nature, some critics contend, occurs on a much more routine basis. Spiders, despite Google News's claims to the contrary, do not operate in a manner that is entirely unfettered by preconceived perceptions. More specifically, the charge being made is that the automated selection of news sources is too narrow, that it recurrently privileges major commercial sites at the expense of alternative, non-profit ones. At the same time, others complain that too many stories appear from unreliable – or openly partisan – outlets which do not uphold 'professional' standards of reporting. Both sides concur that a further concern is the way in which editorial or opinion items, even press releases, can sometimes surface via searches of straight news. Others have lamented the death of the online exclusive, contending that Google News's definition of 'relevance' means that the most recently updated story on a topic is usually prioritized – thereby burying out of sight the original item from the news organization deserving credit for breaking the news. Adjustments are being made by Google to its algorithms in order to remedy these and other concerns, and it concedes that much work remains to be done. In the meantime, as the site evolves, Krishna Bharat, a principal scientist at Google News, reminds users that 'if you don't like the news, go out and make some of your own' (Google Blog, 23 January 2006).

Such words of advice for citizens sound laudable, but are cold comfort for those practising the craft as professionals. 'Who needs reporters?' columnist Howard Kurtz had enquired at the time of Google News's launch. 'Why spend money on whiny, self-centered, 401(k)-obsessed human beings when you can produce a nice news Web site with quiet, easy-to-abuse computers?' (*Washington Post*, 30 September 2002). Underlying Kurtz's tongue-in-cheek response to what he calls 'news on the cheap' are points of tension which have become increasingly pronounced over recent years. In the absence of an original reporting staff, an internal team of reviewers decides where the spiders crawl, making one of the web's most popular news sites remarkably inexpensive to operate. Not surprisingly, many news organizations have expressed their anger over what they perceive to be the 'exploitation' – some calling it 'Napsterisation' – of their content. 'Google, Yahoo! and other search engines are not some new breed of social benefactors of information – they are assuredly commercial, very much for profit organisations and not the new Robin Hoods', argued Gavin O'Reilly, president of the World Association of Newspapers. 'They are building revenue generating businesses from the aggregation of newspaper content, which the newspapers have had to pay for' (cited in *Information World Review*, 1 February 2006). At the same time, it is also worth observing that sites such as Google News and Yahoo! News strive to restrict their links only to established news organizations, seeing in them an intrinsic value which it does not recognize in reports from citizen journalists or bloggers. This 'gate-keeping' strategy may change as they consolidate their provision, but in the meantime it signals that 'news' is being routinely defined in broad accordance with the 'professional' dictates of (predominantly corporate) journalism. Anyone seeking out user-generated forms of reporting will be better served using the companies' general search engines to identify 'amateur', citizen-based alternatives.

Digital futures

Much of this book's discussion has been devoted to examining the ways in which the very users of online news are rewriting the rules which have traditionally governed journalism as a profession. What counts as journalism in the connected, always-on society is open to negotiation, with fluidly changing points of convergence and divergence between its practice in the mainstream and in the margins. To the extent it is possible to discern a 'news agenda' across the mediasphere, one can be assured that ordinary people – whether engaged as self-declared citizen or participant journalists, bloggers or the like – are actively pursuing their own preferred news agendas. Corresponding notions of 'authority', 'credibility' and 'prestige' are in flux, with certain longstanding reportorial principles seeming tired, if not anachronistic, in the eyes of some.

While much of the rhetoric surrounding citizen journalism risks overstating its significance as a grassroots movement storming the ramparts of the news establishment, it remains the case that responses to it from the major news organizations have been typically undertaken with considerable reluctance. Complacency is the problem for some, while trepidation about the prospect of making mistakes means others are delaying making the additional expenditure until the last possible moment. In the assessment of internet analysts Shayne Bowman and Chris Willis (2005), 'the greater threat to the longevity of established news media might not be a future that's already arrived – it might be their inability to do anything about it'. The key factors involved, they suggest, stem from the fact that the impact of the internet is being underestimated. As a result, the necessary investment in new technologies, with some notable exceptions, is happening much too slowly. 'Bureaucratic inertia, hierarchical organizational structure, and a legacy mentality', they argue, 'have paralyzed many news organizations from developing a meaningful strategy in this dynamic information age'. Administrative uncertainty similarly characterizes the almost reluctant response of some organizations to the demands of interactivity with users. Enhanced forms of audience participation will influence, by definition, which news stories are covered, how, and why, a not altogether welcome development in the eyes of some. For advocates such as Dan Gillmor, founder of the non-profit Center for Citizen Media, there is no choice in practical terms, however. He argues that the 'former audience' has been effectively invited into the newsroom, which means that news organizations must stop lecturing and instead commit to establishing a genuine dialogue with their users. 'There is the absolute democratisation of the media with the [ability of] anyone who has access to increasingly professional and cheap tools of production to publish to a global audience', he points out. 'The "former audience" know more than we do and once we embrace that, we can get in to some powerful journalism' (cited in *The Guardian*, 1 February 2006). In recognizing that listening is a necessary component of any meaningful conversation, it follows that important insights into how best to manage change will come from users themselves.

It is precisely this dialogical – 'We the Media' – principle that informs the online provision of the BBC. Citizen-generated content is an important and growing feature of BBC News Online operation, as shown in previous chapters, a commitment understood to be derivative of its public service ethos. 'We always need to push boundaries, be different and be distinctive', Pete Clifton, head of BBC News Interactive, insists. 'We can't stand still' (cited in Journalism.co.uk, 19 October 2005). One important way in which the site is facilitating such efforts is by making its content – ranging from software to archive material – available for use by other sites, including those managed by ordinary citizens. 'Much of the innovation on the Internet comes from the bedroom, not the boardroom', Tom Loosemore, head of new media foresight at the BBC, observes. 'We want to promote innovation on the Web by enabling people outside the Corporation to create new contexts and experiences around our content' (cited in *New Media Age*, 26 May 2005). Relaxing restrictions means, in turn, that digital items can be remixed and repackaged. It also opens up new ways to make online news available to users, such as via radio players that can download audio files. Radio Five Live podcasts, for example, have proven sufficiently successful to warrant a wide array of podcast packages being developed. Experiments are similarly underway with an interactive media player (touted as an 'iTunes for the broadcast industry'), so that television news will find a home on different platforms. 'It is all about control and convenience', suggests BBC interactive project manager Sarah

Pragg (cited in *The Guardian*, 1 February 2006). And also about accentuating the relevance of today's public service journalism for tomorrow's digital citizens.

Further initiatives underway include Digital Storytelling, where short films made by users can be inserted into the news. 'It takes the tools of digital media production into communities across the United Kingdom', the BBC's Richard Sambrook (2005) explains, 'enabling people to tell their stories in their own way'. By organizing 'local workshops, held in a portable studio, 10 people at a time learn new skills such as crafting scripts, recording voices, laying down music, and editing stills and video'. Also pertinent here is the development of community television via broadband, where ultra-local content is provided by reporters – within the BBC and from ordinary members of the public – equipped with digital camera and laptop computer. Meanwhile, the BBC's Action Network (formerly called iCan) is a website offering a civic space for participants to exchange viewpoints and information (including briefing material and databases provided by the BBC) with a view to establishing a dialogue about community issues and problems. These examples, drawn from amongst several others, briefly illustrate some of the ways in which the BBC's news operation is being reinvigorated. 'The BBC holds a license from the government that enables it to experiment with citizen journalism and social networks', Sambrook points out. 'This circumstance allows it to try out things that commercial broadcasters, with an eye to the bottom line and share value, would not attempt.' Moreover, while he acknowledges that these and related types of initiatives are merely the first steps in what is 'likely to be a long journey into new territory', he is confident that they will 'help those who receive our news to contribute to our services as we witness fundamental realignment of the relationship between broadcaster and the public'.

Much can be gained from considering the relative strengths and limitations of the BBC's efforts in other national contexts, especially those where there is little by way of a public service tradition. In the US, for example, where public broadcasting draws relatively small audiences (albeit influential ones), insufficient resources have been available to translate the strength of its news reporting to their online counterparts to an adequate extent. Many critics – from both government and corporate realms – maintain that commercial news sites more than satisfy public demand. Others contend that state involvement in online news is an inappropriate use of taxpayers' monies and, moreover, poses a threat to freedom of expression that only a market-based system can adequately preserve. Some claim to detect a 'liberal' or 'pro-big government' bias in content, which they insist is out of step with popular opinion. In response, advocates of publicly funded sites highlight what they perceive to be the shortcomings of advertiser-oriented journalism, suggesting that the range, depth and diversity on offer by sites such as BBC News Online make plain precisely why the pressures of the 'bottom line and share value' need to be alleviated. The public interest is being poorly served, they argue, due to the commodification of news by owners intent on cutting expenditures and maximizing revenues.

How best to realize the ideals of public service in journalism is a matter of intense debate, of course, but the BBC's innovative ideas have been attracting attention in places such as the US for some time now. In praising the BBC for 'leading the way as it so often does', Gillmor (2004) maintains that no major journalism organization has done more to involve its audience. 'While news companies make it their mission to inform the public', he writes, 'few have made it a mission to arm them with tools they can use to make a public ruckus' (2004: 125). Similarly impressed with how the Corporation empowers citizens to make their own news is blogger Jeff Jarvis of BuzzMachine. In particular, he applauds its commitment to 'share the knowledge', such as the posting of free training modules and educational guidelines on topics such as video-making and photography. The future of news, Jarvis believes, is about sharing:

> By teaching those who care to learn, the BBC is building an army of news-gatherers in the world. One of them could be there when the huge story happens. One of them will be inspired to go out and report a story. And that video will end up on the air – on the BBC or on the internet or elsewhere – and we're all better informed.

At the same time, he adds, US broadcasters – he mentions NPR, PRI, and PBS – should be doing something similar.

> I'll argue that the wise commercial station – and newspaper – should be doing this, too, because it will produce more news and improve the reporting of that news reporting at a lower cost, while also taking down the barriers that have been built up between the press and its public. It's good journalism. It's good citizenship. And it's good business. (BuzzMachine, 16 June 2005)

At a time when journalistic integrity and profit are recurrently being defined as mutually exclusive, especially where investigative reporting is concerned, it is vital that exemplars of good practice be emulated wherever possible. Too often the pressures of the marketplace being brought to bear on online news are working to narrow the spectrum of possible viewpoints to those which advertisers are inclined to support, thereby engendering a form of censorship that confuses the quantity of the news provision with its quality.

Re-inventing traditions

For reasons which will be made apparent, I wish to bring this book to a close by noting the recent death of veteran journalist and news anchor, David Brinkley. Brinkley's television career began in 1951 as a correspondent with the *Camel News Caravan*, where he played a key part in developing television news in the US. In October 1956, the *Caravan* was replaced by *The Huntley-Brinkley Report*, which featured co-anchors Brinkley in Washington, DC and Chet Huntley in New York City. As the NBC network's flagship television newscast, it was widely credited for pioneering a number of the features so familiar to us today. Following Brinkley's retirement in 1970, the programme was renamed *NBC Nightly News*.

On the occasion of Brinkley's death on 11 June 2003, Tom Brokaw, then the anchor of *NBC Nightly News*, recalled: 'David Brinkley was an icon of modern broadcast journalism, a brilliant writer who could say in a few words what the country needed to hear during times of crisis, tragedy and triumph' (cited in Haberman 2003). Evidently years earlier, when asked in an interview what he thought his legacy to television news would be, Brinkley had remarked: '[E]very news program on the air looks essentially as we started it (with *The Huntley-Brinkley Report*). We more or less set the form for broadcasting news on television which is still used. No one has been able to think of a better way to do it' (cited in Waite 2003). In an essay adapted from his memoirs, however, Brinkley's (2003) views on the current state of television news could hardly have been more critical. He wrote:

> TV anchors and reporters serve the useful function of delivering the goods, attractively wrapped in the hope of attracting some millions of people to tune in. In recent decades, I fear, the wrapping has sometimes become too attractive and much television news, in response to economic pressures, competition and perhaps a basic lack of commitment to the integrity and value of the enterprise, has become so trivial and devoid of content as to be little different from entertainment programming. But even at its best, television news is driven less by the ideology of those who deliver it than by the pressures of the medium itself. And as a result, individual journalists, from the anchors to the local news beat reporters, are all constrained in their power by the skepticism of a public that from the beginning saw in television something closer to the tradition of entertainment (movies, theater and the like) than to the tradition of the press. (Brinkley 2003)

These words, written by someone who played such a significant part in helping to consolidate the conventions of television journalism, deserve careful attention. Not only do they constitute a warning about the future direction of television news, but Brinkley also makes the crucial point that it is 'the pressures of the medium itself' which are necessarily shaping its ongoing configuration. That is to say, the basic tensions engendered 'from the beginning' between the 'tradition of entertainment' and the 'tradition of the press' continue to inform its development, for better and – clearly in his view – for worse.

My rationale for discussing Brinkley's views is likely becoming clear by now. It is my contention that we are currently witnessing a similar process of consolidation where the forms, practices and epistemologies of online news are concerned. The types of issues he touched upon regarding the early days of television news resound in current debates about how best to realize the extraordinary potential of the internet, not least with respect to – using his phrase – its 'useful function of delivering the goods' for diverse publics around the globe. As this book has sought to show, news sites are hardly immune from the types of economic pressures, competition from rival news organizations, and concerns about reportorial commitment and integrity which his words highlight in relation to television news. Arguably more challenging to discern, however, are the 'pressures of the medium itself' associated with online news, namely because of its still relatively inchoate status. And yet, to the extent that these pressures are tacitly characterized as taken-for-granted features of the medium, they become all the more difficult to change.

While this book has endeavoured to examine a multiplicity of distinctive strategies for online reporting, strategies which can vary markedly from one place to the next, it is my perception overall that news sites are beginning to share more similarities than differences. This is so, in my view, not only in their appearance but also, more troublingly, in their preferred definitions of what counts as news and how best to report it. One of the reasons Brinkley's words resonate so powerfully for me is that I believe online news is slowly becoming more closely aligned with the 'attractive wrapping' of commercial television, when I am convinced that it needs to reaffirm a stronger commitment to the public service ethos of the investigative press and broadcaster. As I have sought to demonstrate over the course of this book, to better understand the imperatives shaping this contested, always uneven development, a historical perspective is invaluable. It is my belief that it will enhance our ability to envisage new, innovative ways of improving the quality of online news for tomorrow, before it is too late.

Notes

Chapter 1 Introduction

1   A 'blog' (short for 'weblog') is a website, typically operated by a single in-
    dividual, which serves as an online diary or journal. The customary format
    sees each new entry placed at the top of the page, its posting being instantly
    time- and date-stamped. Please see Chapter 3 for a detailed discussion.

2   The word 'tsunami' is from the Japanese *tsu*, 'harbour', and *nami*, 'waves'.

3   The term 'citizen journalism' may be a relatively recent innovation, but
    several precedents of practice come to mind. Examples include the silent, 8
    mm 'home movie' recording of John F. Kennedy's assassination; the cam-
    corder videotape of Rodney King being beaten by the Los Angeles police; or
    digital photographs of US soldiers abusing Iraqi prisoners in Abu Ghraib gaol,
    amongst others.

4   Moreover, as journalist Yuki Noguchi has pointed out, the 'personal, visceral
    feel of those pictures inspired well-wishers to open their checkbooks to sup-
    port philanthropy in unprecedented numbers' (*Washington Post*, 8 July 2005).

Chapter 2 The rise of online news

1   Further to this point about a 'high-speed telecommunications link', we need
    to note that in 1995 most modems transmitted data at 14.4 or 28.8 Kbps – in
    other words, rather slowly by today's broadband standards. Still, this was a
    marked improvement in users' personal 'surfing' experience. Ten years earlier,
    as Mark Nollinger (1995) recalls, 'going online was about as far from most
    folks' idea of a good time as it could possibly get. Modems were exotic, pricey
    accessories. Even if you had one, there wasn't a whole lot you could do with
    it. Information highway? Forget about it – a scattered collection of dead-end
    streets was more like it. The Internet was just beginning to emerge from the
    clutches of the Pentagon, and the entire commercial online market consisted
    of a paltry 500,000 pioneering propeller heads, scrolling text at 300 baud and
    spending an arm and a leg for the privilege. Signing on was complicated,
    expensive, and dull' (see also Naughton 1999).

Chapter 4 Covering the crisis: online journalism on September 11

[1]   Dan Rather made his comments during an interview with Madeleine Holt on the BBC's *Newsnight* programme, broadcast 16 March 2002. The full quotation reads: 'What we are talking about here – whether one wants to recognise it or not, or call it by its proper name or not – is a form of self-censorship. It starts with a feeling of patriotism within oneself. It carries through with a certain knowledge that the country as a whole – and for all the right reasons – felt and continues to feel this surge of patriotism within themselves. And one finds oneself saying: "I know the right question, but you know what? This is not exactly the right time to ask it".' Rather then continues: 'I worry that patriotism run amok will trample the very values that the country seeks to defend [. . .] In a constitutional republic, based on the principles of democracy such as ours, you simply cannot sustain warfare without the people at large understanding why we fight, how we fight, and have a sense of accountability to the very top.' For a critical assessment of the news reporting on September 11, see the essays in Zelizer and Allan (2002).

[2]   Evidence provided in a report prepared by the Pew Internet and American Life Project helps to contextualize these accounts. The study's data were collected via a daily tracking survey of people's use of the internet in the US. Specifically, telephone interviews were conducted among a random sample of 1226 adults, aged 18 and older (some 663 of whom were internet users), between September 12 and September 13. The results for such a limited study need to be treated with caution, not least due to the usual sorts of qualifications where opinion surveys are concerned (sampling error, interpretations of question wording, practical difficulties), yet may be broadly suggestive of certain types of patterns. The findings highlighted the difficulties internet users experienced in reaching certain news sites on the day of the attacks:

> About 43% of them said they had problems getting to the sites they wanted to access. Of those who had trouble, 41% kept trying to get to the same site until they finally reached it; 38% went to other sites, 19% gave up their search. [. . .] A high proportion of Internet users were actively surfing to get all the information they could about the crisis; 58% of those seeking news online were going to multiple Web sites in their hunt for information. (Pew Internet and American Life Project 2001: 4)

In general terms, however, the authors of the report stressed that 'Internet users were just like everyone else in the population in their devotion to getting most of their news from television' (Pew Internet and American Life Project 2001: 3). Consequently, these findings appear to confirm the assumption that for most internet users, online news provided a helpful supplement to television, by far their primary resource for news about the tragedy.

3   It is worth noting that advertising messages remained a constant feature on many news sites, despite the fact that their presence slowed the loading time of some pages quite considerably. Amongst those sites that eliminated most of their advertising was USAToday.com, which retained only one small advertisement on its homepage. Washingtonpost.com cleared its homepage of all advertisements but loaded them with individual stories (Langfield 2001a). In contrast, network television newscasts in the US did not interrupt their coverage with advertising on September 11, nor for a good part of September 12.

Chapter 6 Online reporting of the war in Iraq: bearing witness

1   Fisk, as noted in the previous chapter, has seen his surname turned into a verb – 'Fisking' – by some bloggers as a form of shorthand to describe the critical practice of deconstructing a published news item on a point by point basis. A somewhat sceptical Brendan O'Neill (2003) comments: 'Fisk is now a kind of mythical figure, that strange British journalist who dares to say the unthinkable – a view which, it has to be said, is often out of proportion to any biting insight on Fisk's part.' Evidently it is fair to say that for some Fisking is a way to challenge mainstream journalism's hegemony, while for others it is little more than an opportunity to engage in a politically partisan rant.

2   Prior to the launch of al-Jazeera's website in January 2001, Arabic speakers were typically most interested in CNN.com (www.arabic.cnn.com) when looking for news online. Since the September 11 attacks, however, the page views for the Arabic-language site operated by al-Jazeera reportedly grew from about 700,000 a day to 3 million, with more than 40 per cent of visitors logging on from the US (*The Mercury News*, 28 February 2003).

3   Evidently, MSNBC set down 'a few understandable stipulations', which Kevin Sites described in his blog as: '1) I'm here because NBC News has hired me to be here, therefore the observations and experiences in Iraq that I relate to you this blog would probably not happen without them. 2) They have the right of first refusal on anything that I write that relates to this assignment. That means I run it by them and if they want it they will publish it on MSNBC.COM. It will be republished here. 3) If it's something they're not interested in or not directly related to an assignment they've paid me to do— it can appear here first. I think that's fair and bypasses any of the editorial oversight and ownership issues that we encountered in the first run of kevinsites.net.'

4   An example of the 'corrective power' of the medium's interactivity, to use

Allbritton's (2003) phrase, revolved around Fisk's report in *The Independent* newspaper of an incident where a bomb exploded in a crowded Baghdad marketplace, killing many individuals in the vicinity. In the report in question, Fisk cites the Western numerals painted on a metal fragment found nearby. According to Welch (2003), 'Australian blogger Tim Blair, a free-lance journalist, reprinted the partial numbers and asked his military-knowledgeable readers for insight. Within twenty-four hours, more than a dozen readers with specialized knowledge (retired Air Force, former Naval Air Systems Command employees, others) had written in describing the weapon (U.S. high-speed antiradiation missile), manufacturer (Raytheon), launch point (F-16), and dozens of other minute details not seen in press accounts days and weeks later. Their conclusion, much as it pained them to say so: Fisk was probably right.'

5 'For a source to be considered acceptable to this project', an explanatory statement on the website states, 'it must comply with the following standards: (1) site updated at least daily; (2) all stories separately archived on the site, with a unique url; (3) source widely cited or referenced by other sources; (4) English Language site; (5) fully public (preferably free) web-access. The project relies on the professional rigour of the approved reporting agencies. It is assumed that any agency that has attained a respected international status operates its own rigorous checks before publishing items (including, where possible, eye-witness and confidential sources).'

6 'The truth about who is being killed by the US air strikes', Patrick Cockburn, correspondent for *The Guardian* newspaper, pointed out, 'is difficult to ascertain exactly because Islamic militants make it very dangerous for journalists to go to places recently attacked. Bodies are buried quickly and wounded insurgents do not generally go to public hospitals. But, where the casualties can be checked, many of those who die or are injured have proved to be innocent civilians' (*The Guardian*, 18 September 2004).

7 Regarding methodological considerations, the authors write: 'The results in this report are based on data from telephone interviews conducted by Princeton Survey Research Associates from May 15 to June 17, 2004, among a sample of 2,200 adults, 18 and older. For results based on the total sample, one can say with 95% confidence that the error attributable to sampling is plus or minus 2 percentage points. For results based Internet users (n=1,399), the margin of sampling error is plus or minus 3 percentage points.'

8 One exception to this general rule was a statement made by US Brigadier General Mark Kimmitt, the senior military spokesperson in Iraq, in the aftermath of a particularly violent round of fighting in Fallujah. Asked what he would tell Iraqis about televised images 'of Americans and coalition soldiers killing innocent civilians', he replied: 'Change the channel' (cited in *The New York Times*, 12 April 2004). For useful studies of war reporting more generally, see Thussu and Freedman (2003); Allan and Zelizer (2004); Paterson and Sreberny (2004); Seib (2004); Tumber and Palmer (2004); Cottle (2006).

9   This relative silence was briefly interrupted by a study published by the *Lancet* medical journal in October 2004. The findings of the research team, led by Les Roberts of the Johns Hopkins Bloomberg School of Public Health in Baltimore, suggested that about 100,000 Iraqi civilians (half of them women and children) had died in Iraq since the invasion. The study's data was based on information gathered from door-to-door household surveys (33 clusters of 30 households each across the country) concerning births and deaths since January 2002. Press reports highlighted the study's findings (see, for example, *The Guardian*, 29 October 2004; *Washington Post*, 29 October 2004), but they did not receive sustained attention.

Chapter 8 Citizen journalists on the scene: the London bombings and Hurricane Katrina

1   For a copy of the statement, see: http://www.london.gov.uk/mayor/ mayor_statement_070705.jsp

2   Criticism of a different sort was expressed by the Chartered Institute of Journalists, who condemned the use of such images by the media as 'totally unacceptable' and 'bordering on the irresponsible'. Singled out for particular scorn was ITV's London News Tonight due to its appeals to viewers: 'Register with us, so we can contact you when a news story breaks in your area, because we want you, the viewer, to feel a part of the exciting world of news-gathering.' Chief amongst the concerns expressed was the television companies' apparent 'disregard for the danger they may be subjecting their viewers to in their attempt to obtain picture material' (cited in *Press Gazette*, 2 August 2005).

Chapter 9 New directions

1   Just as the newspaper evolves into a 'multi-platform product', new strategies are being devised to sell 'wireless media products' to users of mobile telephones. So-called 'news alerts' are proving increasingly popular with people inclined to follow events closely. Speaking at the time of the CBS Corporation's launch of its mobile subscription service, chief executive Leslie Moonves remarked: 'You're literally going to be able to see an explosion in Baghdad a couple of minutes after it happens, right from CBS News' (cited in *The New York Times*, 27 February 2006). Meanwhile, next-generation phones are already starting to appear, equipped to allow full streaming of live newscasts.

Bibliography

Agrawal, R. (1995) Getting the word out, *The Quill*, 83(6): 32.

Allan, S. (2002) Reweaving the internet: online news of September 11, in B. Zelizer and S. Allan (eds) *Journalism After September 11*. London and New York: Routledge.

Allan, S. (2004a) *News Culture*, 2nd edn. Maidenhead and New York: Open University Press.

Allan, S. (2004b) The culture of distance: online reporting the Iraq war, in S. Allan and B. Zelizer (eds) *Reporting War: Journalism in Wartime*. London and New York: Routledge.

Allan, S. (ed.) (2005) *Journalism: Critical Issues*. Maidenhead and New York: Open University Press.

Allan, S. (2006) Local news, global politics: reporting the London bomb attacks, in B. Franklin (ed.) *Local Media: Local Journalism in Context*. London and New York: Routledge.

Allan, S. and Zelizer, B. (eds) (2004) *Reporting War: Journalism in Wartime*. London and New York: Routledge.

Allbritton, C. (2003) Blogging from Iraq, *Nieman Reports*, Fall, 57(3): 82–5.

Andrews, P. (2003) Is blogging journalism?, *Nieman Reports*, Fall, 57(3): 63–4.

Arora, N. (2006) Searching questions, *The Guardian*, 13 February.

Bearak, B. (2005) The day the sea came, *The New York Times*, 27 November.

Billmon (2004) Blogging sells, and sells out, *Los Angeles Times*, 26 September.

Blair, T. (2001) Internet performs global role, supplementing TV, *Online Journalism Review*, 11 September.

Blood, R. (2000) Weblogs: a history and perspective, posted to *Rebecca's Pocket*, 7 September.

Blood, R. (ed.) (2002) *We've Got Blog*. Cambridge, MA: Perseus.

Boczkowski, P.J. (2004) *Digitizing the News: Innovation in Online Newspapers*. Cambridge, MA: The MIT Press.

Borden, D.L. and Harvey, K. (1998) *The Electronic Grapevine: Rumor, Reputation, and Reporting in the New On-Line Environment*. Mahwah, NJ: Lawrence Erlbaum.

Bowman, S. and Willis, C. (2005) The future is here, but do news media companies see it?, *Nieman Reports*, Winter, 59(4): 6–10.

Brinkley, D. (2003) On being an anchorman, *The New York Times*, 14 June.

Brown, M. (2005) Abandoning the news, *Carnegie Corporation of New York*, 3(2): Spring.

Bryant, S. (2003) Blogs build community in ways traditional journalism can't, journalists.org, 15 November (accessed 26 February 2006).

Carter, C. and Allan, S. (2005) Hearing their voices: young people, citizenship and online news, in A. Williams and C. Thurlow (eds) *Talking Adolescence: Perspectives on Communication in the Teenage Years*. New York: Peter Lang.

Cavanaugh, T. (2001a) The backlash that almost wasn't, *Online Journalism Review*, 14 September.

Cavanaugh, T. (2001b) Another voice: net generates sound and fury, *Online Journalism Review*, 21 September.

Colombo, S. (2005) Latimes.com introduces blogs, with more changes on the way, *Online Journalism Review*, 27 May.

Compton, J.R. (2004) *The Integrated News Spectacle*. New York and Berlin: Peter Lang.

Connell, J. (2003) Weblog Central explained, msnbc.com, 30 March.

Cottle, S. (2006) *Mediatized Conflict*. Maidenhead and New York: Open University Press.

Daou, P. (2005) The triangle: limits of blog power, Salon.com, 19 September.

Dodge, T. (2003) An Iraqi in cyberspace, *The Times Literary Supplement*, 24 October.

Dotinga, R. (2005) Write the news yourself!, *Christian Science Monitor*, 20 June.

Douglas, S.J. (2005) The margins go mainstream, *In These Times*, 24 October.

Elmer-Dewitt, P. (1995) Welcome to cyberspace, *Time*, 1 March.

Franke-Ruta, G. (2005) Blogged down, *American Prospect*, 9 March.

French, H.W. (2003) Online newspaper shakes up Korean politics, *The New York Times*, 6 March.

Froomkin, D. (2004) Ideas for online publications, *Online Journalism Review*, 26 May.

Gaines, J.R. (1995) From the Managing Editor, *Time*, 1 March.

Gann, D. (2004) Inside dope: Mark Halperin and the transformation of the Washington establishment, *The New Yorker*, 25 October.

Garfield, B. (2005) Interview with Rony Abovitz, *On the Media*, WNYC Radio, 18 February.

Gauntlett, D. (ed.) (2000) *Rewiring Media Studies for the Digital Age*. London: Arnold.

Gibson, W. (1984) *Neuromancer*. London: Ace Books.

Gillmor, D. (2003) Moving toward participatory journalism, *Nieman Reports*, Fall, 57(3): 79–80.

Gillmor, D. (2004) *We the Media: Grassroots Journalism by the People, for the People*. Sebastopol, CA: O'Reilly.

Gladwell, M. (2000) *The Tipping Point: How Little Things Can Make a Big Difference*. London: Abacus.

Glaser, M. (2003a) For bloggers, NYT story was fit to print, *Online Journalism Review*, 10 June.

Glaser, M. (2003b) Reading between the lines in Iraqi blogs and newspapers, *Online Journalism Review*, 7 November.

Glaser, M. (2004a) A tale of two rumors: how Reagan, Kerry news spread online, *Online Journalism Review*, 16 June.

Glaser, M. (2004b) To their surprise, bloggers are force for change in big media, GlobalEcho.org, 7 June.

Glaser, M. (2005) NOLA.com blogs and forums help save lives after Katrina, *Online Journalism Review*, 13 September.

Glasner, J. (2001) Net slows in wake of attacks, *Wired News*, 11 September.

Glasner, J. (2004a) Wikipedia creators move into news, *Wired*, 29 November.

Glasner, J. (2004b) All the news that's fit to Wiki, *Wired*, 22 April.

Grabowicz, P. (2003) Weblogs bring journalists into a larger community, *Nieman Reports*, Fall, 57(3): 74–76.

Gunter, B. (2003) *News and the Net*. Mahwah, NJ: Lawrence Erlbaum.

Haberman, L. (2003) David Brinkley dies, *E! Online News*, 12 June.

Hall, J. (2001) *Online Journalism: A Critical Primer*. London: Pluto.

Halperin, M., Wilner, E. and Ambinder, M. (2002) Man bites dog: and this time, the GOP is the dog, *The Note*, 6 December.

Hanson, C. (1997) The dark side of online scoops, *Columbia Journalism Review*, May/June.

Hassan, R. (2004) *Media, Politics and the Network Society*. Maidenhead: Open University Press.

Hewitt, G. (2003) The war on the web, cooltech.iafrica.com, 25 March (accessed 26 February 2006).

Huffington, A. (2002) In praise of making a stink, ariannaonline.com, 19 December.

Huffington, A. (2004) A mash note to the blogosphere, Salon.com, 7 April.

Iskandar, A. and El-Nawawy, M. (2004) Al-Jazeera and war coverage in Iraq: the quest for contextual objectivity, in S. Allan and B. Zelizer (eds) *Reporting War: Journalism in Wartime*. London and New York: Routledge.

Jackson, D.S. (1995) Extra! readers talk back!, *Time*, 1 March.

Jensen, M. (2003) A brief history of weblogs, *Columbia Journalism Review*, September–October.

Kahney, L. (2000) The web the way it was, *Wired*, 23 February.

Kahney, L. (2001a) Who said the web fell apart?, *Wired News*, 12 September.

Kahney, L. (2001b) Amateur newsies top the pros, *Wired News*, 15 September.

Kahney, L. (2003) Media watchdogs caught napping, *Wired News*, 17 March.

Katz, J. (1997a) Scoop story, *Wired News*, 4 March.

Katz, J. (1997b) Deaths in the family, *Hotwired*, 31 March.

Katz, J. (1998) Nothing quite like Slashdot.org – experience it!, freedomforum.org, 6 November.

Katz, J. (1999) Here come the weblogs, Slashdot.org, 24 May.

Katz, J. (2001) Net: our most serious news medium?, Slashdot.org, 11 October.

Kawamoto, K. (ed.) (2003) *Digital Journalism: Emerging Media and the Changing Horizons of Journalism*. Lanham, MD: Rowman & Littlefield.

Kim, T. and Lee, S. (2005) *Media Big Bang: Challenge and Change in the Media World.* trans. Y. Lee, Seoul: Communication Books.

King, B. (2001) Tech sites pick up the news, *Wired News*, 11 September.

Klam, M. (2004) Fear and laptops on the campaign trail, *The New York Times Magazine*, 26 September.

Koch, T. (1991) *Journalism for the 21st Century: Online Information, Electronic Databases, and the News.* Westport, CT and London: Praeger.

Kramer, S.D. (2002) The perfect news incubator, *Online Journalism Review*, 18 December.

Kurtz, H. (2005) CNN's Jordan resigns over Iraq remarks, *Washington Post*, 12 February.

Langfield, A. (2001a) When web sites caught up, then ran far, *Online Journalism Review*, 11 September.

Langfield, A. (2001b) Commercial sites struggle to keep current, *Online Journalism Review*, 12 September.

Langfield, A. (2001c) New news lethargy, *Online Journalism Review*, 21 December.

Lasica, J.D. (2001a) A scorecard for net news ethics, *Online Journalism Review*, 20 September.

Lasica, J.D. (2001b) Online news on a tightrope, *Online Journalism Review*, 1 November.

Lasica, J.D. (2003) Blogs and journalism need each other, *Nieman Reports*, Fall, 57(3): 70–4.

Lasica, J.D. (2005) Citizens' media gets richer, *Online Journalism Review*, 7 September.

Lennon, S. (2003) Blogging journalists invite outsider's reporting inside, *Nieman Reports*, Fall, 57(3): 76–79.

Levy, S. (2003) Bloggers delight, *Newsweek Web Exclusive*, msnbc.com, 28 March.

Madsen, M.E. (2004) Blogs, journalism and democracy, *Extended Phenotype*, 11 May.

Mandel, C. (2005) Readers become the reporters with launch of Wikinews website, *Calgary Herald*, 16 September.

Mapes, M. (2005) 60 Minutes is going down! *Vanity Fair*, December.

Masson, S. (2004) The blogosphere: bloggers in their own words, *Quadrant* magazine, June.

Matheson, D. (2004) Weblogs and the epistemology of the news: some trends in online journalism, *New Media and Society*, 6(4): 493–518.

Matheson, D. and Allan, S. (2006) Weblogs and the war in Iraq, in P. Golding and G. Murdock (eds) *Unpacking Digital Dynamics.* Cresskill, NJ: Hampton.

Mayes, I. (2001a) News travels, *The Guardian*, 22 September.

Mayes, I. (2001b) Worlds apart, *The Guardian*, 13 October.

Mernit, S. (2003) Kevin Sites and the blogging controversy, *Online Journalism Review*, 3 April.

Meyer, P. (2004) *The Vanishing Newspaper: Saving Journalism in the Information Age.* Columbia, MO: University of Missouri Press.

Miller, R. (2001) From niche site to news portal: how Slashdot survived the attack, *Online Journalism Review*, 14 September.

Murdoch, R. (2005) Speech to American Society of Newspaper Editors, press release, Newscorp.com, 13 April.

Naughton, J. (1999) *A Brief History of the Future: The Origins of the Internet*. London: Phoenix.

Nollinger, M. (1995) America, Online!, *Wired News*, September.

Oakes, C. (1995) Shock waves: communication about Oklahoma City bombing on the internet, *Los Angeles Magazine*, 40(6): 112.

O'Leary, S. (2001) Rumors of grace and terror, *Online Journalism Review*, 5 October.

Olafson, S. (2003) A reporter is fired for writing a weblog, *Nieman Reports*, Fall, 57(3): 91–92.

Olsen, T.G. (1995) Cyberhoax!, *Columbia Journalism Review*, 34(3): 12.

O'Neill, B. (2003) Gone to the blogs, *Spiked-Online*, 14 January.

Outing, S. (2001a) Attacks lessons for news web sites, *Editor and Publisher*, 19 September.

Outing, S. (2001b) The first shock of history, *Poynter.Org*. 5 November.

Packer, G. (2004) The revolution will not be blogged, *Mother Jones*, May–June.

Paterson, C. and Sreberny, A. (eds) (2004) *International News in the Twenty-First Century*. Eastleigh, Hants: John Libbey / University of Luton Press.

Paton, D. (1999) War of words: virtual media versus mainstream press, *Christian Science Monitor*, 3 December.

Pavlik, J.V. (2001) *Journalism and New Media*. New York: Columbia University Press.

Pein, C. (2005) Blog-gate, *Columbia Journalism Review*, January–February.

Perrone, J.L. (1998) Spotlight on the Beeb, *Online Journalism Review*, 22 July.

Pew Internet and American Life Project (2001) How Americans used the internet after the terror attack, 15 September.

Pew Internet and American Life Project (2003) The internet and the Iraq war, project report, 1 April.

Pew Internet and American Life Project (2004) The internet as a unique news source, 8 July.

Polier, A. (2004) The education of Alexandra Polier, *New York* magazine, 7 June.

Raeste, J.-P. (2005) In South Korea, every citizen is a reporter, *Helsingin Sanomat*, 8 January.

Raphael, J. (2001) Media critics see web role emerge, *Online Journalism Review*, 18 September.

Raynsford, J. (2003) Blogging: the new journalism?, Journalism.co.uk, 25 March.

Regan, T. (2003) Weblogs threaten and inform traditional journalism, *Nieman Reports*, Fall, 57(3): 68–70.

Rheingold, H. (2002) *Smart Bombs: The Next Social Revolution*. Cambridge, MA: Basic Books.

Rheingold, H. (2003) Moblogs seen as a crystal ball for a new era in online journalism, *Online Journalism Review*, 9 July.

Rosenberg, S. (1999) Fear of links, Salon.com, 28 May.

Rosenberg, S. (2002) Much ado about blogging, *Salon.com*, 10 May.

Runett, R. (2001) Clicking from coast to coast during a crisis, *American Press Institute.org*, 12 September.

Salter, L. (2003) Democracy, new social movements, and the internet: a Habermasian analysis, in M. McCaughey and M.D. Ayers (eds) *Cyberactivism*. New York and London: Routledge.

Salwen, M.B., Garrison, B., and Driscoll, P.D. (eds) (2005) *Online News and the Public*. Mahwah, NJ: Lawrence Erlbaum.

Sambrook, R. (2005) Citizen journalism and the BBC, *Nieman Reports*, Winter, 59(4): 13–16.

Sambrook, R. (2006) How the net is transforming news, *BBC News Online*, 20 January.

Schechter, D. (2003) Blogging the war away, *Nieman Reports*, Summer: 90–2.

Schechter, D. (2005) Helicopter journalism, Mediachannel.org, 5 January.

Schofield, J. (2004) Hacks of all trades, *The Guardian*, 22 July.

Seelye, K.Q. (2005) Snared in the web of a Wikipedia liar, *The New York Times*, 4 December.

Seib, P. (2001) *Going Live: Getting the News Right in a Real-Time, Online World*. Lanham, MD: Rowman & Littlefield.

Seib, P. (2004) *Beyond the Front Lines: How the News Media Cover a World Shaped by War*. New York: Palgrave Macmillan.

Senft, T.M. (2000) Baud girls and cargo cults, in A. Herman and T. Swiss (eds) *The World Wide Web*. New York: Routledge.

Shepard, A.C. (2005) Upheaval on *Los Angeles Times* editorial pages, *The New York Times*, 13 June.

Sifry, D. (2006) State of the blogosphere, *Technorati*, 6 February.

Smith, S. (2006) MSNBC.com, *OMMA: The Magazine of Online Media, Marketing and Advertising*, February.

Smolkin, R. (2004) The expanding blogosphere, *American Journalism Review*, June–July.

Srinivas, S. (2005) Online citizen journalists respond to South Asian disaster, *Online Journalism Review*, 7 January.

Thorsen, E. (2005) Wikinews: The common sense of a neutral point of view, Unpublished MA Thesis, School of Cultural Studies, University of the West of England, Bristol.

Thussu, D.K. and Freedman, D. (eds) (2003) *War and the Media*. London: Sage.

Toolan, B. (2003) An editor acts to limit a staffer's weblog, *Nieman Reports*, Fall, 57(3): 92–93.

Trammell, K.D. (2005) Slogging, and blogging, through Katrina, *Washington Post*, 3 September.

Trippi, J. (2004) *The Revolution Will Not Be Televised*. New York: Regan Books.

Tumber, H. and Palmer, J. (2004) *The Media at War: The Iraq Crisis*. London: Sage.

Ulmanu, A. (2005) Collective power: 'Smart mobs' connect, share information on net, *Online Journalism Review*, 10 June.

Wagstaff, J. (2004) Korea's new crusaders, *Far Eastern Economic Review*, 7 October.

Waite, C.H. (2003) David Brinkley, *The Museum of Broadcast Communications*, www.museum.tv/archives.

Warner, B. (2003) War bloggers get reality check, msnbc.com, 9 April.

Weaver, J. (2003) Iraq war a milestone for web news, msnbc.com, 1 April.

Weissman, R. (1999) Democracy is in the streets, *Multinational Monitor*, December.

Welch, M. (2003) Blogworld: the new amateur journalists weigh in, *Columbia Journalism Review*, 5, September / October.

Wendland, M. (2001) Overloaded internet fails info-starved Americans, *Poynter.-Org.* 11 September.

Whitney, J. (2005) What's the matter with IndyMedia?, *LiP Magazine*, 31 July.

Wilkin, P. and Lacy, M. (eds) (2006) *Global Politics in the Information Age*. Manchester: Manchester University Press.

Will, G.F. (2005) Unread and unsubscribing, *Washington Post*, 24 April.

Williams, R. (1958) Culture is ordinary, in R. Gable (ed.) (1989) *Resources of Hope*. London: Verso.

Winston, B. (2005) *Messages: Free Expression, Media and the West from Gutenberg to Google*. London: Routledge.

Zelizer, B. and Allan, S. (eds) (2002) *Journalism After September 11*. London and New York: Routledge.

Index